'OVER THE LAND AND OVER THE SEA'

EDWARD LEAR was born in London in 1812. The twentieth in a family of twenty-one children, he was largely brought up by his sister Ann. His first project as a young artist, to make drawings of the parrots in the London Zoo, established his reputation as an ornithological illustrator and led to his being taken on by the Earl of Derby to produce illustrations of the menagerie at Knowsley Hall, near Liverpool. It was while working at Knowsley that Lear began to write nonsense verse, to entertain the Earl's children. In 1846 he was engaged to give a series of drawing lessons to Queen Victoria. Lear became a successful artist, an associate of the Pre-Raphaelite circle, and had work accepted by the Royal Academy, but his health was poor, and he was prone to depression; the death of Ann in 1861 was particular distressing to him. Throughout his life he travelled widely in southern Europe and further afield in Egypt, the Holy Land and India, writing and painting. In 1870 Lear built a house in San Remo, where he died in 1888.

PETER SWAAB studied at Cambridge, Harvard and New York universities, and is currently Senior Lecturer in English at University College London.

Fyfield*Books* aim to make available some of the great classics of British and European literature in clear, affordable formats, and to restore often neglected writers to their place in literary tradition.

Fyfield*Books* take their name from the Fyfield elm in Matthew Arnold's 'Scholar Gypsy' and 'Thyrsis'. The tree stood not far from the village where the series was originally devised in 1971.

> *Roam on! The light we sought is shining still.*
> *Dost thou ask proof? Our tree yet crowns the hill,*
> *Our Scholar travels yet the loved hill-side*

from 'Thyrsis'

EDWARD LEAR

'Over the Land and Over the Sea'
Selected Nonsense and Travel Writings

Edited with an introduction by
PETER SWAAB

'And we'd go to the Dee, and the Jelly Bo Lee,
Over the land, and over the sea; –
    Please take me a ride! O do!'
    Said the Duck to the Kangaroo.
        from 'The Duck and the Kangaroo'

FyfieldBooks

CARCANET

First published in Great Britain in 2005 by
Carcanet Press Limited
Alliance House
Cross Street
Manchester M2 7AQ

Introduction and editorial matter © Peter Swaab 2005
Illustrations on pp. 115, 122 by permission of the British Library; on pp. 121,
128, 154, 167, 218, 236, 245, 297, 305, 319 by permission of the Syndics of the
Cambridge University Library; on p. 235 by permission of Vivien Noakes

A CIP catalogue record for this book is available from the British Library
ISBN 1 85754 759 4

The publisher acknowledges financial assistance from Arts Council England

Typeset by XL Publishing Services, Tiverton
Printed and bound in England by SRP Ltd, Exeter

Contents

List of Illustrations   vii
Acknowledgements   viii
Introduction   ix
Selected Further Reading   xxv

Nonsense Writings

Eclogue   4
'When the light dies away on a calm summer's eve'   6
Ode to the little China Man   7
The Hens of Oripò   8
Limericks from *A Book of Nonsense* (1846 and1855)   9
Limericks from *A Book of Nonsense* (1861)   22
'She sits upon her Bulbul'   28
The Duck and the Kangaroo   28
The Story of the Four Little Children Who Went Round the
    World   30
Growling Eclogue   43
The Owl and the Pussy-cat   47
The Broom, the Shovel, the Poker, and the Tongs   49
The Daddy Long-legs and the Fly   51
Nonsense Cookery   54
Nonsense Botany (1)   56
The Jumblies   58
The Nutcrackers and the Sugar-tongs   61
Mr and Mrs Discobbolos   62
The Courtship of the Yonghy-Bonghy-Bò   64
Limericks from *More Nonsense, Pictures, Rhymes, Botany, Etc.*
    (1872)   68
Nonsense Botany (2)   79
'Cold are the crabs that crawl on yonder hill'   82
The Scroobious Pip   83
The Quangle Wangle's Hat   87
The Pobble who has no Toes   89
The Akond of Swat   90
The Cummerbund: An Indian Poem   94
The Pelican Chorus   96

The Two Old Bachelors   98
The Dong with a Luminous Nose   100
Nonsense Trees   103
'Mrs Jaypher found a wafer'   106
The Later History of the Owl and the Pussy-cat   106
'O dear! how disgusting is life!'   107
'How pleasant to know Mr Lear!'   108
Mr and Mrs Discobbolos: Second Part   109
Some Incidents in the Life of my Uncle Arly   111
'He only said "I'm very weary"'   113

Travel Writings

from the Prospectus to *Views in Rome and Its Environs: Drawn
    from Nature and on Stone* (1841)   115
from *Illustrated Excursions in Italy*,Volumes I and II (1846) 121
from *Journals of a Landscape Painter in Albania, Etc.* (1851) 167
from *Journals of a Landscape Painter in Southern Calabria,
    Etc.* (1852)   235
'A Leaf from the Journals of a Landscape Painter' (1858, 1897) 281
from *Views in the Seven Ionian Islands* (1863)   297
from *Journal of a Landscape Painter in Corsica* (1870)   305

Appendix: Lear and Natural History   341

Index of Nonsense Verse First Lines   349
Index of Places   351

List of Illustrations

Lear's drawing for the title page of the 1846 and 1855
editions of *A Book of Nonsense*   1

Title page to *Views in Rome and Its Environs* (1841), Lear's
lithograph of the castle of Ostia   115

Title page to *Illustrated Excursions in Italy* (1846), Lear's
lithograph of Santa Maria di Collemaggio, Aquila   121

Map of the Three Abruzzi, from *Illustrated Excursions in Italy*
(1846)   122

Music of the Pifferari, from the Appendix to *Illustrated
Excursions in Italy* (1846)   128

Lear's lithograph of the Pass of Anversa, plate 24 from
Illustrated Excursions in Italy (1846)   154

Map of Albania, from *Journals of a Landscape Painter in
Albania, Etc.* (1851)   167

Lear's lithograph of Khimára from *Journals of a Landscape
Painter in Albania, Etc.* (1851)   218

Drawing by Lear (probably early 1850s), from Vivien Noakes,
Edward Lear: The Life of a Wanderer (1968). Reproduced by
permission of Vivien Noakes   235

Map of part of the Kingdom of Naples, province of Calabria
Ulteriore Prima, from *Journals of a Landscape Painter in
Southern Calabria, Etc.* (1852)   236

Lear's lithograph of Palizzi, plate 3 from *Journals of a
Landscape Painter in Southern Calabria, Etc.* (1852)   245

Lear's drawing from letter to Chichester Fortescue (March 9,
1858), on the necessity for firearms practice before
travelling to the Middle East, from *The Letters of Edward
Lear*, ed. Lady Strachey (1907)   281

Lear's lithograph of the view from 'One Gun Battery', Corfú,
title page to *Views in the Seven Ionian Islands* (1863)   297

Map of Corsica, from *Journal of a Landscape Painter in Corsica*
(1870)   305

Lear's lithograph of Sarténé, plate 5 from *Journal of a
Landscape Painter in Corsica* (1870)   319

Lear's drawing for 'V' in a nonsense alphabet drawn in 1870,
published in *More Nonsense, Pictures, Rhymes, Botany, Etc.*
(1872)   341

Acknowledgements

The illustrations on pages 115 and 122 are reproduced by permission of the British Library; those on pages 121, 128, 154, 167, 218, 236, 245, 297, 305, and 319 by permission of the Syndics of the Cambridge University Library; and that on page 235 by permission of Vivien Noakes. I would also like to thank Vivien Noakes for permission to reproduce the 'Ode to the little China man' and its illustration, and the poem 'O dear! how disgusting is life!'; *Poetry Review*, for 'When the light dies away on a calm summer's eve'; and Marie-Lou Legg, for permission to quote from the unpublished typescript 'The Road to San Remo: The Pilgrimage of Edward Lear' by Humphrey Jennings.

I would like to thank the following for help and suggestions: James Ball; Lesley Benjamin; Charles Cox; Greg Dart; Jonathan Edmondson; T. Lux Feininger and the late Pat Feininger; Graeme and Fiona Frost; Philip Horne; Kevin Jackson; Alison Light; Anna Monticelli; Katharine Morton; Patrizia Oliver; A.F. Paddock; Allen Reddick; Peter Robinson; Ornella Trevisan; Henry Woudhuysen; and Melissa Zeiger. Andrew McDonald has been an indispensable help and a fine guide to Lear as painter and draughtsman. My thanks to Judith Willson of Carcanet Press for her expertise and imagination in editing this book. Finally, I would like to acknowledge Vivien Noakes for her indispensable books on Lear and for her generous advice.

Introduction

Edward Lear was one of the most gifted and adventurous travel writers of his time, though most of his readers are too young to know him in this guise. Of the seniors who have felt curious about his travel writing there must be many who have found, as I have, that the books are extremely difficult to get hold of. The first of his four travel journals (1846) has never been reprinted (not even excerpts), and none of the four has been in print for many years. This edition aims to make Lear available again as a travel writer, and to show his nonsense and travel writings alongside each other as twin areas of his versatile creative life.

The remarkable thing is that until now these two sides of Lear's writing life have never been brought together in a single volume. But what, after all, is nonsense poetry if not a poetry of departures, always departing from our usual norms, often in stories of voyaging and questing? And what is travel writing if not a series of encounters with the extraordinary and often absurd? Looking at Lear's writing as a whole makes better sense of its individual parts, and gives us the chance to see the interconnectedness of his career. In working on this edition I found I was following in the distinguished footsteps of the English filmmaker Humphrey Jennings, who in the 1940s put together a sort of biography-cum-anthology of Lear, stitching together source materials from his nonsense, letters and journals. Jennings argued that we should see his work as a multifaceted whole: 'we should cease to regard him as a not very successful landscape painter who wrote children's books in his spare time, which grown ups find amusing and to which some people would go so far as to give the name "poetry"… In place of this picture I see the life of Lear as a whole – the so-called Nonsense poetry filling an increasing part of it as he got older – and being increasingly absolutely an expression of himself' ('The Road to San Remo: The Pilgrimage of Edward Lear').

Lear as Poet

The first of Lear's poems which survives is an 'Eclogue', written in 1825 when his family were forced by financial difficulties to leave their home in Highgate. He was 13 at the time. A parody of William

Collins's 'Hassan – the Camel Driver', it brings together the worlds of suburban London and the exotic east: he was in a way moved to be a travel writer from the first. He also had the wit and character at 13 to put humour to work as a way of dealing with bad times (just as he would at 55 in his next, 'growling', eclogue, which looks wryly at the moans and groans of the grumpy old men Lear and J.A. Symonds). Exile and rootlessness were to remain central to his experience and his writing. 'My Sweet Home is no longer mine', was his traditional title for a poem of 1838, in a melting idiom suggesting how far his early sensibility was influenced by Tom Moore and Byron, orthodox tastes of the late Romantic moment of his adolescence. Lear's vocation as poet was to produce new, comic variations on the Romantic themes of yearning, alienation and adventure.

A Book of Nonsense was published in 1846 under the pseudonym 'Derry down Derry'. It comprised seventy-three 'nonsenses', as Lear called them, or 'limericks', as they came to be known (the word is first recorded in 1898), written while he was working at Knowsley Hall as a zoological illustrator. This had been his professional field since he was 17, first at the newly opened zoological gardens in Regent's Park in London, and later working mainly with John Gould on the grand ornithological books which were fashionable at the time. Lord Derby had been impressed by Lear's superb and innovative volume of parrot lithographs, and engaged him to draw his 'menagerie' near Liverpool. In the evenings Lear often entertained the children of the house with poems and games, and it was his celebrity with the children that brought him to his employer's attention, and led to his promotion from downstairs status as employee to upstairs one as house-guest.

Some of the limericks present a sort of menagerie too, a collection of unusual specimens. The rigid outlines of Lear's limericks make the poems into miniature life stories, classifying the habitat and chief characteristics of the specimen in question, duly illustrated in the accompanying drawing. First, the species, generally an old man or old person, but sometimes a young lady: 'There was an Old Person'. Next, their habitat: 'of Blythe'. Then, their chief identifying behaviour: 'Who cut up his meat with a scythe'. After this we generally see how they interact with their fellows ('When they said "Well! I never!" – he cried, "Scythes for ever!"'), and return to a summary in the final line: 'That lively old person of Blythe'.

Looking at the scientific texts alongside Lear's zoological illustrations (some of the former are included as the Appendix on 'Lear and Natural History'), one can see details which might well have appealed to a young man with a sense of the absurd. In *A Monograph of the Ramphastidae, or Family of Toucans* by John Gould (1834), one of the toucans 'is extremely shy, ... keeping to the tops of the highest trees, and exercising the utmost wariness and caution', as well it might, since its scientific observers meant it no good (kidnap or killing would be its fate). 'It is said', Gould noted, 'to be extremely partial to the banana.' Another of the toucans presents a natural enigma, with 'peculiar markings of the mandibles, which in some measure resemble Hebrew characters'. Among the observers of these rare birds are the bipeds Professor Wagler and Dr Such. A few years later, in *The Birds of Europe* (1837), we find an Egyptian vulture which has strayed into Somerset and unluckily found a dead sheep: 'with the flesh of which it was so gorged, as to be either incapable of flight, or, at all events, unwilling to exert itself sufficiently to effect its escape; it was therefore shot with little difficulty'. There is also an owl with an eloquent melancholy night-song, but when it 'accidentally wanders abroad by day, it is so dazzled by the sun that it becomes stupid, and may be easily taken'. Other books observe an emu which 'has somehow lost an eye', another emu unwilling to breed in England, and turtles both tame and fearsome. One species of turtle found in India is 'so tenacious of life' that 'their heads bite vigorously after being completely disssevered from their bodies'. Some of these far-fetched and colourful creatures, with their weird, dubious and various ways, could be seen as the precursors of the hybrid and sometimes grotesque heroes of Lear's nonsense poems. The very Victorian activities of global exploration and scientific classification suggest a structure for the discoveries of the nonsense world, in Lear's botanies and alphabets as well as in his narrative poems.

Lear's limericks have sometimes been conceived in romantic terms. Aldous Huxley found them part of an 'eternal struggle between the genius or the eccentric and his fellow-beings'. George Orwell homed in on the Old Man of Whitehaven:

There was an Old Man of Whitehaven,
Who danced a quadrille with a Raven;
But they said – 'It's absurd, to encourage this bird!'
So they smashed that Old Man of Whitehaven.

'To smash somebody just for dancing a quadrille with a raven is exactly the kind of thing that "They" would do', Orwell remarked. But maybe this Old Man's offence is even worse: he doesn't just dance with the raven, but is thought more subversively to 'encourage' it (him? her?), and where might *that* end? Quoth the Raven 'Give me more'? People from white havens shouldn't dance with black birds; and *two* creatures have no business to dance a *quad*rille: both semantic and mathematical proprieties are offended. Orwell chose a good example, but his generalizing sense of 'They' owes more to his 1984 than to Lear's 1849 (or so). Ina Rae Hark has noted that what W.H. Auden called 'the legions of cruel inquisitive They' are on the offensive in only about 20 of the first series of 112 limericks; and in the second series of 100 they tend to be less offensive still. She picks out six types of limerick plots in which 'they' variously figure. 'They' may be: hostile and quell the old man; hostile but themselves quelled; hostile but provoked; neutral but rebutted; friendly and approving; sympathetic and helpful – hardly, then, a uniform protest about relations between the individual and society. The old men, moreover, are not always geniuses; sometimes they are boors, lunatics or self-harmers. The violence and irrationality in the poems don't belong only to 'they'. Nor do the stories always pit an alienated individual against a repressive society. The outcomes are very various, sometimes happy but rather more often not, sometimes anarchic, at others law-abiding, sometimes cheery, at others blithely murderous. Hark has assembled some interesting statistics on the components of the limericks: 169 out of the 212 have an old man or old person, 28 a young lady, and 10 a young person. The figure's place of origin is named in 172, and only 14 fail to reinstate him or her there in the last line. 'They' figure in fewer than half the poems, and 'they' are never killed. About one poem in five includes eating or drinking, and a similar number involve animals, more of these in the second series. About a quarter of the first series threaten death, but far fewer than this in the second series. Within the collections one gets a sense of fate as chancy: natural selection in the nonsense world is ruled by the forces of alliteration and rhyme and the sound of the hometown, the luck of the draw or the luck of the alphabet, with such logic as these have but not a whit more.

The brevity of the poems wards off pathos and keeps them out of the deeper waters they often suggest. Lear had found a laconic poetic form which suited his penchant for touching on his darker feelings but not dwelling on them; it would, for instance, take little to turn this passage (from an 1862 letter written in Corfu) into a limerick: 'There is a man in a boat here under the window – who catches fish all and every day with a long 5 pronged fork: a waistcoat and drawers being his dress. Why should I not do the same?'

There was an Old Man of Corfu
Who caught fish with a fork all day through.
When they said 'Can't you shift?', he replied 'No, I'll drift!',
That stubborn Old Man of Corfu.

Lear would have done better, especially with line two (easily improved by relocating the old man to New York), but even this amateur effort shows a possible fit between his cast of mind and the shape of the limerick – especially in conjunction with his drawings, which could here supply the waistcoat and drawers and each prong of the fork. The key is the externalization of that plaintive question 'Why should I not do the same?' Instead of the melancholy hint at an inertia like that of Tennyson's Mariana or his lotos-eaters, the limerick gives a brisk plot of self-will rebuffing friendly (or irritable) concern.

All of Lear's poems were originally published with his own illustrations (as they are also in this edition), and the limericks in particular cannot be separated from the drawings. The image often lightens the poem, as for instance with the Old Man of Whitehaven, where we see the dancing, not the smashing, and where the Old Man's bird-like hair and the wings of his coat suggest that he and the bird are well paired. They gaze raptly at each other, too. Thomas Byrom has argued that the drawings, especially in the second series, give us 'a minor sublime' and depict a 'radiant affinity between man and nature'. Certainly the drawings defy gravity, often in both senses, with plenty of dancing and tiptoe and rising off the ground. His figures are wonderfully dynamic and vivid in gesture. In her book on Lear's birds, Susan Hyman suggests that 'It is in his nonsense rather than his landscapes that Lear reveals himself most clearly as a trained naturalist.'

Nonsense poetry is by definition a departure from the normal, and it often takes travel as its subject. It may be English literature's closest counterpart to the French *'poésie de départs'* – the poetry of departures. Many of Lear's later poems are stories of escape, not just 'The Owl and the Pussy-cat', but among others 'The Daddy

Long-legs and the Fly' and 'The Nutcrackers and the Sugar-tongs'. They mingle an aggressively disenchanted sense of home with a woozier hope, sometimes gratified, for an enchanted elsewhere. When Auden writes in his poem on Lear that 'affection was miles away', he catches a dual aspect of such travel literature, implying both that affection was miles away from his ordinary life, a painful absence, but also that affection had its real and genuine life miles away, available as a far prospect for the imagination. Poems like Carroll's *The Hunting of the Snark* and Lear's 'The Jumblies' catch something about the character of islanders going to sea in search of such satisfactions of elsewhere. The mysterious compulsiveness of British imperial globe-trotting is no less captivating in these poems than in such acknowledged Victorian masterpieces as Tennyson's 'Ulysses' and Browning's 'Childe Roland to the Dark Tower Came'. Take the Jumblies:

> They went to sea in a Sieve, they did,
>   In a Sieve they went to sea:
> In spite of all their friends could say,
> On a winter's morn, on a stormy day,
>   In a Sieve they went to sea!
> And when the Sieve turned round and round,
> And every one cried, 'You'll all be drowned!'
> They called aloud, 'Our Sieve ain't big,
> But we don't care a button! we don't care a fig!
>   In a Sieve we'll go to sea!'
>   Far and few, far and few,
>   Are the lands where the Jumblies live;
>   Their heads are green, and their hands are blue,
>   And they went to sea in a Sieve.

Unlike Lear's limerick seafarers, there is a collective here, a jumble of Jumblies. The escape has turned entirely sociable: they aren't moony solitaries. It is a comradely idyll without leaders and rank, in which everyone has the same impulse at the same time. It makes a contrast with the rigid stratifications of Lewis Carroll's crew in *The Hunting of the Snark*, who all begin with the letter 'B', but are divided by their professions (butcher, baker, bellman and so on), and by the fact that some of them wish to kill others. The map in Carroll's poem is 'a perfect and absolute blank', and the Snark turns out to be insolubly enigmatic (like 'The Scroobious Pip' and 'The Akond of Swat' in later poems by Lear), but 'The Jumblies' is not so philosophically exercised. We may not know where they are going, or why, or for how long, and there is no sign that they do either, but 'we don't care a button! We don't care a fig!': the heart of the matter is the call to go. It is not the best time, as their gloomy friends and the grim weather make clear, but the Jumblies and their makeshift vessel are buoyant in spite of the worst the world can do, and in spite of the usual laws regulating the behaviour of sieves. Theirs might be thought a romantically idiotic venture, and perhaps it is kept afloat by a literary tradition of inspired lunacy going back to Wordsworth's comic masterpiece 'The Idiot Boy'. The idea is that you don't have to be sensible to get places. Their sieve is able to go round and round, and also to go forward to the 'lands where the Jumblies live', evoked by Lear as a sort of luxury supermarket.

> They sailed to the Western Sea, they did,
>   To a land all covered with trees,
> And they bought an Owl, and a useful Cart,
> And a pound of Rice, and a Cranberry Tart,
>   And a hive of silvery Bees

– who soon rhyme with 'no end of Stilton Cheese'. The nay-saying friends are proven guilty of what economists call 'Excessive Risk Aversiveness', though as is their conservative wont they don't say so. 'The Jumblies' is unusual in finishing in conciliatory style with a *poésie de retours*, with a look ahead to a new generation recruited by their promotion of seafaring. The refrain, however, continues to imagine them elsewhere: 'Far and few, far and few, / Are the lands where the Jumblies live', we hear again at the end, with an ungrammatical twist on Lear's crucial word 'far'.

The Jumblies' heads are green and their hands are blue, but we know little else about them. In particular, neither the poem nor the illustration tells us whether they are boy Jumblies (as maritime convention might suggest) or girl Jumblies. The poem has much of the lure of romanticism, but none of the complications of sex, complications which are so common elsewhere in the literature of exotic travel. Like much of the best children's literature, 'The Jumblies' takes pleasure in a moment before sexuality makes its presence unignorable.

In his other longer poems and stories, Lear's travellers who set off together tend to be odd couples. The Owl and the Pussy-cat, for instance, are creatures who have very few links in life, the main one – a taste for mice – being softened and vegetarianised to mince and quince. Yet although they make an odd couple, they are not so odd as to think themselves disqualified from marriage and its formal recognitions. As in 'The Jumblies', the regular world is left behind, but its ways are not entirely repudiated. It is only in a partial sense that Victorian nonsense – 'a conservative-revolutionary genre' as Jean-Jacques Lecercle calls it – can be thought of as protest literature. Dancing in the honeymoonlight which bathes the poem, the Owl and the Pussy-cat more wistfully, but less pessimistically, get on terms with another Victorian classic, Matthew Arnold's 'Dover Beach'. Arnold's is also a seaside honeymoon poem, but his newlyweds watch 'ignorant armies clash by night' instead of dancing by the light of the moon.

Lear's unfinished sequel, generally known as 'The Later History of the Owl and the Pussy-cat', gives us a male owl, but in the original poem he mixes the signals. The owl does the serenading, and takes the ring, as a groom might; but the pussy proposes, and stands on the right in the illustrations to the second and third verses – also as a groom might. The poem is not so much a gender-bender as a gender-transcender. If you can marry across species, why worry about gender? (Other escapee couples in Lear, such as Mr Daddy Long-legs and Mr Floppy Fly, and the Nutcrackers and the Sugar-tongs, also fail to fit the Mr and Mrs norm). Lear imagines for us a world where such impossibilities can happen:

> What a beautiful Pussy you are,
>   You are,
>   You are!
> What a beautiful Pussy you are!

It is the third 'You are!', with its exultant exclamation mark, which makes this such a grand cry of amazement and happiness. Omit the line and the rhythm is smoothed, but much of the magic is gone.

Nonsense writing can be a place where such extraordinary intimacies can flourish, but always within the boundaries of the self-consciously fantastical genre, and sometimes within limits evoked by the nonsense narratives themselves. Compare the epithalamium of Lear's Owl and Pussy-cat, left to their future with our blessing, with this poignant episode from Lewis Carroll's *Through the Looking-Glass, and What Alice Found There*:

So they walked on together through the wood, Alice with her

arms clasped lovingly round the soft neck of the Fawn, till they
came out again into another open field, and here the Fawn gave
a sudden bound into the air, and shook itself free from Alice's
arms. 'I'm a Fawn!' it cried out in a voice of delight, 'and, dear
me! you're a human child!' A sudden look of alarm came into
its beautiful brown eyes, and in another moment it had darted
away at full speed.

Alice stood looking after it, almost ready to cry with vexation
at having lost her dear little fellow-traveller so suddenly.
'However, I know my name now', she said, 'that's *some* comfort.
Alice – Alice – I won't forget it again. And now, which of these
finger-posts ought I to follow, I wonder?'

Carroll's magic wood is a loving place, but it depends on its
inhabitants not remembering who they are. The Fawn is delighted
to rediscover its normal self even though this means abandoning
poor Alice, and Alice with characteristic mettle puts her vexation
behind her and starts afresh on her way.

Lear's lovelorn figures are less consolable, especially in his
darker, later poems, which include spectacularly unhappy
versions of romantic love. Nonsense writing often includes
creatures with unfortunate structures of desire (like those of its
foremost exponents, Lear, Carroll and Housman): they may be
abandoned by their loved one, like the Dong with the Luminous
Nose (of whom *The Spectator* in 1887 pointed out that his was a
'nonsense version of the love of Nausicaa for Ulysses, only that the
sexes are inverted'); their timing may be out, as with the Yonghy-
Bonghy-Bò; or they may be too narcissistically bound up in
themselves and their jobs to have much time for intimacy, like
many of Lewis Carroll's creatures in the Alice books, including the
Cheshire Cat, Humpty Dumpty, and the White Knight. The adult
implication that all desire can be seen as a nonsense gives these
writings an emotional charge, and a place alongside other
children's literature fearful of the burdens of adulthood, including
Kipling's *Jungle Books* and Barrie's *Peter Pan*.

The fact that the nonsense world includes versions of life's
misfits, mismatches and bereavements is one of the things that
stops it from being quaint or winsome. Indeed, the *Saturday Review*
in 1888 suggested that Lear's subjects 'gallantly bear their
eccentricities and nobly disregard any of those inconveniences
which ensue upon the indulgence of personal eccentricity', quite

bringing him into line with the traditions of Victorian high stoicism. Lear had many reasons not to feel at home with himself: besides what biographical evidence suggests was for him an unhappy homosexual orientation, he was afflicted from childhood by epilepsy, which he concealed from almost all of his friends; and by chronic depression, which he called 'the morbids', as though it had some sort of life of its own. His last major poem, 'Some Incidents in the Life of my Uncle Arly', encodes the circumstances of his life and sets them to notes of beautifully controlled pathos. His other writings can at times be astonishingly fierce. Mr Discobbolos, for instance, lives on top of a wall (like Tennyson's St Simeon Stylites up his pillar) and eventually dynamites himself, along with his wife and twelve kids: 'Let the wild bee sing and the blue bird hum! / For the end of our lives has certainly come!', he announces in lines of creepy psycho sublimity. For their detonation Lear borrows a cadence from Tennyson's comparably demented *Maud*: 'And the mortified mountain echoed again / To the sounds of an awful fall!' Again, in one of his prose children's stories, 'The History of the Seven Families of the Lake Pipple-Popple', he sends seven lots of seven children tearfully out on their voyages: that makes no fewer than forty-nine childish voyagers, and every last one is killed off, mostly eaten, leaving the various predators, Lear tells us, to return to 'their respective homes full of joy and respect, sympathy, satisfaction, and disgust'. Children often enjoy a good dose of violence and disaster in their reading, but you might think twice before reading this to the more sensitive souls.

Lear as Travel Writer

When he gave up his work as a zoological illustrator, Lear turned to landscape painting for a livelihood, so he had a professional reason to keep on the move in the search for new views to depict. His published journals represent a small fraction of the ground he covered, nearly always on foot, which included Crete, Corsica, Egypt, Sinai, Palestine, India, as well as many regions of Greece and Italy. He really was a remarkable traveller. 'In an age that abounded in travel writers and travel painters', Susan Hyman argues, 'he was both, leaving a visual and verbal record of foreign lands that was unique in his own time and possibly unequalled in any other.' Commercial considerations were not his only spur. As Vivien Noakes brings out in her biography, he took pleasure in travel for its own sake and for its benefits to his state of mind: 'Lear always enjoyed walking – it was the most certain way of keeping off attacks of epilepsy – and he found the world a happier place when he was outside and on the move.' He seems himself to have thought of Wanderlust remedially: 'if you are absolutely alone in the world, and likely to be so, then move about continually and never stand still', he wrote to Chichester Fortescue in 1859: 'I therefore think I shall be compulsed and more especially by the appearance of things on the horizon'. If it was a matter of being 'compulsed', then it was a mostly happy and willing compulsion. Even in his bleakest misery after the death of his beloved older sister Ann in 1861, his mind turned to the prospect of travel for relief from grief and solitude:

> I am all at sea and do not know my way an hour ahead.
> I shall be so terribly alone.
> Wandering about a little may do some good perhaps.
>   (Letter to Fortescue, March 18 1861)

The temper of the journals is generally buoyant and high-spirited, alive with Lear's pleasure in incident and encounter, which sometimes gives them a Pickwickian charm; and with his appreciation of beautiful surroundings, which at its best leads to descriptions of Coleridgean precision and emotion. 'The Elements – trees, clouds, etc., – silence... seem to have far more part with me or I with them, than mankind', he wrote in 1862, but on his travels he had no need to choose between sociability and sublimity.

There are two particularly vivid accounts of Lear at work as a landscape painter. The first is by Charles Church, describing Lear in Thermopylae in 1848, a few months before the trip recorded in the *Journals of a Landscape Painter in Albania, Etc.*:

> he was at work all the time, from three o'clock in the morning, only resting during the midheat – among the crowds in the market place, among the soldiers, only intent upon his work, with infinite patience and unflagging good humour and coolness.

The other account, from Lear's later years, is by his young friend and pupil, Hubert Congreve, and also suggests his speed and concentration:

> When we came to a good subject, Lear would sit down, and

taking his block from George [his servant Giorgio Kokali], would lift his spectacles, and gaze for several minutes at the scene through a monocular glass he always carried; then, laying down the glass, and adjusting his spectacles, he would put on paper the view before us, mountain range, villages and foreground, with a rapidity and accuracy that inspired me with awestruck admiration.

Both the rapidity and accuracy were legacies of his scientific experience as a painter of live animals. Jeremy Maas makes the interesting claim that 'no artist understood the geological characteristics of strange wild landscape so well' as Lear, once again suggesting the formative importance of his background as a trained observer in the sciences. Lear's reputation as an artist is still changing, but the majority opinion is that the oil paintings on which he rested his greatest hopes sadly lack the vitality and delicacy of his watercolours, which he would make by laying washes of colour over these rapidly executed drawings. With an output estimated by Vivien Noakes at around 300 oils and over 10,000 watercolours, Lear takes his place, whatever else may be true, as one of the hardest workers even of Victorian times.

To read Lear's journals in sequence is to witness the period of most dramatic expansion in European tourism. In the excursions to the Abruzzi, Calabria and Albania, he is a traveller, frequently the first Englishman that local people have met. 'England', he is told in Calabria in 1847, 'is a very small place… about the third part of the size of the city of Rome.' He is thought to be a nonsensical figure with his discomfort and his sketchbook. But by the time of the last journal in Corsica in 1868, he is recognizably a tourist, recommending places to stay, and meeting fellow-travellers. But in the earlier books he is entirely dependent on letters of introduction, and he encounters revolution, cholera, two murders, bandits and a fire.

His method as a traveller combined preparation and improvisation. He would diligently research the available literature on the region in question, and furnish himself with letters of introduction from the great and the good; but he also allowed himself to digress if something unforeseen beckoned, like the great 'festa' in Tagliacozzo in the *Illustrated Excursions in Italy*, where he fell into a bed of broccoli while helping, or trying to help, put out a fire. 'Put yourself, as a predestinarian might say, calmly into the dice-box of small events, and be shaken out whenever circumstances may ordain', he tells himself in Saloníki, sounding for a moment like Fitzgerald's Omar Khayyam. Socially, he found himself in a curious position, at one moment knocking on the door of the wealthiest landowner in a region, at the next bedding down in hovels. Lear enjoyed the sponsoring friendship of Britain's high colonial administrators, though perhaps his position as professional artist meant that he was never quite on equal terms with them; but in his travels he mostly preferred to avoid the insulating effects of wealthy hospitality and, no less importantly, the social duties of a house-guest. Hans Magnus Enzensberger aptly describes his floating status as 'that of the déclassé' ('*die des Deklassierten*'). He chose 'liberty, hard living, and filth', as he puts it in the Albania journals, over 'luxury and inconvenience', and the journals communicate a studentish pleasure in roughing it, abetted by the younger companions with whom he often chose to travel.

The journals themselves are full of haunting evocations:

> August 13th, 1843. The cool valley of Antrodoco is in deep shade till late in the morning. I was sauntering by the brawling river, when a little boy passed me carrying a dead fox. 'It is delightful food (*cibo squisito*)', said he, 'either boiled or roast'; – said I, 'I wish you joy.' (*Illustrated Excursions*)

There is something touching about the exchange of courtesies here, with Lear the pupil to his young pastoral guide. Humphrey Jennings, who included this passage in 'The Road to San Remo', finely notes what a '*mediaeval* picture Lear's travel journals present – like going into the *past* – the "incommodo" and cut-offness of most of the people'. This sometimes finds expression in a piercingly heightened sense of the kindness and hospitality of strangers in far-off places, as in this short paragraph:

> I wandered down to the river Liris, through a beautiful oak wood; dwelling much on the memory of such frequent hospitalities; such warm-hearted people; such primitive mountain homes. (*Illustrated Excursions*)

The Albanian journals are particularly interesting for the encounters between a predominantly Moslem culture and an undogmatically Christian author. Lear was sometimes militantly anti-clerical, sounding in one passage of his journals like Shelley or Blake – 'for in all ages the Priest has been the advocate of lying, the promoter of darkness and hatred, the antagonist of light and progress'; but he was generally respectful of the varieties of religious faith, including both Islam and Judaism. In one astonishing incident in Elbassán, a religious clash born of the Islamic prohibition on figurative art dissolves into wild laughter:

> when I had sketched such of the principal buildings as they could recognize, a universal shout of 'Shaitan!' ['Devil!'] burst from the crowd; and, strange to relate, the greater part of the mob put their fingers into their mouths and whistled furiously, after the manner of butcher-boys in England. Whether this was a sort of spell against my magic I do not know; but the absurdity of sitting still on a rampart to make a drawing, while a great crowd of people whistled at me with all their might, struck me so forcibly that, come what might of it, I could not resist going off into convulsions of laughter, an impulse the Gheghes seemed to sympathize with, as one and all shrieked with delight, and the ramparts resounded with hilarious merriment. (*Journals in Albania, Etc.*)

For an epileptic to use the phrase 'convulsions of laughter' shows the high-wrought pitch of this moment, and 'shrieked with delight' has an alarming intensity, but it is an extraordinary evocation of absurdity producing sympathy. Other moments of cultural friendship also emerge from Lear's ability to imagine, as if he were an outsider to himself, what he looks like:

> We halted at the *khan* of Episkopí, close to a stream full of capital watercresses which I began to gather and eat with some bread and cheese, an act which provoked the Epirote bystanders of the village to ecstatic laughter and curiosity... One brought a thistle, a second a collection of sticks and wood, a third some grass; a fourth presented me with a fat grasshopper – the whole scene was acted amid shouts of laughter, in which I joined as loudly as any. We parted amazingly good friends, and the wits of Episkopí will long remember the Frank who fed on weeds out of the water. (*Journals in Albania, Etc.*)

Here he is the eccentric old man of the limericks, and 'they' humour him, enjoying the presence of the foreign creature and his nonsensical diet.

A number of the best moments in the journals involve wildlife, often in literal or metaphorical collision with the human.

Something falls on his head in an Albanian khan: 'flomp – miaw – fizz! – an accidental cat had tumbled from some unexplored height'. 'Flomp – miaw – fizz'! Has anybody better caught the essence of falling cat? Or of moths – 'big frizzly moths, bustling into my eyes and face'? Or of dignified absurdity – 'a solitary elder sits, in the enjoyment of tobacco and serenity, and looking in his blue and yellow robes very like an encaged macaw'? These examples all come from the Albania journal; in the Calabrian one we are asked 'Does a mullet plough? Can a prawn give milk?', questions of the sort more usually found in schoolbooks, with the answer no, or in nonsense writing, with the answer yes. One of the touching encounters in Corsica involves a solemn goatherd boy who wants to reciprocate the kindness of Lear, who had given him two loaves of bread:

> 'Perhaps,' says he, 'you might be pleased to know the names of my goats: one is Black-nose, another Silver-spot, that is Grey-foot, and this is Cippo. Cippo is quite the best goat in these parts, and likes to be talked to – *come un Cristiano* – just like a Christian – perhaps even, if you stand still, she may let you scratch the end of her nose and I will call her at once if you choose to try.'

'The children are grave and thinking little animals', he wrote to Emily Tennyson, about his Corsican travels. Lear's humanity often emerges from his sense of a creatureliness we share across cultures.

'By degrees I want to topographize and typographize all the journeyings of my life', he wrote to Lady Waldegrave on 9 January 1868. He did not do so, and left many of his journals to the care of his executor and friend Franklin Lushington without having published them or prepared them for the press. Some of the travel writings have been edited and published since his death, notably the journals in Crete and India, but this edition has chosen to represent Lear as travel writer only by what he published in his lifetime. There has been one exception to the rule, the 'Journey to Petra', which was published with an introduction by Lushington, and with his authority, in *Macmillan's Magazine* in 1897. Lear's letters and unpublished journals are full of interest and offer many pleasures, but the guiding editorial principle in this book has been to represent his writings as they might have been seen by his contemporaries.

Note on the Text

The selection of nonsense writings follows the texts and the chronology used in Vivien Noakes's 2001 Penguin edition of Lear's *Complete Verse and Other Nonsense*. Excerpts from the travel journals are taken from the first editions: some of the punctuation conventions (mainly for quotations and parentheses) have been modernized, and the italicizing of foreign words and phrases has been standardized. Dates have been added at the start of journal entries, and locations when these are not obviously specified. Sets of four asterisks signify passages omitted from within a single journal entry. A few of the place-names occur in different versions: Lear was not completely consistent in his use of place-names, and many of these changed both within his time and between his time and now, especially in the *Journals of a Landscape Painter in Albania, Etc.*

I have arranged the journal extracts as far as I could to give the outlines of a coherent narrative. Footnotes have been kept to a minimum, but none of the travel journals has been edited until now, and I have tried to supply what a modern reader is likely to need to follow the abridged text, and to understand Lear's references to people, places and events. Lear's own footnotes are indicated by superscript numbers, and mine by superscript asterisks.

With the exception of the magazine article 'A Leaf from the Journals of a Landscape Painter', all of the travel excerpts come from illustrated books. This edition reproduces the itinerary maps and one of the lithographs from the *Illustrated Excursions in Italy* and from each of the three *Journals of a Landscape Painter*. It also reproduces the illustrated title-pages of *Views in Rome and its Environs, Illustrated Excursions in Italy* and *Views of the Seven Ionian Islands*. Although the *Views in Rome* and *Views of the Seven Ionian Islands* were essentially books of lithographs, I have included brief excerpts from the accompanying or related texts so as to give a sample of all the travel books Lear published in his lifetime.

Selected Further Reading

Works by Edward Lear

A Book of Nonsense (1846), by 'Derry down Derry', new edition 1855, new enlarged edition 1861
Nonsense Songs, Stories, Botany, and Alphabets (1871)
More Nonsense, Pictures, Rhymes, Botany, Etc. (1872)
Laughable Lyrics, A Fourth Book of Nonsense Poems, Songs, Botany, Music, Etc. (1877)

Views in Rome and its Environs: Drawn from Nature and on Stone (1841)
Illustrated Excursions in Italy (2 volumes, 1846)
Journals of a Landscape Painter in Albania, Etc. (1851)
Journals of a Landscape Painter in Southern Calabria, Etc. (1852)
Views in the Seven Ionian Islands (1863)
Journal of a Landscape Painter in Corsica (1870)

Nonsense Songs and Stories (1895)
Queery Leary Nonsense, edited by Lady Strachey (1911)
Teapots and Quails, edited by Angus Davidson and Philip Hofer (1953)
The Complete Verse and Other Nonsense, edited by Vivien Noakes (2001)

Letters of Edward Lear, edited by Lady Strachey (1907)
Later Letters of Edward Lear, edited by Lady Strachey (1911)
Selected Letters of Edward Lear, edited by Vivien Noakes (1988)

Selected Travel Journals of Edward Lear , edited by Herbert Van Thal (1952)
Edward Lear's Indian Journal, edited by Ray Murphy (1953)
Edward Lear: The Cretan Journal, edited by Rowena Fowler (Athens, 1984)
Edward Lear in the Levant: Travels in Albania, Greece, and Turkey in Europe 1848–1849, edited by Susan Hyman (1988)
Edward Lear: The Corfu Years: A Chronicle Presented through his Letters and Journals, edited by Philip Sherrard (1988)

Works about Lear and Nonsense Writing

Byrom, Thomas, *Nonsense and Wonder: The Poems and Cartoons of Edward Lear* (1977)

Colley, Ann C., *Edward Lear and the Critics* (1993)

Davidson, Angus, *Edward Lear: Landscape Painter and Nonsense Poet* (1938)

Empson, William, *Some Versions of Pastoral* (1935)

Enzensberger, Hans Magnus, *Edward Lears Kompletter Nonsensus* (1977)

Hark, Ina Rae, *Edward Lear* (1982)

Haughton, Hugh, *The Chatto Book of Nonsense Verse* (1989)

Hyman, Susan, *Edward Lear's Birds* (1980)

Lehmann, John, *Edward Lear and his World* (1977)

Lecercle, Jean-Jacques, *Philosophy of Nonsense: The Intuitions of Victorian Nonsense Literature* (1994)

Levi, Peter, *Edward Lear* (1995)

Noakes, Vivien, *Edward Lear 1812–1888* (1985, the catalogue of the Royal Academy exhibition of 1985)

Noakes, Vivien, *Edward Lear: The Life of a Wanderer* (1968, fourth edition 2004)

Noakes, Vivien, *The Painter Edward Lear* (1991)

Pitman, Ruth, *Edward Lear's Tennyson* (1988)

Sewell, Elizabeth, *The Field of Nonsense* (1952)

Nonsense Writings

There was an old Derry down Derry,
Who loved to see little folks merry;
   So he made them a Book,
    And with laughter they shook,
At the fun of that Derry down Derry!

Nonsense Writings

Lear published his first *Book of Nonsense* in 1846 under the pseudonym 'Derry down Derry'. It contained seventy-three illustrated limericks, printed as three-line verses of diminishing length. A second edition came out in 1855, and a third was published under Lear's own name in 1861, adding forty-three new limericks and cancelling three rather fierce ones ('Kildare', 'New York' and the 'Sailor of Compton', all included here).

His next, more miscellaneous nonsense books were *Nonsense Songs, Stories, Botany, and Alphabets* (1871); *More Nonsense, Pictures, Rhymes, Botany, Etc.* (1872), which included one hundred more limericks; and *Laughable Lyrics: A Fourth Book of Nonsense Poems, Songs, Botany, Music, Etc.* (1877). The posthumous collections *Nonsense Songs and Stories* (1895), *Queery Leary Nonsense* (1911), edited by Lady Strachey, and *Teapots and Quails* (1953), edited by Angus Davidson and Philip Hofer, contained some previously unpublished nonsense writings. Vivien Noakes's superb Penguin edition of the *Complete Verse and Other Nonsense* (2001) includes a considerable amount of materials and versions previously uncollected or unpublished.

This selection is arranged chronologically in order of composition, following the sequence suggested by Vivien Noakes.

Eclogue*

Vide Collins 'Hassan – or the Camel Driver'

In dreary silence down the bustling road
The Lears – with all their goods and chattels rode;
Ten carts of moveables went on before,
And in the rear came half-a-dozen more;
A Hackney-coach the Lears themselves enshrouds
To guard them from the gaze of vulgar crowds.
The vehicle has reached the turnpike gate, –
Where wond'ring toll-men, – throngs of people wait; –
The loaded carts their dusty way pursue, –
Shrill squeak the wheels, – dark London was in view.
With grief heart-rending then, those mournful folk
Thrice sighed – thrice wiped their eyes – as thus they spoke:
'Sad was the hour – and luckless was the day
When first from Bowman's Lodge we bent our way! –

'How little half the woes can we foresee,
Of that thrice odious New Street where we flee! –
Bethink thee Mother! – can we ever find
Half room enough for all these goods behind? –
Soon must those carts their precious loads resign, –
Then, what but noise and trouble shall be thine! –
Ye banished furnitures, that once did bear
In our last Halls a more than equal share,
Here, where no dark rooms shew their craving door,
Or mildewed lumberrooms make place for more,
In vain ye hope the comfort – space – to know,
Which dark rooms large or lumberrooms bestow, –
Here closets only – dwarfish rooms are found,
And scanty inconvenience rules around.
Sad was the hour and luckless was the day
When first from Bowman's Lodge we bent our way!
'What noisome thought could urge our parents so –

---

*   Lear's earliest surviving poem, written when he was 13. It is closely modelled
     on William Collins's 'Hassan – or the Camel Driver' (1742), also 86 lines long.
     The Lears had been forced by financial difficulties to leave the family home,
     Bowman's Lodge in Highgate.

To leave the country and to London go!
The rural scene to change for houses, brown,
And barter health for the thick smoke of town!
What demon tempts him from our home to go
In horrid New Street to pour forth our woe? –
Oft – oft we've hoped this hour we ne'er might see,
Yet London – now at last we come to thee!
Oh! why was New Street so attractive made, –
Or why our Dad so easily betrayed?
Why heed we not as swift we ride along
The farewell peal of Highgate bells ding dong, –
Or wherefore think the flowery hedges hide, –
The grunting pigs, and fowls in speckled pride?
Why think we these less pleasing to behold
Than dirty streets which lead to houses old!
Sad was the hour and luckless was the day
When first from Bowman's Lodge we bent our way!

'Oh! cease our fears! all grumbling as we go,
While thought creates unnumbered scenes of woe, –
What if the mobs in all their ire we meet!
Oft in the dust we trace their crowded feet, –
And fearful – oft when day's November light
Yields up her yellow reign to gas-lit night,
By mischief roused they scour the streets, and fly,
While radical reform is all they cry:
Before them Death with fire directs their way,
Fills the loud yell and guides them to their prey.
Sad was the hour and luckless was the day
When first from Bowman's Lodge we bent our way.

'At that dread hour the noise of fire shall sweep –
If aught of rest we find, upon our sleep,
Or some rude thief bounce through the window – smash –
And wake our dozings with a hideous crash,
Thrice happy they – the Catharine Street poor –
From wish of town – from dread of fire secure!
They tempt no New Street, and no thieves they find! –
No carts of goods have they – before – behind! –
Sad was the hour and luckless was the day
When first from Bowman's Lodge we bent our way!

'Oh! Hapless Lears! – for that your care hath won, –
The large sidegarden will be most undone! –
Big swelled our hearts, on this same mournful day
When low the plants drooped down – as thus they seemed to
                                                        say; –
"Farewell! ye Lears whom fruits could not detain! –
Whom flowrets drooping buds implored in vain! –
Yet as ye go may every blow fall down,
Weak as those buds on each receiving crown, –
So may ye see nor care – nor grievous fuss, –
Nor e're be cast to earth – to die like us! –"
Ah! might we safely to our home return –
Say to our garden – "Cease – no longer mourn! –"
Ah! might we teach our hearts to lose their fears,
And linger there our yet remaining years!'
They said – and ceased: lamenting o'er the day,
When first from Bowman's Lodge they bent their way.

'When the light dies away on a calm summer's eve'

When the light dies away on a calm summer's eve
And the sunbeams grow faint and more faint in the west,
How we love to look on, till the last trace they leave
Glows alone like a blush upon modesty's breast! –
Lonely streak! dearer far than the glories of day
Seems thy beauty – 'mid silence and shadow enshrined, –
More bright as its loneliness passes away –
And leaves twilight in desolate grandeur behind! –
So when grief has made lonely and blighted our lot,
And her icy cold chain o'er our spirits has cast,
Will not memory oft turn to some thrice hallowed spot,
That shines out like a star among years that are past?
Some dream that will wake in a desolate heart,
Every chord into music that long has been hushed,
Mournful echo! – soon still – for it tolls with a smart,
That the joys which first woke it, are long ago crushed!

Ode to the little China Man

Who art thou – sweet little China Man? –
    Your name I want to know
With your lovely face so pale and wan –
    With a high diddle diddledy do. –

Your high cheek bones: – your screwed up mouth,
    How beautiful they be! –
And your eyes that ogle from north to south,
    With a high diddle diddledy dee! –

And your cultivated eyebrows too! –
    That depend from either eye! –
(I'm sure it's a fashion entirely new!) –
    With a high diddle diddledy di! –

But ev'ry one – (as the Frenchman said) –
    Ev'ry one to his way, –
(When he boiled in a pipkin his grandmother's head,)
    With a high diddle diddledy da! –

Int'resting Mortal! – Whence art thou? –
    In figure surpassed by few! –
Tell us thy name – is it 'Chum-chu-wow'? –
    With a high diddle diddledy du? –

The little man fetched a sort of a sneer –
    As he made his sage reply –
While he twisted his eyebrow round his ear,
    With a high diddle diddledy dy. –

'Good folks' – (and he shook his noddle-ding-dong)
    'It's enough for you to know –
That in spite of my eyebrows – two feet long –
    I'm Miss Eliza's beau!!' –*

---

*   The poem was written for Eliza Drewitt, probably in 1830.

The Hens of Oripò*

The agèd hens of Oripò,
    They tempt the stormy sea;
Black, white and brown, they spread their wings,
    And o'er the waters flee;
And when a little fish they clutch
    Athwart the wave so blue,
They utter forth a joyful note, –
    A cock-a-doodle-doo!
O! Oo! Oripò – Oo! the hens of Oripò!

The crafty hens of Oripò,
    They wander on the shore,
Where shrimps and winkles pick they up,
    And carry home a store;
For barley, oats, or golden corn,
    To eat they never wish,
All vegetably food they scorn,
    And only seek for fish.
O! Oo! Oripò – Oo! the hens of Oripò!

The wily hens of Oripò,
    Black, white and brown and gray,
They don't behave like other hens;
    In any decent way.
They lay their eggs among the rocks,
    Instead of in the straw,
. . . .
    . . . .
O! Oo! Oripò – Oo! the hens of Oripò!

The nasty hens of Oripò,
    With ill-conditioned zeal,
All fish defunct they gobble up,
    At morn or evening meal.
Whereby their eggs, as now we find,

. . . .

A fishlike ancient smell and taste
    Unpleasant cloth pervade.
O! Oo! Oripò – Oo! the hens of Oripò!

---

* An unfinished poem, written on 16 June 1848, during Lear's Greek tour. 'Oripò'
is the Euripos, the narrow waterway between Euboea and mainland Greece.

Limericks from A Book of Nonsense *(1846 and 1855)*

There was a Young Lady of Bute,
Who played on a silver-gilt flute;
She played several jigs, to her uncle's white pigs,
That amusing Young Lady of Bute.

There was an Old Person of Chester,
Whom several small children did pester;
They threw some large stones, which broke most of his bones,
And displeased that Old Person of Chester.

There was a Young Lady whose eyes,
Were unique as to colour and size;
When she opened them wide, people all turned aside,
And started away in surprise.

There was an Old Man of Berlin,
Whose form was uncommonly thin;
Till he once, by mistake, was mixed up in a cake,
So they baked that Old Man of Berlin.

There was an Old Person of Tartary,
Who divided his jugular artery;
But he screeched to his wife, and she said, 'Oh, my life!
Your death will be felt by all Tartary!'

There was an Old Man of Corfu,
Who never knew what he should do;
So he rushed up and down, till the sun made him brown,
That bewildered Old Man of Corfu.

There was a Young Lady of Tyre,
Who swept the loud chords of a lyre;
At the sound of each sweep, she enraptured the deep,
And enchanted the city of Tyre.

There was a Young Lady of Hull,
Who was chased by a virulent Bull;
But she seized on a spade, and called out – 'Who's afraid!'
Which distracted that virulent Bull.

There was an Old Person of Gretna,
Who rushed down the crater of Etna;
When they said, 'Is it hot?' He replied, 'No, it's not!'
That mendacious Old Person of Gretna.

There was an Old Man of Peru,
Who never knew what he should do;
So he tore off his hair, and behaved like a bear,
That intrinsic Old Man of Peru.

There was a Young Lady of Troy,
Whom several large flies did annoy;
Some she killed with a thump, some she drowned at the pump,
And some she took with her to Troy.

There was a Young Lady of Norway,
Who casually sat in a doorway;
When the door squeezed her flat, she exclaimed, 'What of that?'
This courageous Young Lady of Norway.

There was a Young Lady of Sweden,
Who went by the slow train to Weedon;
When they cried, 'Weedon Station!' she made no observation,
But thought she should go back to Sweden.

There was an Old Person of Ischia,
Whose conduct grew friskier and friskier;
He danced hornpipes and jigs, and ate thousands of figs,
That lively Old Person of Ischia.

There was an Old Person of Troy,
Whose drink was warm brandy and soy;
Which he took with a spoon, by the light of the moon,
In sight of the city of Troy.

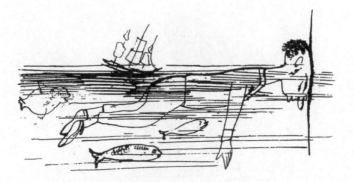

There was an Old Sailor of Compton,
Whose vessel a rock it once bump'd on;
The shock was so great, that it damaged the pate
Of that singular Sailor of Compton.

There was a Young Lady of Dorking,
Who bought a large bonnet for walking;
But its colour and size, so bedazzled her eyes,
That she very soon went back to Dorking.

There was an Old Man of Cape Horn,
Who wished he had never been born;
So he sat on a chair, till he died of despair,
That dolorous Man of Cape Horn.

There was an Old Man of New York,
Who murdered himself with a fork;
But nobody cried though he very soon died, –
For that silly Old Man of New York.

There was an Old Man of the Nile,
Who sharpened his nails with a file;
Till he cut off his thumbs, and said calmly, 'This comes –
Of sharpening one's nails with a file!'

There was a Young Lady of Parma,
Whose conduct grew calmer and calmer;
When they said, 'Are you dumb?' she merely said, 'Hum!'
That provoking Young Lady of Parma.

There was an Old Man of Kildare,
Who climbed into a very high chair;
When he said, –'Here I stays, – till the end of my days,'
That immovable Man of Kildare.

There was an Old Person whose legs,
Bore a striking resemblance to pegs;
When they said, 'Can you toddle?' he answered – 'I waddle,
What else *should* I do with my legs?'

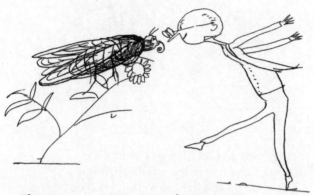

There was an Old Person who said, 'See!
I have found a most beautiful bee!'
When they said, 'Does it buzz?' he answered, 'It *does*,
I never beheld such a bee!'

There was an Old Person whose mirth,
Induced him to leap from the earth;
But in leaping too quick, he exclaimed 'I'm too sick
To leap any more from the earth.'

There was an Old Man who said 'O! –
Let us come where the humble bees grow!
There are no less than five sitting still on a hive,
Singing songs to their children below.'

Limericks from A Book of Nonsense *(1861)*

There was an Old Man with a beard,
Who said, 'It is just as I feared! –
Two Owls and a Hen, four Larks and a Wren,
Have all built their nests in my beard!'

There was a Young Lady whose bonnet,
Came untied when the birds sate upon it;
But she said, 'I don't care! all the birds in the air
Are welcome to sit on my bonnet!'

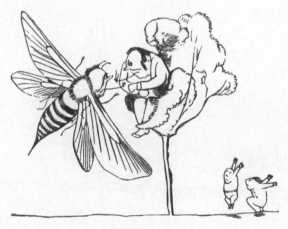

There was an Old Man in a tree,
Who was horribly bored by a Bee;
When they said, 'Does it buzz?' he replied, 'Yes it does!
It's a regular brute of a Bee!'

There was a Young Lady of Portugal,
Whose ideas were excessively nautical;
She climbed up a tree, to examine the sea,
But declared she would never leave Portugal.

There was an Old Person of Philæ,
Whose conduct was scroobious and wily;
He rushed up a Palm, when the weather was calm,
And observed all the ruins of Philæ.

There was a Young Lady of Lucca,
Whose lovers completely forsook her;
She ran up a tree, and said, 'Fiddle-de-dee!'
Which embarrassed the people of Lucca.

There was an Old Person of Cromer,
Who stood on one leg to read Homer;
When he found he grew stiff, he jumped over the cliff,
Which concluded that Person of Cromer.

There was an Old Man of Whitehaven,
Who danced a quadrille with a Raven;
But they said – 'It's absurd, to encourage this bird!'
So they smashed that Old Man of Whitehaven.

There was an Old Man who said, 'Hush!
I perceive a young bird in this bush!'
When they said –'Is it small?' He replied –'Not at all!
It is four times as big as the bush!'

There was an Old Person of Anerly,
Whose conduct was strange and unmannerly;
He rushed down the Strand, with a Pig in each hand,
But returned in the evening to Anerly.

There was an Old Man who said, 'Well!
Will *nobody* answer this bell?
I have pulled day and night, till my hair has grown white,
But nobody answers this bell!'

'She sits upon her Bulbul'

She sits upon her Bulbul
    Through the long long hours of night –
And o'er the dark horizon gleams
    The Yashmack's fitful light.
The lone Yaourt sails slowly down
    The deep and craggy dell –
And from his lofty nest, loud screams
    The white-plumed Asphodel.

The Duck and the Kangaroo

Said the Duck to the Kangaroo,
    'Good gracious! how you hop!
Over the fields and the water too,
    As if you never would stop!
My life is a bore in this nasty pond,
And I long to go out in the world beyond!
    I wish I could hop like you!'
    Said the Duck to the Kangaroo.

'Please give me a ride on your back!'
    Said the Duck to the Kangaroo.
'I would sit quite still, and say nothing but "Quack,"
    The whole of the long day through!
And we'd go to the Dee, and the Jelly Bo Lee,
Over the land, and over the sea; –
    Please take me a ride! O do!'
    Said the Duck to the Kangaroo.

Said the Kangaroo to the Duck,
  'This requires some little reflection;
Perhaps on the whole it might bring me luck,
  And there seems but one objection,
Which is, if you'll let me speak so bold,
Your feet are unpleasantly wet and cold,
  And would probably give me the roo-
  matiz!' said the Kangaroo.

Said the Duck, 'As I sate on the rocks,
  I have thought over that completely,
And I bought four pairs of worsted socks
  Which fit my web-feet neatly.
And to keep out the cold I've bought a cloak,
And every day a cigar I'll smoke,
  All to follow my own dear true
  Love of a Kangaroo!'

Said the Kangaroo, 'I'm ready!
   All in the moonlight pale;
But to balance me well, dear Duck, sit steady!
   And quite at the end of my tail!'
So away they went with a hop and a bound,
And they hopped the whole world three times round;
   And who so happy, – O who,
   As the Duck and the Kangaroo?

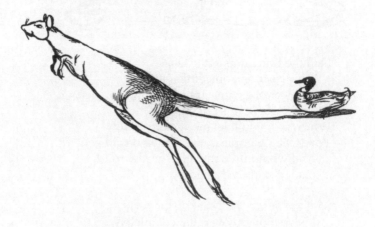

The Story of the Four Little Children Who Went Round the World

Once upon a time, a long while ago, there were four little people whose names were

VIOLET,   SLINGSBY,   GUY, and LIONEL;

and they all thought they should like to see the world. So they bought a large boat to sail quite round the world by sea, and then they were to come back on the other side by land. The boat was painted blue with green spots, and the sail was yellow with red stripes; and when they set off, they only took a small Cat to steer and look after the boat, besides an elderly Quangle-Wangle, who had to cook the dinner and make the tea; for which purposes they took a large kettle.

For the first ten days they sailed on beautifully, and found plenty to eat, as there were lots of fish, and they had only to take them out of the sea with a long spoon, when the Quangle-Wangle instantly cooked them, and the Pussy-cat was fed with the bones, with which she expressed herself pleased on the whole, so that all the party were very happy.

During the day-time, Violet chiefly occupied herself in putting saltwater into a churn, while her three brothers churned it violently, in the hope that it would turn into butter, which it seldom, if ever did; and in the evening they all retired into the Tea-kettle, where they all managed to sleep very comfortably, while Pussy and the Quangle-Wangle managed the boat.

After a time they saw some land at a distance; and when they came to it, they found it was an island made of water quite surrounded by earth. Besides that, it was bordered by evanescent isthmusses with a great Gulf-stream running about all over it, so that it was perfectly beautiful, and contained only a single tree, 503 feet high.

When they had landed, they walked about, but found to their great surprise, that the island was quite full of veal-cutlets and chocolate-drops, and nothing else. So they all climbed up the single high tree to discover, if possible, if there were any people; but having remained on the top of the tree for a week, and not seeing anybody, they naturally concluded that there were no inhabitants, and accordingly when they came down, they loaded the boat with two thousand veal-cutlets and a million of chocolate drops, and these afforded them sustenance for more than a month, during which time they pursued their voyage with the utmost delight and apathy.

After this they came to a shore where there were no less than sixty-five great red parrots with blue tails, sitting on a rail all of a row, and all fast asleep. And I am sorry to say that the Pussy-cat and the Quangle-Wangle crept softly and bit off the tail-feathers of all the sixty-five parrots, for which Violet reproved them both severely.

Notwithstanding which, she proceeded to insert all the feathers, two hundred and sixty in number, in her bonnet, thereby causing it to have a lovely and glittering appearance, highly prepossessing and efficacious.

The next thing that happened to them was in a narrow part of the sea, which was so entirely full of fishes that the boat could go on no further; so they remained there about six weeks, till they had eaten nearly all the fishes, which were Soles, and all ready-cooked and covered with shrimp sauce, so that there was no trouble whatever. And as the few fishes who remained uneaten complained of the cold, as well as of the difficulty they had in getting any sleep on account of the extreme noise  made by the Arctic Bears and the Tropical Turnspits which frequented the neighbourhood in great numbers, Violet most amiably knitted a small woollen frock for several of the fishes, and Slingsby administered some opium drops to them, through which kindness they became quite warm and slept soundly.

Then they came to a country which was wholly covered with immense Orange-trees of a vast size, and quite full of fruit. So they all landed, taking with them the Tea-kettle, intending to gather some of the Oranges and place them in it. But while they were busy about this, a most dreadfully high wind rose, and blew out most of the Parrot-tail feathers from Violet's bonnet. That, however, was nothing compared with the calamity of the Oranges falling down on their heads by millions and millions, which thumped and bumped and bumped and thumped them all so seriously that they were obliged to run as hard as they could for their lives, besides that the sound of the Oranges rattling on the Tea-kettle was of the most fearful and amazing nature.

Nevertheless they got safely to the boat, although considerably vexed and hurt; and the Quangle-Wangle's right foot was so knocked about, that he had to sit with his head in his slipper for at least a week.

This event made them all for a time rather melancholy, and

perhaps they might never have become less so, had not Lionel with a most praiseworthy devotion and perseverance, continued to stand on one leg and whistle to them in a loud and lively manner, which diverted the whole party so extremely, that they gradually recovered their spirits, and agreed that whenever they should reach home they would subscribe towards a testimonial to Lionel, entirely made of Gingerbread and Raspberries, as an earnest token of their sincere and grateful infection.

After sailing on calmly for several more days, they came to another country, where they were much pleased and surprised to

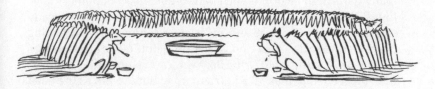

see a countless multitude of white Mice with red eyes, all sitting in a great circle, slowly eating Custard Pudding with the most satisfactory and polite demeanour.

And as the Four Travellers were rather hungry, being tired of eating nothing but Soles and Oranges for so long a period, they held a council as to the propriety of asking the Mice for some of their Pudding in a humble and affecting manner, by which they could hardly be otherwise than gratified. It was agreed therefore that Guy should go and ask the Mice, which he immediately did; and the result was that they gave [him] a Walnut-shell only half full of Custard diluted with water. Now, this displeased Guy, who said, 'Out of such a lot of Pudding as you have got, I must say you might have spared a somewhat larger quantity!' But no sooner had he finished speaking than all the Mice turned round at once, and sneezed at him in an appalling and vindictive manner, (and it is

impossible to imagine a more scroobious and unpleasant sound than that caused by the simultaneous sneezing of many millions of angry Mice,) so that Guy rushed back to the boat, having first shied his cap into the middle of the Custard Pudding, by which means he completely spoiled the Mice's dinner.

By-and-by the Four Children came to a country where there were no houses, but only an incredibly innumerable number of large bottles without corks, and of a dazzling and sweetly susceptible blue colour. Each of these blue bottles contained a Blue-Bottle-Fly, and all these interesting animals live continually together in the most copious and rural harmony, nor perhaps in many parts of the world is such perfect and abject happiness to be found. Violet, and Slingsby, and Guy, and Lionel, were greatly struck with this singular and instructive settlement, and having previously asked permission of the Blue-Bottle-Flies (which was most courteously granted), the Boat was drawn up to the shore and they proceeded to make tea in front of the Bottles; but as they had no tea-leaves, they merely placed some pebbles in the hot water,

and the Quangle-Wangle played some tunes over it on an Accordion, by which of course tea was made directly, and of the very best quality.

The Four Children then entered into conversation with the Blue-Bottle-Flies, who discoursed in a placid and genteel manner, though with a slightly buzzing accent, chiefly owing to the fact that they each held a small clothes-brush between their teeth which naturally occasioned a fizzy extraneous utterance.

'Why,' said Violet, 'would you kindly inform us, do you reside in bottles? and if in bottles at all, why not rather in green or purple, or indeed in yellow bottles?'

To which questions a very aged Blue-Bottle-Fly answered, 'We found the bottles here all ready to live in, that is to say, our great-great-great-great-great-grandfathers did, so we occupied them at once. And when the winter comes on, we turn the bottles upside-down, and consequently rarely feel the cold at all, and you know very well that this could not be the case with bottles of any other colour than blue.'

'Of course it could not,' said Slingsby, 'but if we may take the liberty of inquiring, on what do you chiefly subsist?'

'Mainly on Oyster-patties,' said the Blue-Bottle-Fly, 'and, when these are scarce, on Raspberry Vinegar and Russian leather boiled down to a jelly.'

'How delicious!' said Guy.

To which Lionel added, 'Huzz!' and all the Blue-Bottle-Flies said 'Buzz!'

At this time, an elderly Fly said it was the hour for the Evening-song to be sung; and on a signal being given all the Blue-Bottle-Flies began to buzz at once in a sumptuous and sonorous manner, the melodious and mucilaginous sounds echoing all over the waters, and resounding across the tumultuous tops of the transitory Titmice upon the intervening and verdant mountains, with a serene and sickly suavity only known to the truly virtuous. The Moon was shining slobaciously from the star-bespringled sky, while her light irrigated the smooth and shiny sides and wings and backs of the Blue-Bottle-Flies with a peculiar and trivial splendour, while all nature cheerfully responded to the cerulæan and conspicuous circumstances.

In many long-after years, the Four little Travellers looked back to that evening as one of the happiest in all their lives, and it was already past midnight, when – the Sail of the Boat having been set up by the Quangle-Wangle, the Tea-kettle and Churn placed in their respective positions, and the Pussy-cat stationed at the Helm – the Children each took a last and affectionate farewell of the Blue-Bottle-Flies, who walked down in a body to the water's edge to see the Travellers embark.

As a token of parting respect and esteem, Violet made a curtsey quite down to the ground, and stuck one of her few remaining

Parrot-tail feathers into the back hair of the most pleasing of the Blue-Bottle-Flies, while Slingsby, Guy, and Lionel offered them three small boxes, containing respectively, Black Pins, Dried Figs, and Epsom Salts: and thus they left that happy shore for ever.

Overcome by their feelings, the Four little Travellers instantly jumped into the Tea-kettle, and fell fast asleep. But all along the shore for many hours there was distinctly heard a sound of severely suppressed sobs, and of a vague multitude of living creatures using their pocket-handkerchiefs in a subdued simultaneous snuffle – lingering sadly along the wallopping waves as the boat sailed farther and farther away from the Land of the Happy Blue-Bottle-Flies.

Nothing particular occurred for some days after these events, except that as the Travellers were passing a low tract of sand, they perceived an unusual and gratifying spectacle, namely, a large number of Crabs and Crawfish – perhaps six or seven hundred – sitting by the water-side, and endeavouring to disentangle a vast heap of pale pink worsted, which they moistened at intervals with a fluid composed of Lavender-water and White-wine Negus.

'Can we be of any service to you, O crusty Crabbies?' said the Four Children.

'Thank you kindly,' said the Crabs, consecutively. 'We are trying to make some worsted Mittens, but do not know how.'

On which Violet, who was perfectly acquainted with the art of mitten-making, said to the Crabs, 'Do your claws unscrew, or are they fixtures?'

'They are all made to unscrew,' said the Crabs, and forthwith they deposited a great pile of claws close to the boat, with which Violet uncombed all the pale pink worsted, and then made the loveliest Mittens with it you can imagine. These the Crabs, having resumed and screwed on their claws, placed cheerfully upon their wrists, and walked away rapidly on their hind-legs, warbling songs with a silvery voice and in a minor key.

After this the Four little People sailed on again till they came to a vast and wide plain of astonishing dimensions, on which nothing whatever could be discovered at first; but as the Travellers walked onward, there appeared in the extreme and dim distance a single object, which on a nearer approach and on an accurately cutaneous inspection, seemed to be somebody in a large white wig sitting on an arm-chair made of Sponge Cakes and Oyster-shells. 'It does not quite look like a human being,' said Violet, doubtfully; nor could they make out what it really was, till the Quangle-Wangle (who had previously been round the world), exclaimed softly in a loud voice, 'It is the Co-operative Cauliflower!'

And so in truth it was, and they soon found that what they had taken for an immense wig was in reality the top of the cauliflower, and that he had no feet at all, being able to walk tolerably well with a fluctuating and graceful movement on a single cabbage stalk, an accomplishment which naturally saved him the expense of stockings and shoes.

Presently, while the whole party from the boat was gazing at him with mingled affection and disgust, he suddenly arose, and in a somewhat plumdomphious manner hurried off towards the setting sun, – his legs supported by two superincumbent confidential cucumbers, and a large number of Waterwagtails

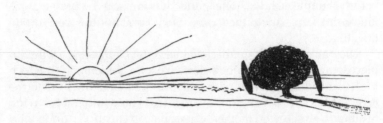

proceeding in advance of him by three-and-three in a row – till he finally disappeared on the brink of the western sky in a crystal cloud of sudorific sand.

So remarkable a sight of course impressed the Four Children very deeply; and they returned immediately to their boat with a strong sense of undeveloped asthma and a great appetite.

Shortly after this the Travellers were obliged to sail directly below some high overhanging rocks, from the top of one of which, a particularly odious little boy, dressed in rose-coloured knickerbockers, and with a pewter plate upon his head, threw an enormous Pumpkin at the boat, by which it was instantly upset.

But this upsetting was of no consequence, because all the party knew how to swim very well, and in fact they preferred swimming about till after the moon rose, when the water growing chilly, they sponge-taneously entered the boat. Meanwhile the Quangle-Wangle threw back the Pumpkin with immense force, so that it hit the rocks where the malicious little boy in rose-coloured knickerbockers was sitting, when, being quite full of Lucifer-matches, the Pumpkin exploded surreptitiously into a thousand bits, whereon the rocks instantly took fire, and the odious little boy became unpleasantly hotter and hotter and hotter, till his knickerbockers were turned quite green, and his nose was burned off.

Two or three days after this had happened, they came to another place, where they found nothing at all except some wide and deep pits full of Mulberry Jam. This is the property of the tiny Yellow-nosed Apes who abound in these districts, and who store up the Mulberry Jam for their food in winter, when they mix it with pellucid pale periwinkle soup, and serve it out in Wedgwood China bowls, which grow freely all over that part of the country. Only one of the Yellow-nosed Apes was on the spot, and he was fast asleep: yet the Four Travellers and the Quangle-Wangle and Pussy were so terrified by the violence and sanguinary sound of his snoring, that they merely took a small cupful of the Jam, and returned to re-embark in their Boat without delay.

What was their horror on seeing the boat (including the Churn and the Tea-kettle), in the mouth of an enormous Seeze Pyder, an aquatic and ferocious creature truly dreadful to behold, and happily only met with in these excessive longitudes. In a moment the beautiful boat was bitten into fifty-five-thousand-million-hundred-billion bits; and it instantly became quite clear that Violet, Slingsby, Guy, and Lionel could no longer preliminate their voyage by sea.

The Four Travellers were therefore obliged to resolve on pursuing their wanderings by land, and very fortunately there happened to pass by at that moment, an elderly Rhinoceros, on which they seized; and all four mounting on his back, the Quangle-Wangle sitting on his horn and holding on by his ears, the Pussy-cat swinging at the end of his tail, they set off, having only four small beans and three pounds of mashed potatoes to last through their whole journey.

They were, however, able to catch numbers of the chickens and turkeys, and other birds who incessantly alighted on the head of the Rhinoceros for the purpose of gathering the seeds of the rhododendron plants which grew there, and these creatures they cooked in the most translucent and satisfactory manner, by means of a fire lighted on the end of the Rhinoceros' back. A crowd of Kangaroos and Gigantic Cranes accompanied them, from feelings of curiosity and complacency, so that they were never at a loss for company, and went onward as it were in a sort of profuse and triumphant procession.

Thus, in less than eighteen weeks, they all arrived safely at home, where they were received by their admiring relatives with joy tempered with contempt; and where they finally resolved to carry out the rest of their travelling plans at some more favourable opportunity.

As for the Rhinoceros, in token of their grateful adherence, they had him killed and stuffed directly, and then set him up outside the door of their father's house as a Diaphanous Doorscraper.

Growling Eclogue

Composed at Cannes, December 8th, 1867

(Interlocutors – Mr Lear and Mr and Mrs Symonds)*

Edwardus – What makes you look so black, so glum, so cross?
        Is it neuralgia, headache, or remorse?

Johannes – What makes you look as cross, or even more so?
        Less like a man than is a broken Torso?

E. – What if my life is odious, should I grin?
     If you are savage, need I care a pin?

J. – And if I suffer, am I then an owl?
    May I not frown and grind my teeth and growl?

E. – Of course you may; but may not I growl too?
    May I not frown and grind my teeth like you?

J. – See Catherine comes! To her, to her,
    Let each his several miseries refer;
    She shall decide whose woes are least or worst,
    And which, as growler, shall rank last or first.

Catherine – Proceed to growl, in silence I'll attend,
        And hear your foolish growlings to the end;
        And when they're done, I shall correctly judge
        Which of your griefs are real or only fudge.
        Begin, let each his mournful voice prepare,
        (And, pray, however angry, do not swear!)

J. – We came abroad for warmth, and find sharp cold!
    Cannes is an imposition, and we're sold.

E. – Why did I leave my native land, to find
    Sharp hailstones, snow, and most disgusting wind?

---

* John Addington Symonds and Catherine Symonds (who appear also in the
Journal of a Landscape Painter in Corsica – see below, p. 311).

J. – What boots it that we orange trees or lemons see,
      If we must suffer from *such* vile inclemency?

E. – Why did I take the lodgings I have got,
      Where all I don't want is: – all I want not?

J. – Last week I called aloud, O! O! O! O!
      The ground is wholly overspread with snow!
      Is that at any rate a theme for mirth
      Which makes a sugar-cake of all the earth?

E. – Why must I sneeze and snuffle, groan and cough,
      If my hat's on my head, or if it's off?
      Why must I sink all poetry in this prose,
      The everlasting blowing of my nose?

J. – When I walk out the mud my footsteps clogs,
      Besides, I suffer from attacks of dogs.

E. – Me a vast awful bulldog, black and brown,
      Completely terrified when near the town;
      As calves, perceiving butchers, trembling reel,
      So did *my* calves the approaching monster feel.

J. – Already from two rooms we're driven away,
      Because the beastly chimneys smoke all day:
      Is this a trifle, say? Is this a joke?
      That we, like hams, should be becooked in smoke?

E. – Say! what avails it that my servant speaks
      Italian, English, Arabic, and Greek,
      Besides Albanian: if he don't speak French,
      How can he ask for salt, or shrimps, or tench?

J. – When on the foolish hearth fresh wood I place,
      It whistles, sings, and squeaks, before my face:
      And if it does unless the fire burns bright,
      And if it does, yet squeaks, how can I write?

E. – Alas! I needs must go and call on swells,
      That they may say, 'Pray draw me the Estrelles.'*

---

* 'Estrelles': hills above Cannes.

On one I went last week to leave a card,
The swell was out – the servant eyed me hard:
'This chap's a thief disguised,' his face expressed:
If I go there again, may I be blest!

J. – Why must I suffer in this wind and gloom?
Roomattics in a vile cold attic room?

E. – Swells drive about the road with haste and fury,
As Jehu drove about all over Jewry.
Just now, while walking slowly, I was all but
Run over by the Lady Emma Talbot,
Whom not long since a lovely babe I knew,
With eyes and cap-ribbons of perfect blue.

J. – Downstairs and upstairs, every blessed minute,
There's each room with pianofortes in it.
How can I write with noises such as those?
And, being always discomposed, compose?

E. – Seven Germans through my garden lately strayed,
And all on instruments of torture played;
They blew, they screamed, they yelled: how can I paint
Unless my room is quiet, which it ain't?

J. – How can I study if a hundred flies
Each moment blunder into both my eyes?

E. – How can I draw with green or blue or red,
If flies and beetles vex my old bald head?

J. – How can I translate German Metaphys-
ics, if mosquitoes round my forehead whizz?

E. – I've bought some bacon, (though it's much too fat,)
But round the house there prowls a hideous cat:
Once should I see my bacon in her mouth,
What care I if my rooms look north or south?

J. – Pain from a pane in one cracked window comes,
Which sings and whistles, buzzes, shrieks and hums;

In vain amain with pain the pane with this chord
I fain would strain to stop the beastly *dis*cord!

E. – If rain and wind and snow and such like ills
Continue here, how shall I pay my bills?
For who through cold and slush and rain will come
To see my drawings and to purchase some?
And if they don't, what destiny is mine?
How can I ever get to Palestine?

J. – The blinding sun strikes through the olive trees,
When I walk out, and always makes me sneeze.

E. – Next door, if all night long the moon is shining,
There sits a dog, who wakes me up with whining.

Cath. – Forbear! You both are bores, you've growled enough:
No longer will I listen to such stuff!
All men have nuisances and bores to afflict 'um:
Hark then, and bow to my official dictum!

For you, Johannes, there is most excuse,
(Some interruptions are the very deuce,)
You're younger than the other cove, who surely
Might have some sense – besides, you're somewhat poorly.
This therefore is my sentence, that you nurse
The Baby for seven hours, and nothing worse.

For you, Edwardus, I shall say no more
Than that your griefs are fudge, yourself a bore:
Return at once to cold, stewed, minced, hashed mutton –
To wristbands ever guiltless of a button –
To raging winds and sea, (where don't you wish
Your luck may ever let you catch one fish?) –
To make large drawings nobody will buy –
To paint oil pictures which will never dry –
To write new books which nobody will read –
To drink weak tea, on tough old pigs to feed –
Till spring-time brings the birds and leaves and flowers,
And time restores a world of happier hours.

The Owl and the Pussy-cat

The Owl and the Pussy-cat went to sea
In a beautiful pea-green boat,
They took some honey, and plenty of money,
Wrapped up in a five-pound note.
The Owl looked up to the stars above,
And sang to a small guitar,
'O lovely Pussy! O Pussy, my love,
What a beautiful Pussy you are,
You are,
You are!
What a beautiful Pussy you are!'

Pussy said to the Owl, 'You elegant fowl!
How charmingly sweet you sing!
O let us be married! too long we have tarried:
But what shall we do for a ring?'
They sailed away, for a year and a day,
To the land where the Bong-tree grows,
And there in a wood a Piggy-wig stood,
With a ring at the end of his nose,
His nose,
His nose,
With a ring at the end of his nose.

'Dear Pig, are you willing to sell for one shilling
    Your ring?' Said the Piggy, 'I will.'
So they took it away, and were married next day
    By the Turkey who lives on the hill.
They dined on mince, and slices of quince,
    Which they ate with a runcible spoon;
And hand in hand, on the edge of the sand,
    They danced by the light of the moon,
        The moon,
        The moon,
They danced by the light of the moon.

The Broom, the Shovel, the Poker, and the Tongs

The Broom and the Shovel, the Poker and Tongs,
   They all took a drive in the Park,
And they each sang a song, Ding-a-dong, Ding-a-dong,
   Before they went back in the dark.
Mr Poker he sate quite upright in the coach,
   Mr Tongs made a clatter and clash,
Miss Shovel was dressed all in black (with a brooch),
   Mrs Broom was in blue (with a sash).
      Ding-a-dong! Ding-a-dong!
      And they all sang a song!

'Oh Shovely so lovely!' the Poker he sang,
   You have perfectly conquered my heart!
Ding-a-dong! Ding-a-dong! If you're pleased with my song,
   I will feed you with cold apple tart!
When you scrape up the coals with a delicate sound,
   You enrapture my life with delight!
Your nose is so shiny! your head is so round!
   And your shape is so slender and bright!
      Ding-a-dong! Ding-a-dong!
      Ain't you pleased with my song?'

'Alas! Mrs Broom !' sighed the Tongs in his song,
  'O is it because I'm so thin,
And my legs are so long – Ding-a-dong! Ding-a-dong!
  That you don't care about me a pin?
Ah! fairest of creatures, when sweeping the room,
  Ah! why don't you heed my complaint!
Must you needs be so cruel, you beautiful Broom,
  Because you are covered with paint?
     Ding-a-dong! Ding-a-dong!
     You are certainly wrong!'

Mrs Broom and Miss Shovel together they sang,
  'What nonsense you're singing to-day!'
Said the Shovel, 'I'll certainly hit you a bang!'
  Said the Broom, 'And I'll sweep you away!'
So the Coachman drove homeward as fast as he could,
  Perceiving their anger with pain;
But they put on the kettle, and little by little,
  They all became happy again.
     Ding-a-dong! Ding-a-dong!
     There's an end of my song!

The Daddy Long-legs and the Fly

Once Mr Daddy Long-legs,
    Dressed in brown and grey,
Walked about upon the sands
    Upon a summer's day;
And there among the pebbles,
    When the wind was rather cold,
He met with Mr Floppy Fly,
    All dressed in blue and gold.
And as it was too soon to dine,
They drank some Periwinkle-wine,
And played an hour or two, or more,
At battlecock and shuttledore.

Said Mr Daddy Long-legs
    To Mr Floppy Fly,
'Why do you never come to court?
    I wish you'd tell me why.
All gold and shine, in dress so fine,
    You'd quite delight the court.
Why do you never go at all?
    I really think you *ought*!
And if you went, you'd see such sights!
Such rugs! and jugs! and candle-lights!
And more than all, the King and Queen,
One in red, and one in green!'

'O Mr Daddy Long-legs,'
    Said Mr Floppy Fly,
'It's true I never go to court,
    And I will tell you why.

If I had six long legs like yours,
    At once I'd go to court!
But oh! I can't, because *my* legs
    Are so extremely short.
And I'm afraid the King and Queen
(One in red, and one in green)
Would say aloud, "You are not fit,
You Fly, to come to court a bit!"'

'O Mr Daddy Long-legs,'
    Said Mr Floppy Fly,
'I wish you'd sing one little song!
    One mumbian melody!
You used to sing so awful well
    In former days gone by,
But now you never sing at all;
    I wish you'd tell me why:
For if you would, the silvery sound
Would please the shrimps and cockles round,
And all the crabs would gladly come
To hear you sing, "Ah, Hum di Hum!"'

Said Mr Daddy Long-legs,
    'I can never sing again!
And if you wish, I'll tell you why,
    Although it gives me pain.
For years I cannot hum a bit,
    Or sing the smallest song;
And this the dreadful reason is,
    My legs are grown too long!
My six long legs, all here and there,
Oppress my bosom with despair;
And if I stand, or lie, or sit,
I cannot sing one single bit!'

So Mr Daddy Long-legs
    And Mr Floppy Fly
Sat down in silence by the sea,
    And gazed upon the sky.
They said, 'This is a dreadful thing!
    The world has all gone wrong,

Since one has legs too short by half,
   The other much too long!
One never more can go to court,
Because his legs have grown too short;
The other cannot sing a song,
Because his legs have grown too long!'

Then Mr Daddy Long-legs
   And Mr Floppy Fly
Rushed downward to the foamy sea
   With one sponge-taneous cry;
And there they found a little boat,
   Whose sails were pink and grey;
And off they sailed among the waves,
   Far, and far away.
They sailed across the silent main,
And reached the great Gromboolian plain;
And there they play for evermore
At battlecock and shuttledore.

Nonsense Cookery

Extract from the *Nonsense Gazette,* for August, 1870.

Our readers will be interested in the following communications from our valued and learned contributor, Professor Bosh, whose labours in the fields of Culinary and Botanical science, are so well known to all the world. The first three Articles richly merit to be added to the Domestic cookery of every family; those which follow, claim the attention of all Botanists, and we are happy to be able through Dr Bosh's kindness to present our readers with Illustrations of his discoveries. All the new flowers are found in the valley of Verrikwier, near the lake of Oddgrow, and on the summit of the hill Orfeltugg.

THREE RECEIPTS FOR DOMESTIC COOKERY TO MAKE AN
AMBLONGUS PIE
Take 4 pounds (say 4½ pounds) of fresh Amblongusses, and put them in a small pipkin.

Cover them with water and boil them for 8 hours incessantly, after which add 2 pints of new milk, and proceed to boil for 4 hours more.

When you have ascertained that the Amblongusses are quite soft, take them out and place them in a wide pan, taking care to shake them well previously.

Grate some nutmeg over the surface, and cover them carefully with powdered gingerbread, curry-powder, and a sufficient quantity of Cayenne pepper.

Remove the pan into the next room, and place it on the floor. Bring it back again, and let it simmer for three-quarters of an hour. Shake the pan violently till all the Amblongusses have become of a pale purple colour.

Then, having prepared the paste, insert the whole carefully, adding at the same time a small pigeon, 2 slices of beef, 4 cauliflowers, and any number of oysters.

Watch patiently till the crust begins to rise, and add a pinch of salt from time to time.

Serve up in a clean dish, and throw the whole out of the window as fast as possible.

TO MAKE CRUMBOBBLIOUS CUTLETS

Procure some strips of beef, and having cut them into the smallest possible slices, proceed to cut them still smaller, eight or perhaps nine times.

When the whole is thus minced, brush it up hastily with a new clothes-brush, and stir round rapidly and capriciously with a salt-spoon or a soup-ladle.

Place the whole in a saucepan, and remove it to a sunny place, – say the roof of the house if free from sparrows or other birds, – and leave it there for about a week.

At the end of that time add a little lavender, some oil of almonds, and a few herring-bones; and then cover the whole with 4 gallons of clarified crumbobblious sauce, when it will be ready for use.

Cut it into the shape of ordinary cutlets, and serve up in a clean tablecloth or dinner-napkin.

TO MAKE GOSKY PATTIES

Take a Pig, three or four years of age, and tie him by the off-hind leg to a post. Place 5 pounds of currants, 3 of sugar, 2 pecks of peas, 18 roast chestnuts, a candle, and six bushels of turnips, within his reach; if he eats these, constantly provide him with more.

Then procure some cream, some slices of Cheshire cheese, four quires of foolscap paper, and a packet of black pins. Work the whole into a paste, and spread it out to dry on a sheet of clean brown waterproof linen.

When the paste is perfectly dry, but not before, proceed to beat the Pig violently, with the handle of a large broom. If he squeals, beat him again.

Visit the paste and beat the Pig alternately for some days, and ascertain if at the end of that period the whole is about to turn into Gosky Patties.

If it does not then, it never will; and in that case the Pig may be let loose, and the whole process may be considered as finished.

Nonsense Botany (1)

Baccopipia Gracilis　　　　Bottlephorkia Spoonifolia

Cockatooca Superba　　　　Fishia Marina

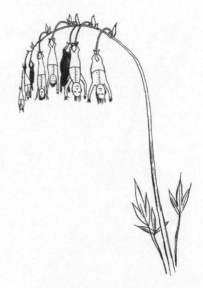

Guittara Pensilis

Manypeeplia Upsidownia

Phattfacia Stupenda

Piggiawiggia Pyramidalis

Plumbunnia Nutritiosa   Pollybirdia Singularis

The Jumblies

They went to sea in a Sieve, they did,
   In a Sieve they went to sea:
In spite of all their friends could say,
On a winter's morn, on a stormy day,
   In a Sieve they went to sea!
And when the Sieve turned round and round,
And every one cried, 'You'll all be drowned!'

They called aloud, 'Our Sieve ain't big,
But we don't care a button! we don't care a fig!
   In a Sieve we'll go to sea!'
     Far and few, far and few,
       Are the lands where the Jumblies live
      Their heads are green, and their hands are blue,
       And they went to sea in a Sieve.

They sailed away in a Sieve, they did,
   In a Sieve they sailed so fast,
With only a beautiful pea-green veil
Tied with a riband by way of a sail,
   To a small tobacco-pipe mast;
And every one said, who saw them go,
'O won't they be soon upset, you know!
For the sky is dark, and the voyage is long,
And happen what may, it's extremely wrong
   In a Sieve to sail so fast!'
     Far and few, far and few,
       Are the lands where the Jumblies live;
      Their heads are green, and their hands are blue,
       And they went to sea in a Sieve.

The water it soon came in, it did,
   The water it soon came in;
So to keep them dry, they wrapped their feet
In a pinky paper all folded neat,
   And they fastened it down with a pin.
And they passed the night in a crockery-jar,
And each of them said, 'How wise we are!
Though the sky be dark, and the voyage be long,
Yet we never can think we were rash or wrong,
   While round in our Sieve we spin!'
     Far and few, far and few,
       Are the lands where the Jumblies live;
      Their heads are green, and their hands are blue,
       And they went to sea in a Sieve.

And all night long they sailed away;
   And when the sun went down,
They whistled and warbled a moony song

To the echoing sound of a coppery gong,
    In the shade of the mountains brown.
'O Timballo! How happy we are,
When we live in a sieve and a crockery-jar,
And all night long in the moonlight pale,
We sail away with a pea-green sail,
    In the shade of the mountains brown!'
        Far and few, far and few,
            Are the lands where the Jumblies live;
            Their heads are green, and their hands are blue,
                And they went to sea in a Sieve.

They sailed to the Western Sea, they did,
    To a land all covered with trees,
And they bought an Owl, and a useful Cart,
And a pound of Rice, and a Cranberry Tart,
    And a hive of silvery Bees.
And they bought a Pig, and some green Jack-daws,
And a lovely Monkey with lollipop paws,
And forty bottles of Ring-Bo-Ree,
    And no end of Stilton Cheese.
        Far and few, far and few,
            Are the lands where the Jumblies live;
            Their heads are green, and their hands are blue,
                And they went to sea in a Sieve.

And in twenty years they all came back,
    In twenty years or more,
And every one said, 'How tall they've grown!
For they've been to the Lakes, and the Torrible Zone,
    And the hills of the Chankly Bore!'
And they drank their health, and gave them a feast
Of dumplings made of beautiful yeast;
And every one said, 'If we only live,
We too will go to sea in a Sieve, –
    To the hills of the Chankly Bore!'
        Far and few, far and few,
            Are the lands where the Jumblies live;
            Their heads are green, and their hands are blue,
                And they went to sea in a Sieve.

The Nutcrackers and the Sugar-tongs

The Nutcrackers sate by a plate on the table,
    The Sugar-tongs sate by a plate at his side;
And the Nutcrackers said, 'Don't you wish we were able
    Along the blue hills and green meadows to ride?
Must we drag on this stupid existence for ever,
    So idle and weary, so full of remorse, –
While every one else takes his pleasure, and never
    Seems happy unless he is riding a horse?

'Don't you think we could ride without being instructed?
    Without any saddle, or bridle, or spur?
Our legs are so long, and so aptly constructed,
    I'm sure that an accident could not occur.
Let us all of a sudden hop down from the table,
    And hustle downstairs, and each jump on a horse!
Shall we try? Shall we go? Do you think we are able?'
    The Sugar-tongs answered distinctly, 'Of course!'

So down the long staircase they hopped in a minute,
    The Sugar-tongs snapped, and the Crackers said 'crack!'
The stable was open, the horses were in it;
    Each took out a pony, and jumped on his back.
The Cat in a fright scrambled out of the doorway,
    The Mice tumbled out of a bundle of hay,
The brown and white Rats, and the black ones from Norway,
    Screamed out, 'They are taking the horses away!'

The whole of the household was filled with amazement,
    The Cups and the Saucers danced madly about,
The Plates and the Dishes looked out of the casement,
    The Salt-cellar stood on his head with a shout,

The Spoons with a clatter looked out of the lattice,
    The Mustard-pot climbed up the Gooseberry Pies,
The Soup-ladle peeped through a heap of Veal Patties,
    And squeaked with a ladle-like scream of surprise.

The Frying-pan said, 'It's an awful delusion!'
    The Tea-kettle hissed and grew black in the face;
And they all rushed downstairs in the wildest confusion,
    To see the great Nutcracker-Sugar-tong race.
And out of the stable, with screamings and laughter,
    (Their ponies were cream-coloured, speckled with brown,)
The Nutcrackers first, and the Sugar-tongs after,
    Rode all round the yard, and then all round the town.

They rode through the street, and they rode by the station,
    They galloped away to the beautiful shore;
In silence they rode, and 'made no observation,'
    Save this: 'We will never go back any more!'
And still you might hear, till they rode out of hearing,
    The Sugar-tongs snap, and the Crackers say 'crack!'
Till far in the distance their forms disappearing,
    They faded away. – And they never came back!

Mr and Mrs Discobbolos

Mr and Mrs Discobbolos
        Climbed to the top of a wall,
    And they sate to watch the sunset sky
    And to hear the Nupiter Piffkin cry
        And the Biscuit Buffalo call.
They took up a roll and some Camomile tea,
And both were as happy as happy could be –
        Till Mrs Discobbolos said –
        'Oh! W! X! Y! Z!
        It has just come into my head –
Suppose we should happen to fall!!!!!
                Darling Mr Discobbolos!

'Suppose we should fall down flumpetty
    Just like pieces of stone!
  On to the thorns, – or into the moat!
    What would become of your new green coat?
      And might you not break a bone?
It never occurred to me before –
That perhaps we shall never go down any more!'
    And Mrs Discobbolos said –
     'Oh! W! X! Y! Z!
    What put it into your head
To climb up this wall? – my own
             Darling Mr Discobbolos?'

Mr Discobbolos answered, –
    'At first it gave me pain, –
  And I felt my ears turn perfectly pink
  When your exclamation made me think
    We might never get down again!
But now I believe it is wiser far
To remain for ever just where we are.'
    And Mr Discobbolos said,
     'Oh! W! X! Y! Z!'
    It is just come into my head –
– We shall never go down again –
            Dearest Mrs Discobbolos!'

So Mr and Mrs Discobbolos
    Stood up, and began to sing,
  'Far away from hurry and strife
  Here we will pass the rest of life,
    Ding a dong, ding dong, ding!
We want no knives nor forks nor chairs,
No tables nor carpets nor household cares,
    From worry of life we've fled –
    Oh! W! X! Y! Z!
    There's no more trouble ahead,
Sorrow or any such thing –
            For Mr and Mrs Discobbolos!'

The Courtship of the Yonghy-Bonghy-Bò

On the Coast of Coromandel
  Where the early pumpkins blow,
    In the middle of the woods
    Lived the Yonghy-Bonghy-Bò.
Two old chairs, and half a candle, –
One old jug without a handle, –
    These were all his worldly goods,
    In the middle of the woods,
    These were all the worldly goods,
  Of the Yonghy-Bonghy-Bò,
  Of the Yonghy-Bonghy-Bò.

Once, among the Bong-trees walking
  Where the early pumpkins blow,
    To a little heap of stones
    Came the Yonghy-Bonghy-Bò.
There he heard a Lady talking,
To some milk-white Hens of Dorking, –
    ''Tis the Lady Jingly Jones!
    On that little heap of stones
    Sits the Lady Jingly Jones!'
  Said the Yonghy-Bonghy-Bò,
  Said the Yonghy-Bonghy-Bò.

'Lady Jingly! Lady Jingly!
    Sitting where the pumpkins blow,
        Will you come and be my wife?'
    Said the Yonghy-Bonghy-Bò.
'I am tired of living singly, –
On this coast so wild and shingly, –
        I'm a-weary of my life;
        If you'll come and be my wife,
        Quite serene would be my life!'
    Said the Yonghy-Bonghy-Bò,
    Said the Yonghy-Bonghy-Bò.

'On this Coast of Coromandel,
    Shrimps and watercresses grow,
        Prawns are plentiful and cheap,'
    Said the Yonghy-Bonghy-Bò.
'You shall have my chairs and candle,
And my jug without a handle! –
        Gaze upon the rolling deep
        (Fish is plentiful and cheap;)
        As the sea, my love is deep!'
    Said the Yonghy-Bonghy-Bò,
    Said the Yonghy-Bonghy-Bò.

Lady Jingly answered sadly,
    And her tears began to flow, –
        'Your proposal comes too late,
    Mr Yonghy-Bonghy-Bò!
I would be your wife most gladly!'
(Here she twirled her fingers madly,)
        'But in England I've a mate!
        Yes! you've asked me far too late,
        For in England I've a mate,
    Mr Yonghy-Bonghy-Bò!
    Mr Yonghy-Bonghy-Bò!'

'Mr Jones – (his name is Handel, –
    Handel Jones, Esquire, & Co.)
        Dorking fowls delights to send,
    Mr Yonghy-Bonghy-Bò!
Keep, oh! keep your chairs and candle,

And your jug without a handle, –
    I can merely be your friend!
    – Should my Jones more Dorkings send,
    I will give you three, my friend!
  Mr Yonghy-Bonghy-Bò!
  Mr Yonghy-Bonghy-Bò!

'Though you've such a tiny body,
    And your head so large doth grow, –
    Though your hat may blow away,
  Mr Yonghy-Bonghy-Bò!
Though you're such a Hoddy Doddy –
Yet I wished that I could modi-
    fy the words I needs must say!
    Will you please to go away?
    That is all I have to say –
  Mr Yonghy-Bonghy-Bò!
  Mr Yonghy-Bonghy-Bò!'

Down the slippery slopes of Myrtle,
    Where the early pumpkins blow,
    To the calm and silent sea
    Fled the Yonghy-Bonghy-Bò.
There, beyond the Bay of Gurtle,
Lay a large and lively Turtle; –
    'You're the Cove,' he said, 'for me;
    On your back beyond the sea,
    Turtle, you shall carry me!'
  Said the Yonghy-Bonghy-Bò,
  Said the Yonghy-Bonghy-Bò.

Through the silent-roaring ocean
    Did the Turtle swiftly go;
        Holding fast upon his shell
    Rode the Yonghy-Bonghy-Bò.
With a sad primæval motion
Towards the sunset isles of Boshen
        Still the Turtle bore him well.
        Holding fast upon his shell,
        'Lady Jingly Jones, farewell!'
    Said the Yonghy-Bonghy-Bò,
    Said the Yonghy-Bonghy-Bò.

From the Coast of Coromandel,
    Did that Lady never go;
        On that heap of stones she mourns
    For the Yonghy-Bonghy-Bò.
On that Coast of Coromandel,
In his jug without a handle,
        Still she weeps, and daily moans;
        On that little heap of stones
        To her Dorking Hens she moans,
    For the Yonghy-Bonghy-Bò,
    For the Yonghy-Bonghy-Bò.

Limericks from More Nonsense,
Pictures, Rhymes, Botany, Etc. (1872)*

There was an Old Man, who when little,
Fell casually into a kettle;
But, growing too stout, he could never get out,
So he passed all his life in that kettle.

There was an Old Man whose despair
Induced him to purchase a hare;
Whereon one fine day, he rode wholly away,
Which partly assuaged his despair.

---

* Following the Penguin Complete Verse and Other Nonsense, I have changed Lear's
 lower case for 'old man', etc. to be consistent with the earlier series of limericks.

There was an Old Person of Deal,
Who in walking used only his heel;
When they said, 'Tell us why?' – he made no reply;
That mysterious Old Person of Deal.

There was an Old Person in black,
A Grasshopper jumped on his back;
When it chirped in his ear, he was smitten with fear,
That helpless Old Person in black.

There was an Old Man in a barge,
Whose nose was exceedingly large;
But in fishing by night, it supported a light,
Which helped that Old Man in a barge.

There was an Old Man of Dunluce,
Who went out to sea on a goose;
When he'd gone out a mile, he observ'd with a smile,
'It is time to return to Dunluce.'

There was an Old Person of Bree,
Who frequented the depths of the sea;
She nurs'd the small fishes, and washed all the dishes,
And swam back again into Bree.

There was an Old Person of Shields,
Who frequented the vallies and fields;
All the mice and the cats, and the snakes and the rats,
Followed after that Person of Shields.

There was an Old Man who screamed out
Whenever they knocked him about;
So they took off his boots, and fed him with fruits,
And continued to knock him about.

There was an Old Person of Sheen,
Whose expression was calm and serene;
He sate in the water, and drank bottled porter,
That placid Old Person of Sheen.

There was an Old Person of Ware,
Who rode on the back of a bear;
When they ask'd, 'Does it trot?' – he said, 'Certainly not!
He's a Moppsikon Floppsikon Bear!'

There was an Old Man on the Border,
Who lived in the utmost disorder;
He danced with the cat, and made tea in his hat,
Which vexed all the folks on the Border.

There was an Old Man of Dumbree,
Who taught little owls to drink tea;
For he said, 'To eat mice is not proper or nice',
That amiable Man of Dumbree.

There was an Old Person of Grange,
Whose manners were scroobious and strange;
He sailed to St Blubb, in a waterproof tub,
That aquatic Old Person of Grange.

There was an Old Person of Nice,
Whose associates were usually Geese;
They walked out together, in all sorts of weather,
That affable Person of Nice!

There was an Old Person of Blythe,
Who cut up his meat with a scythe;
When they said, 'Well! I never!' – he cried, 'Scythes for ever!'
That lively Old Person of Blythe.

There was an Old Person of Bray,
Who sang through the whole of the day
To his ducks and his pigs, whom he fed upon figs,
That valuable Person of Bray.

There was an Old Person of Crowle,
Who lived in the nest of an owl;
When they screamed in the nest, he screamed out with the rest,
That depressing Old Person of Crowle.

There was a Young Lady whose nose,
Continually prospers and grows;
When it grew out of sight, she exclaimed in a fright,
'Oh! Farewell to the end of my nose!'

There was an Old Man in a tree,
Whose whiskers were lovely to see;
But the birds of the air pluck'd them perfectly bare,
To make themselves nests in that tree.

There was an Old Person of Skye,
Who waltz'd with a Bluebottle fly;
They buzz'd a sweet tune, to the light of the moon,
And entranced all the people of Skye.

There was an Old Person of Harrow,
Who bought a mahogany barrow;
For he said to his wife, 'You're the joy of my life!
And I'll wheel you all day in this barrow!'

Nonsense Botany (2)

Barkia Howlaloudia

Enkoopia Chickabiddia

Jinglia Tinkettlia

Nasticreechia Krorluppia

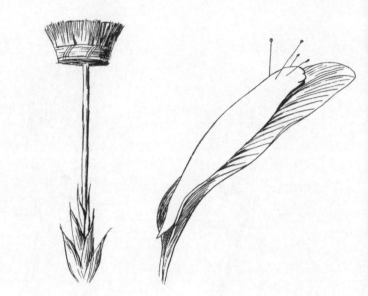

Arthbroomia Rigida   Sophtsluggia Glutinosa

Minspysia Deliciosa   Shoebootia Utilis

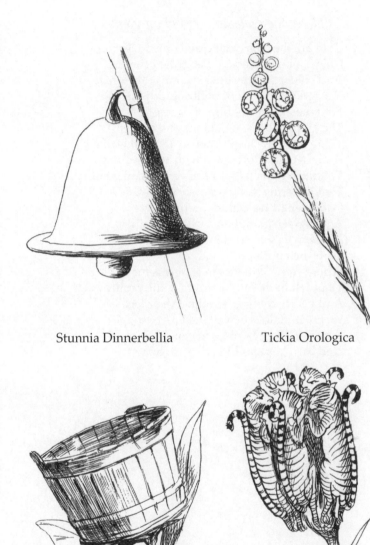

Stunnia Dinnerbellia

Tickia Orologica

Washtubbia Circularis

Tigerlillia Terribilis

'Cold are the crabs that crawl on yonder hill'*

Cold are the crabs that crawl on yonder hill,
Colder the cucumbers that grow beneath
And colder still the brazen chops that wreath
The tedious gloom of philosophic pills!
For when the tardy film of nectar fills
The ample bowls of demons and of men,
There lurks the feeble mouse, the homely hen,
And there the Porcupine with all her quills.
Yet much remains; – to weave a solemn strain
That lingering sadly – slowly dies away,
Daily departing with departing day
A pea-green gamut on a distant plain.
Where wily walruses in congress meet –
Such such is life –
Where early buffaloes in congress meet
Than salt more salt, than sugar still more sweet,
And pearly centipedes adjust their feet
Where buffaloes bewail the loss of soap
Where frantic walruses in clouds elope,
And early pipkins bid adiew to hope.

---

*   Unfinished.

The Scroobious Pip*

The Scroobious Pip went out one day
When the grass was green, and the sky was grey,
Then all the beasts in the world came round
When the Scroobious Pip sate down on the ground.
The Cats and the Dog and the Kangaroo,
The Sheep and the Cow and the Guinea Pig too –
The Wolf he howled, the Horse he neighed,
The little Pig squeaked and the Donkey brayed,
And when the Lion began to roar
There never was heard such a noise before,
And every beast he stood on the tip
Of his toes to look at the Scroobious Pip.

At last they said to the Fox – 'By far
You're the wisest beast – you know you are!
Go close to the Scroobious Pip and say,
"Tell us all about yourself we pray! –
For as yet we can't make out in the least
If you're Fish or Insect, or Bird or Beast."'

---

*   Unfinished.

The Scroobious Pip looked vaguely round
And sang these words with a rumbling sound –
   'Chippetty Flip – Flippetty Chip –
   My only name is the Scroobious Pip.'

The Scroobious Pip from the top of a tree
Saw the distant Jellybolēē, –
And all the birds in the world came there,
Flying in crowds all through the air.
The Vulture and Eagle – the Cock and the Hen,
The Ostrich, the Turkey, the Snipe and Wren,
The Parrot chattered, the Blackbird sung,
And the Owl looked wise but held his tongue,
And when the Peacock began to scream,
The hullabaloo was quite extreme.
And every bird he fluttered the tip
Of his wing as he stared at the Scroobious Pip.

At last they said to the Owl, –'By far
You're [the] wisest Bird – you know you are!
Fly close to the Scroobious Pip and say,
"Explain all about yourself we pray! –
For as yet we have neither seen nor heard
If you're Fish or Insect, Beast or Bird!"'

The Scroobious Pip looked gaily round
And sang these words with a chirpy sound –
   'flippetty chip – Chippetty flip –
   My only name is the Scroobious Pip.'

The Scroobious Pip went into the sea
By the beautiful shore of the Jellybolēē –
All the Fish in the world swam round
With a splashy squashy spluttery sound,
The Sprat, the Herring, the Turbot too,
The Shark, the Sole, and the Mackerel blue,
The ——— spluttered, the Porpoise puffed
——— Flounder ———————
And when the Whale began to spout –
————————————————————

And every Fish he shook the tip

Of his tail as he gazed on the Scroobious Pip.

At last they said to the Whale – 'By far
You're the biggest Fish – you know you are!
Swim close to the Scroobious Pip and say,
"Tell us all about yourself we pray! –
For to know from yourself is our only wish –
Are you Beast or Insect, Bird or Fish?"'

The Scroobious Pip looked softly round
And sang these words with a liquid sound –
 'Plifatty flip – Pliffity flip –
  My only name is the Scroobious Pip.'

The Scroobious Pip sate under a tree
By the silent shores of the Jellybolēe,
All the Insects in all the world
About the Scroobious Pip fluttered and twirled.
Beetles and —— with purple eyes
Gnats and buzztilential Flies –
Grasshoppers, Butterflies, Spiders too,
Wasps and Bees and Dragonfly blue,
And when the Gnats began to hum
—— bounced like a dismal drum –
And every insect curled the tip
Of his snout, and looked at the Scroobious Pip.

At last they said the Ant, – 'By far
You're the wisest Insect – you know you are!
Creep close to the Scroobious Pip and say,
"Tell us all about yourself we pray! –
For we can't find out, and we can't tell why –
If you're Beast or Fish or a Bird or a Fly. –"'

The Scroobious Pip turned quickly round
And sang these words with a whistly sound –
 'Wizziby wip – wizziby wip –
  My only name is the Scroobious Pip.'

Then all the Beasts that walk on the ground
Danced in a circle round and round,

And all the Birds that fly in the air
Flew round and round in a circle there,
And all the Fish in the Jellybolee
Swam in a circle about the sea,
And all the Insects that creep or go
Buzzed in a circle to and fro –
And they roared and sang and whistled and cried
Till the noise was heard from side to side –
        'Chippetty Tip! Chippetty Tip!
        Its only name is the Scroobious Pip.'

The Quangle Wangle's Hat

On the top of the Crumpetty Tree
   The Quangle Wangle sat,
But his face you could not see,
   On account of his Beaver Hat.
For his Hat was a hundred and two feet wide,
With ribbons and bibbons on every side,
And bells, and buttons, and loops, and lace,
So that nobody ever could see the face
     Of the Quangle Wangle Quee.

The Quangle Wangle said
   To himself on the Crumpetty Tree, –
'Jam; and jelly; and bread;
   Are the best of food for me!
But the longer I live on this Crumpetty Tree,
The plainer than ever it seems to me
That very few people come this way
And that life on the whole is far from gay!'
     Said the Quangle Wangle Quee.

But there came to the Crumpetty Tree,
  Mr and Mrs Canary;
And they said, – 'Did ever you see
  Any spot so charmingly airy?
May we build a nest on your lovely Hat?
Mr Quangle Wangle, grant us that!
O please let us come and build a nest
Of whatever material suits you best,
        Mr Quangle Wangle Quee!'

And besides, to the Crumpetty Tree
  Came the Stork, the Duck, and the Owl;
The Snail, and the Bumble-Bee,
  The Frog, and the Fimble Fowl;
(The Fimble Fowl, with a Corkscrew leg;)
And all of them said, – 'We humbly beg,
We may build our homes on your lovely Hat, –
Mr Quangle Wangle, grant us that!
        Mr Quangle Wangle Quee!'

And the Golden Grouse came there,
  And the Pobble who has no toes, –
And the small Olympian bear, –
  And the Dong with a luminous nose.
And the Blue Baboon, who played the flute, –
And the Orient Calf from the Land of Tute, –
And the Attery Squash, and the Bisky Bat, –
All came and built on the lovely Hat
        Of the Quangle Wangle Quee.

And the Quangle Wangle said
  To himself on the Crumpetty Tree, –
'When all these creatures move
  What a wonderful noise there'll be!'
And at night by the light of the Mulberry moon
They danced to the Flute of the Blue Baboon,
On the broad green leaves of the Crumpetty Tree,
And all were as happy as happy could be,
        With the Quangle Wangle Quee.

The Pobble who has no Toes

The Pobble who has no toes
   Had once as many as we;
When they said, 'Some day you may lose them all;' –
   He replied, – 'Fish fiddle de-dee!'
And his Aunt Jobiska made him drink,
Lavender water tinged with pink,
For she said, 'The World in general knows
There's nothing so good for a Pobble's toes!'

The Pobble who has no toes,
   Swam across the Bristol Channel;
But before he set out he wrapped his nose,
   In a piece of scarlet flannel.
For his Aunt Jobiska said, 'No harm
Can come to his toes if his nose is warm;
And it's perfectly known that a Pobble's toes
Are safe, – provided he minds his nose.'

The Pobble swam fast and well,
   And when boats or ships came near him
He tinkledy-binkledy-winkled a bell,
   So that all the world could hear him.
And all the Sailors and Admirals cried,
When they saw him nearing the further side, –
'He has gone to fish for his Aunt Jobiska's
Runcible Cat with crimson whiskers!'

But before he touched the shore,
    The shore of the Bristol Channel,
A sea-green Porpoise carried away
    His wrapper of scarlet flannel.
And when he came to observe his feet,
Formerly garnished with toes so neat,
His face at once became forlorn
On perceiving that all his toes were gone!

And nobody ever knew
    From that dark day to the present,
Whoso had taken the Pobble's toes,
    In a manner so far from pleasant.
Whether the shrimps or crawfish grey,
Or crafty Mermaids stole them away –
Nobody knew; and nobody knows
How the Pobble was robbed of his twice five toes!

The Pobble who has no toes
    Was placed in a friendly Bark,
And they rowed him back, and carried him up,
    To his Aunt Jobiska's Park.
And she made him a feast at his earnest wish
Of eggs and buttercups fried with fish; –
And she said, – 'It's a fact the whole world knows,
That Pobbles are happier without their toes.'

The Akond of Swat*

Who, or why, or which, or *what*, Is the Akond of SWAT?

Is he tall or short, or dark or fair?
Does he sit on a stool or a sofa or chair   or SQUAT,
        The Akond of Swat?

Is he wise or foolish, young or old?
Does he drink his soup and his coffee cold   or HOT,
        The Akond of Swat?

---

*   Lear's note: 'For the existence of this potentate see Indian newspapers, *passim*. The proper way to read the verses is to make an immense emphasis on the monosyllabic rhymes, which indeed ought to be shouted out by a chorus.'

Does he sing or whistle, jabber or talk,
And when riding abroad does he gallop or walk   or TROT,
                    The Akond of Swat?

Does he wear a turban, a fez, or a hat?
Does he sleep on a mattress, a bed, or a mat   or a COT,
                    The Akond of Swat?

When he writes a copy in round-hand size,
Does he cross his T's and finish his I's   with a DOT,
                    The Akond of Swat?

Can he write a letter concisely clear
Without a speck or a smudge or smear   or BLOT,
                    The Akond of Swat?

Do his people like him extremely well?
Or do they, whenever they can, rebel   or PLOT,
                  At the Akond of Swat?

If he catches them then, either old or young,
Does he have them chopped in pieces or hung   or *shot*,
                    The Akond of Swat?

Do his people prig in the lanes or park?
Or even at times, when days are dark   GAROTTE,
                  O the Akond of Swat!

Does he study the wants of his own dominion?
Or doesn't he care for public opinion   a JOT,
                    The Akond of Swat?

To amuse his mind do his people show him
Pictures, or anyone's last new poem   or WHAT,
                  For the Akond of Swat?

At night if he suddenly screams and wakes,
Do they bring him only a few small cakes   or a LOT,
                  For the Akond of Swat?

Does he live on turnips, tea, or tripe?
Does he like his shawl to be marked with a stripe or a DOT,
                                    The Akond of Swat?

Does he like to lie on his back in a boat
Like the lady who lived in that isle remote,   SHALOTT,
                                    The Akond of Swat?

Is he quiet, or always making a fuss?
Is his steward a Swiss or a Swede or a Russ   or a SCOT,
                                    The Akond of Swat?

Does he like to sit by the calm blue wave?
Or to sleep and snore in a dark green cave   or a GROTT,
                                    The Akond of Swat?

Does he drink small beer from a silver jug?
Or a bowl? or a glass? or a cup? or a mug?   or a POT,
                                    The Akond of Swat?

Does he beat his wife with a gold-topped pipe,
When she lets the gooseberries grow too ripe   or ROT,
                                    The Akond of Swat?

Does he wear a white tie when he dines with friends,
And tie it neat in a bow with ends   or a KNOT,
                                    The Akond of Swat?

Does he like new cream, and hate mince-pies?
When he looks at the sun does he wink his eyes   or NOT,
                                    The Akond of Swat?

Does he teach his subjects to roast and bake?
Does he sail about on an inland lake   in a YACHT,
                                    The Akond of Swat?

Someone, or nobody, knows I wot
Who or which or why or what
                                    Is the Akond of Swat!

The Cummerbund

An Indian Poem

She sate upon her Dobie,
　　To watch the Evening Star,
And all the Punkahs as they passed,
　　Cried, 'My! how fair you are!'
Around her bower, with quivering leaves,
　　The tall Kamsamahs grew,
And Kitmutgars in wild festoons
　　Hung down from Tchokis blue.

Below her home the river rolled
　　With soft meloobious sound,
Where golden-finned Chuprassies swam,
　　In myriads circling round.
Above, on tallest trees remote,
　　Green Ayahs perched alone,
And all night long the Mussak moan'd
　　Its melancholy tone.

And where the purple Nullahs threw
　　Their branches far and wide, –
The silvery Goreewallahs flew
　　In silence, side by side, –
The little Bheesties' twittering cry
　　Rose on the flagrant air,
And oft the angry Jampan howled
　　Deep in his hateful lair.

She sate upon her Dobie, –
　　She heard the Nimmak hum, –
When all at once a cry arose, –
　　'The Cummerbund is come!'
In vain she fled: – with open jaws
　　The angry monster followed,
And so, (before assistance came),
　　That Lady Fair was swollowed.

They sought in vain for even a bone
　　Respectfully to bury, –
They said, – 'Hers was a dreadful fate!'
　　(And Echo answered 'Very.')
They nailed her Dobie to the wall,
　　Where last her form was seen,
And underneath they wrote these words,
　　In yellow, blue, and green: –

'Beware, ye Fair! Ye Fair, beware!
　　Nor sit out late at night, –
Lest horrid Cummerbunds should come,
　　And swollow you outright.'

The Pelican Chorus

King and Queen of the Pelicans we;
No other Birds so grand we see!
None but we have feet like fins!
With lovely leathery throats and chins!
    Ploffskin, Pluffskin, Pelican jee!
    We think no Birds so happy as we!
    Plumpskin, Ploshkin, Pelican jill!
    We think so then, and we thought so still!

We live on the Nile. The Nile we love.
By night we sleep on the cliffs above;
By day we fish, and at eve we stand
On long bare islands of yellow sand.
And when the sun sinks slowly down
And the great rock walls grow dark and brown,
When the purple river rolls fast and dim
And the Ivory Ibis starlike skim,
Wing to wing we dance around, –
Stamping our feet with a flumpy sound, –
Opening our mouths as Pelicans ought,
And this is the song we nightly snort; –
    Ploffskin, Pluffskin, Pelican jee!
    We think no Birds so happy as we!
    Plumpskin, Ploshkin, Pelican jill!
    We think so then, and we thought so still!

Last year came out our Daughter, Dell;
And all the Birds received her well.
To do her honour, a feast we made
For every bird that can swim or wade.
Herons and Gulls, and Cormorants black,
Cranes, and Flamingos with scarlet back,
Plovers and Storks, and Geese in clouds,
Swans and Dilberry Ducks in crowds.
Thousands of Birds in wondrous flight!
They ate and drank and danced all night,
And echoing back from the rocks you heard
Multitude-echoes from Bird and Bird, –
    Ploffskin, Pluffskin, Pelican jee!
    We think no Birds so happy as we!
    Plumpskin, Ploshkin, Pelican jill!
    We think so then, and we thought so still!

Yes, they came; and among the rest,
The King of the Cranes all grandly dressed.
Such a lovely tail! Its feathers float
Between the ends of his blue dress-coat;
With pea-green trowsers all so neat,
And a delicate frill to hide his feet, –
(For though no one speaks of it, every one knows,
He has got no webs between his toes!)

As soon as he saw our Daughter Dell,
In violent love that Crane King fell, –
On seeing her waddling form so fair,
With a wreath of shrimps in her short white hair.
And before the end of the next long day,
Our Dell had given her heart away;
For the King of the Cranes had won that heart,
With a Crocodile's egg and a large fish-tart.
She vowed to marry the King of the Cranes,
Leaving the Nile for stranger plains;
And away they flew in a gathering crowd
Of endless birds in a lengthening cloud.
    Ploffskin, Pluffskin, Pelican jee!
    We think no Birds so happy as we!
    Plumpskin, Ploshkin, Pelican jill!
    We think so then, and we thought so still!

And far away in the twilight sky,
We heard them singing a lessening cry, –
Farther and farther till out of sight,
And we stood alone in the silent night!
Often since, in the nights of June,
We sit on the sand and watch the moon; –
She has gone to the great Gromboolian plain,
And we probably never shall meet again!
Oft, in the long still nights of June,
We sit on the rocks and watch the moon; –
–She dwells by the streams of the Chankly Bore,
And we probably never shall see her more.
      Ploffskin, Pluffskin, Pelican jee!
      We think no Birds so happy as we!
      Plumpskin, Ploshkin, Pelican jill!
      We think so then, and we thought so still!

The Two Old Bachelors

Two old Bachelors were living in one house;
One caught a Muffin, the other caught a Mouse.
Said he who caught the Muffin to him who caught the Mouse, –
'This happens just in time! For we've nothing in the house,
Save a tiny slice of lemon and a teaspoonful of honey,
And what to do for dinner – since we haven't any money?
And what can we expect if we haven't any dinner,
But to lose our teeth and eyelashes and keep on growing thinner?'

Said he who caught the Mouse to him who caught the Muffin, –
'We might cook this little Mouse, if we only had some Stuffin'!
If we had but Sage and Onion we could do extremely well,
But how to get that Stuffin' it is difficult to tell!' –

Those two old Bachelors ran quickly to the town
And asked for Sage and Onions as they wandered up and down;
They borrowed two large Onions, but no Sage was to be found
In the Shops, or in the Market, or in all the Gardens round.

But someone said, – 'A hill there is, a little to the north,
And to its purpledicular top a narrow way leads forth; –
And there among the rugged rocks abides an ancient Sage, –
An earnest Man, who reads all day a most perplexing page.
Climb up, and seize him by the toes! – all studious as he sits, –
And pull him down, – and chop him into endless little bits!
Then mix him with your Onion, (cut up likewise into Scraps,) –
When your Stuffin' will be ready – and very good: perhaps.'

Those two old Bachelors without loss of time
The nearly purpledicular crags at once began to climb;
And at the top, among the rocks, all seated in a nook,
They saw that Sage, a-reading of a most enormous book.

'You earnest Sage!' aloud they cried, 'your book you've read
                                        enough in! –
We wish to chop you into bits to mix you into Stuffin'!'

But that old Sage looked calmly up, and with his awful book,
At those two Bachelors' bald heads a certain aim he took; –
And over crag and precipice they rolled promiscuous down, –
At once they rolled, and never stopped in lane or field or town, –
And when they reached their house, they found (beside their
                                        want of Stuffin')
The Mouse had fled; – and, previously, had eaten up the Muffin.

They left their home in silence by the once convivial door.
And from that hour those Bachelors were never heard of more.

The Dong with a Luminous Nose

When awful darkness and silence reign
　Over the great Gromboolian plain,
　　Through the long, long wintry nights; –
When the angry breakers roar
As they beat on the rocky shore; –
　　When Storm-clouds brood on the towering heights
Of the Hills of the Chankly Bore: –

Then, through the vast and gloomy dark,
There moves what seems a fiery spark,
　　A lonely spark with silvery rays
　　Piercing the coal-black night, –
　　A Meteor strange and bright: –
Hither and thither the vision strays,
　　A single lurid light.

Slowly it wanders, – pauses, – creeps, –
Anon it sparkles, – flashes and leaps;
And ever as onward it gleaming goes
A light on the Bong-tree stems it throws.
And those who watch at that midnight hour
From Hall or Terrace, or lofty Tower,
Cry, as the wild light passes along, –

'The Dong! – the Dong!
The wandering Dong through the forest goes!
    The Dong! the Dong!
The Dong with a luminous Nose!'

    Long years ago
The Dong was happy and gay,
Till he fell in love with a Jumbly Girl
    Who came to those shores one day.
For the Jumblies came in a sieve, they did, –
Landing at eve near the Zemmery Fidd
    Where the Oblong Oysters grow,
    And the rocks are smooth and grey.
And all the woods and the valleys rang
With the Chorus they daily and nightly sang, –
        'Far and few, far and few,
        Are the lands where the Jumblies live;
        Their heads are green, and their hands are blue,
        And they went to sea in a sieve.'

Happily, happily passed those days!
        While the cheerful Jumblies staid;
    They danced in circlets all night long,
    To the plaintive pipe of the lively Dong,
        In moonlight, shine, or shade.
For day and night he was always there
By the side of the Jumbly Girl so fair,
With her sky-blue hands, and her sea-green hair.
Till the morning came of that hateful day
When the Jumblies sailed in their sieve away,
And the Dong was left on the cruel shore
Gazing – gazing for evermore, –
Ever keeping his weary eyes on
That pea-green sail on the far horizon, –
Singing the Jumbly Chorus still
As he sate all day on the grassy hill, –
        'Far and few, far and few,
        Are the lands where the Jumblies live;
        Their heads are green, and their hands are blue,
        And they went to sea in a sieve.

But when the sun was low in the West,
　　The Dong arose and said; –
　　– 'What little sense I once possessed
　　Has quite gone out of my head!' –
And since that day he wanders still
By lake and forest, marsh and hill,
Singing – 'O somewhere, in valley or plain
Might I find my Jumbly Girl again!
For ever I'll seek by lake and shore
Till I find my Jumbly Girl once more!'

　　Playing a pipe with silvery squeaks,
　　Since then his Jumbly Girl he seeks,
　　And because by night he could not see,
　　He gathered the bark of the Twangum Tree
　　　　On the flowery plain that grows.
　　　　And he wove him a wondrous Nose, –
　　A Nose as strange as a Nose could be!
Of vast proportions and painted red,
And tied with cords to the back of his head.
　　– In a hollow rounded space it ended
　　With a luminous Lamp within suspended,
　　　　All fenced about
　　　　With a bandage stout
　　　　To prevent the wind from blowing it out; –
　　And with holes all round to send the light,
　　In gleaming rays on the dismal light.

And now each night, and all night long,
Over those plains still roams the Dong;
And above the wail of the Chimp and Snipe
You may hear the squeak of his plaintive pipe
While ever he seeks, but seeks in vain
To meet with his Jumbly Girl again;
Lonely and wild – all night he goes, –
The Dong with a luminous Nose!
And all who watch at the midnight hour,
From Hall or Terrace, or lofty Tower,
Cry, as they trace the Meteor bright,

Moving along through the dreary night, –
    'This is the hour when forth he goes,
    The Dong with a luminous Nose!
    Yonder – over the plain he goes;
        He goes!
        He goes;
    The Dong with a luminous Nose!'

Nonsense Trees

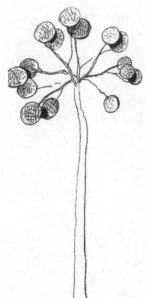

The Biscuit Tree
This remarkable vegetable production has never yet been described or delineated. As it never grows near rivers, nor near the sea, nor near mountains, or vallies, or houses, – its native place is wholly uncertain. When the flowers fall off, and the tree breaks out in biscuits, the effect is by no means disagreeable, especially to the hungry. – If the Biscuits grow in pairs, they do not grow single, and if they ever fall off, they cannot be said to remain on. –

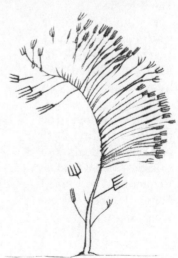

The Clothes-Brush Tree
This most useful natural production does not produce many clothes-brushes, which accounts for those objects being expensive. The omsquombious nature of this extraordinary vegetable it is of course unnecessary to be diffuse upon.

The Fork Tree

This pleasing and amazing Tree never grows above four hundred and sixty-three feet in height, – nor has any specimen hitherto produced above forty thousand silver forks at one time. If violently

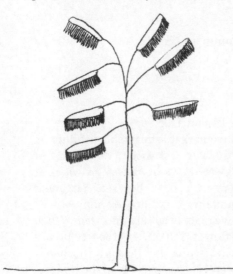

shaken it is most probable that many forks would fall off, – and in a high wind it is highly possible that all the forks would rattle dreadfully, and produce a musical tinkling to the ears of the happy beholder.

The Kite Tree

The Kite Tree is a fearful and astonishing vegetable when all the Kites are agitated by a tremendous wind, and endeavour to escape from their strings. The tree does not appear to be of any particular use to society, but would be frequented by small boys if they knew where it grew.

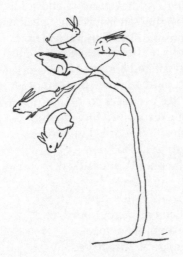

The Rabbit Tree

The Clomjombimbilious Tree   The Dish Tree

'Mrs Jaypher found a wafer'

Mrs Jaypher found a wafer
Which she stuck upon a note;
This she took and gave the cook.
Then she went and bought a boat
Which she paddled down the stream
Shouting, 'Ice produces cream,
Beer when churned produces butter!
Henceforth all the words I utter
Distant ages thus shall note –
From the Jaypher Wisdom-Boat.'

Mrs Jaypher said, 'It's safer,
If you've Lemons in your head,
First to eat a pound of meat,
And then to go at once to bed.
Eating meat is half the battle,
Till you hear the Lemons rattle!
If you don't, you'll always moan;
In a Lemoncolly tone;
For there's nothing half so dread=
=ful, as Lemons in your head!'

The Later History of the Owl and the Pussy-cat*

Our mother was the Pussy-Cat, our father was the Owl,
And so we're partly little beasts and partly little fowl,
The brothers of our family have feathers and they hoot,
While all the sisters dress in fur and have long tails to boot.
    We all believe that little mice,
    For food are singularly nice.

---

* Unfinished drafts written in April 1885. The manuscript is hard to decipher in
  places, and is untitled.

Our mother died long years ago. She was a lovely cat
Her tail was 5 feet long, and grey with stripes, but what of that?
In Sila forest on the East of far Calabria's shore
She tumbled from a lofty tree – none ever saw her more.
Our owly father long was ill from sorrow and surprise,
But with the feathers of his tail he wiped his weeping eyes.
And in the hollow of a tree in Sila's inmost maze
We made a happy home and there we pass our obvious days.

From Reggian Cosenza many owls about us flit
And bring us worldly news for which we do not care a bit.
We watch the sun each morning rise, beyond Tarento's straight;
We go out ———— before it gets too late,
And when the evening shades begin to lengthen from the trees
———————— as sure as bees is bees.
We wander up and down the shore
Or tumble over head and heels, but never, never more,
Can see the far Gromboolian plains
Or weep as we could once have wept o'er many a vanished scene:
This is the way our father moans – he is so very green.

Our father still preserves his voice, and when he sees a star
He often sings ————————————— to that original guitar.
The pot in which our parents took the honey in their boat,
But all the money has been spent, beside the £5 note.
The owls who come and bring us news are often ————
Because we take no interest in poltix of the day

'O dear! how disgusting is life!'

O dear! how disgusting is life!
To improve it O what can we do?
Most disgusting is hustle and strife,
And of all things an ill fitting shoe –
  Shoe
      O bother an ill fitting shoe!

'How pleasant to know Mr Lear!'

From a Photograph.

'How pleasant to know Mr Lear!'
    Who has written such volumes of stuff
Some think him ill-tempered and queer,
    But a few think him pleasant enough.

His mind is concrete and fastidious; –
    His nose is remarkably big; –
His visage is more or less hideous; –
    His beard it resembles a wig.

He has ears, and two eyes, and ten fingers, –
    (Leastways if you reckon two thumbs;)
Long ago he was one of the singers,
    But now he is one of the dumms.

He sits in a beautiful parlour,
    With hundreds of books on the wall;
He drinks a great deal of Marsala,
    But never gets tipsy at all.

He has many friends, laymen and clerical;
    Old Foss is the name of his cat;
His body is perfectly spherical; –
    He weareth a runcible hat.

When he walks in a waterproof white
    The children run after him *so*!
Calling out, – 'He's come out in his night-
    gown, that crazy old Englishman, – O!'

He weeps by the side of the ocean,
    He weeps on the top of the hill;
He purchases pancakes and lotion,
    And chocolate shrimps from the mill.

He reads, but he cannot speak, Spanish;
    He cannot abide ginger-beer. –
Ere the days of his pilgrimage vanish, –
    'How pleasant to know Mr Lear!'

Mr and Mrs Discobbolos
Second Part

Mr and Mrs Discobbolos
    Lived on the top of the wall,
    For twenty years, a month and a day,
    Till their hair had grown all pearly grey,
    And their teeth began to fall.
They never were ill, or at all dejected, –
By all admired, and by some respected,
    Till Mrs Discobbolos said,
    'O W! X! Y! Z!
    It is just come into my head –
We have no more room at all –
    Darling Mr Discobbolos!

'Look at our six fine boys!
        And our six sweet girls so fair!
    Up on this wall they have all been born,
    And not one of the twelve has happened to fall,
        Through my maternal care!
Surely they should not pass their lives
Without any chance of husbands or wives!'
        And Mrs Discobbolos said,
        'O W! X! Y! Z!
        Did it never come into your head
    That our lives must be lived elsewhere,
                Dearest Mr Discobbolos?

'They have never been at a Ball,
        Nor have even seen a Bazaar!
    Nor have heard folks say in a tone all hearty, –
    "What loves of girls (at a garden party)
        Those Misses Discobbolos are!"
Morning and night it drives me wild
To think of the fate of each darling child, – ! –'
        But Mr Discobbolos said,
        'O – W! X! Y! Z!
        What has come into your fiddledum head!
    What a runcible goose you are!
                Octopod Mrs Discobbolos!'

Suddenly Mr Discobbolos
        Slid from the top of the wall;
    And beneath it he dug a dreadful trench, –
    And filled it with Dynamite gunpowder gench, –
        And aloud began to call, –
'Let the wild bee sing and the blue bird hum!
For the end of our lives has certainly come!'
        And Mrs Discobbolos said,
        'O! W! X! Y! Z!
        We shall presently all be dead,
    On this ancient runcible wall, –
                Terrible Mr Discobbolos!'

Pensively, Mr Discobbolos
    Sate with his back to the wall; –
He lighted a match, and fired the train, –
And the mortified mountains echoed again
    To the sounds of an awful fall!
And all the Discobbolos family flew
In thousands of bits to the sky so blue,
    And no one was left to have said,
    'O! W! X! Y! Z!
    Has it come into anyone's head
That the end has happened to all
    Of the whole of the Clan Discobbolos?'

Some Incidents in the Life of my Uncle Arly

O my agèd Uncle Arly! –
Sitting on a heap of Barley
    All the silent hours of night, –
Close beside a leafy thicket: –
On his nose there was a Cricket, –
In his hat a Railway Ticket; –
    (But his shoes were far too tight.)

Long ago, in youth, he squander'd
All his goods away, and wander'd
    To the Timskoop Hills afar.
There, on golden sunsets blazing
Every evening found him gazing, –
Singing, – 'Orb! you're quite amazing!
    How I wonder what you are!'

Like the ancient Medes and Persians,
Always by his own exertions
    He subsisted on those hills; –
Whiles, – by teaching children spelling, –
Or at times by merely yelling, –
Or at intervals by selling
    'Propter's Nicodemus Pills'.

Later, in his morning rambles
He perceived the moving brambles
        Something square and white disclose; –
'Twas a First-class Railway-Ticket
But in stooping down to pick it
Off the ground, – a pea-green Cricket
        Settled on my uncle's Nose.

Never – never more, – oh! never,
Did that Cricket leave him ever, –
        Dawn or evening, day or night; –
Clinging as a constant treasure, –
Chirping with a cheerious measure, –
Wholly to my uncle's pleasure, –
        (Though his shoes were far too tight.)

So, for three-and-forty winters,
Till his shoes were worn to splinters,
        All those hills he wander'd o'er, –
Sometimes silent; – sometimes yelling; –
Till he came to Borly-Melling,
Near his old ancestral dwelling;
        – And he wander'd thence no more.

On a little heap of Barley
Died my agèd Uncle Arly,
        And they buried him one night; –
Close beside the leafy thicket; –
There, – his hat and Railway Ticket; –
There, – his ever faithful Cricket; –
        (But his shoes were far too tight.)

'He only said, "I'm very weary"'

He only said, 'I'm very weary.'
   The rheumatiz he said,
He said, 'It's awful dull and dreary.
   I think I'll go to bed.'

from the prospectus to

Views in Rome and Its Environs:
Drawn from Nature and on Stone
(1841)

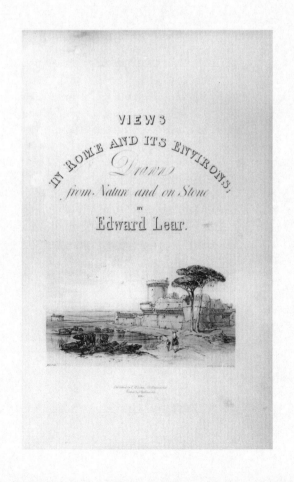

From *the prospectus to* Views in Rome and Its Environs: Drawn from Nature and on Stone *(1841)*

Lear's first travel book was *Views in Rome and Its Environs: Drawn from Nature and on Stone*, published by T. McLean in 1841. It was a lavish folio volume, priced at four guineas, and published by subscription: the list of eminent subscribers was headed by Lear's future pupil, the young Queen Victoria. The published book consisted of twenty-five lithographed views (plus another on the title-page) without accompanying letterpress text. However, to help raise subscribers the publishers had issued a four-page prospectus, and this included brief descriptions of each of the views. The British Library copy of the book has this prospectus bound in with it, which gives some indication of a close tie between the advertised descriptions and the published book. As the book is rare, and the prospectus even more so, I have here included a few extracts, on the grounds that these notes to the views represent Lear's first published travel writings. Internal evidence indicates that they were written by Lear himself, and though they are for the most part functional and impersonal, they give some flavour of the book. Five of the views are set in Rome, and most of the rest are situated within a day's ride of the city: the notes describe local costumes, recommend fine views, supply a little history and explain some of the details in the lithographs. The first description below, of the 'Castle of Ostia', refers to the inset lithograph on the title-page, reproduced above on p. 115.

TITLE-PAGE – CASTLE OF OSTIA

This picturesque remnant of the warlike time of Julius the Second,* stands at the mouth of the Tiber, about eighteen miles from Rome. The once important town of Ostia is now reduced to a miserable village, inhabited but by a few peasants, employed in the adjacent salt-marshes; there are, however, abundant traces of its former extent, scattered in masses of ruin over the neighbouring meadows; and, although wars, and the removal of the port of Rome, by the Emperor Claudian, to the opposite mouth of the river, have caused the fall and desertion of Ostia, yet, as the first Christian Bishopric (its Bishop has the exclusive right of crowning the Pontiff), this melancholy place must continue to bear an interest not possessed by more flourishing spots. The illustration in the title-page of Mr LEAR's volume, is taken at a time when the marshy ground about the Castle is covered with water, and frequented by gloomy-looking buffaloes. The tower of the Castle, with its two pines adjoining, are a conspicuous object in the dreary Campagna which surrounds it.

PLATE 4. CERVARA

This remarkable town is built on one of the very high ranges of mountains between Tivoli and Subiaco; the ascent to it is painfully long; and, from its being overlooked on one side by huge rocks and higher hills, the view from its summit is more circumscribed than one would be led to suppose. Shaded by high rocks, from the east, till the sun is high in the heavens, Cervara is the last town of these mountains that is crimsoned by the western light. Its people wear a costume peculiar to themselves; and the Cervarese woman, with her blue gown, crimson stockings, and high-heeled shoes, is easily recognized at fairs and markets, amongst all her sisters and fair country-women. Cervara is one of the eighteen towns dependent on the Abbacy of Subiaco, and is a place too formidable, from its remote situation, to be often visited by strangers.

PLATE 5. CIVITELLA DI SUBIACO

On the very summit of a high single rock, towering above all its kindred towns, Civitella is an object of view for a great distance: so frequently, in the lonely walks of those beautiful mountains,

---

*   Julius the second: Giuliano della Rovere (1443-1513), Pope Julius II (1503–13).

does the marked form of its rock appear (from its isolated situation) as if near at hand, – though a long journey lies between it and the traveller, – that it has become a proverb among the native peasantry. The narrow town itself, with its church tower, is built on the site of an old Cyclopean town, and commands immense views of the surrounding country; nearly forty towns, of which Roiate is on the left, may be discerned from it. Between are deep vallies, filled with pine and chestnut, where it is shaded even at noon, and beyond are the plains of the Latin valley, with the mountain-ridge of the ancient Volscians. Civitella is about nine miles from Subiaco, and is one of its eighteen dependencies; the scenery in its neighbourhood is unrivalled for extreme beauty and grandeur.

PLATE 6. COLLEPARDO
This little town is but a few miles from the town Alatri, and is perched on the edge of a ravine; it possesses more of the wild and fearful than most of the scenes in the Roman States. A mule-path winds down to the bottom of the glen, (by the huge rock to the right of the figures), and, crossing a stream, ascends to the village of Collepardo, which in itself contains little or no interest; below nothing is seen but enormous rocks and dreary chasms, some of which are well adapted for a hermit's life.

PLATE 7. FRASCATI, FROM VILLA MONDRAGONE, BELONGING TO THE BORGHESI
No two places ever contrasted more strongly than the present and the preceding Plate; for beneath groups of the beautiful pines of Italy, one sees the wide Campagna, stretching to the blue sea; in its centre is the town of Frascati; and the left side (all of which forms part of the territory of ancient Tusculum), is covered with villas, and gardens of pines, cypress and olives; these villas (amongst which is represented that of Falconieri), look towards Rome, and are, in summer, delightful for their abundant foliage and shade. Frascati is about eleven miles from Rome, and is much frequented by Romans on holiday.

PLATE 15. ROME, FROM THE GARDENS OF MONTE PINCIO
This is one of the most beautiful views of modern Rome, taken from the public walk in the Pincian Gardens. The Villa Medici, used now

as the French Academy, is the highest building on the left; then, towards the right, are the Tower of the Villa Malta, the Church of La Trinità, and the Obelisk at the head of the steps leading to the Piazza di Spagna. Beyond, are the long lines of the Pope's summer or Quirinal palace; the Colonna palace, and the pine said to have been planted in its gardens by Rienzi.* Behind it stands the Tower of Nero, and more in the foreground are the houses chiefly occupied by English travellers. On a clear summer's morning it is difficult to imagine a more beautiful scene than this from Monte Pincio.

PLATE 20. FAIR OF SANT' ANATOLIA
On the 10th of July the annual fair, here represented, is held; and great crowds of the peasants, from the mountain towns far and near, flock to it. They meet in a little plain before the Chapel of the Saint (which stands among the trees on the left of the drawing), below the little town of Girano, which is about ten miles from Subiaco. The festival commences over-night; but by sunrise, on the 10th, nothing can be more striking than the variety of brilliant costume which extends over the plain. In the drawing, the time is chosen – as about ten or twelve – when great numbers, becoming weary, sleep on the grass, or prepare a midday meal: the confusion of every possible article of food and furniture which strews the ground, baffles description. All the figures represented were drawn from nature by Mr LEAR, who for several years was in the habit of visiting the fair of Sant' Anatolia.

PLATE 23. TIVOLI, WITH MÆCENAS' VILLA, LOOKING OVER THE CAMPAGNA
No views near Rome can exclude Tivoli from their number, though it has been so often pourtrayed. The town itself – the Villa of Mæcenas, with its crumbling arches – the numerous cascades – the river, winding away to the far Campagna – the vast extent of plain – and the rich olives that adorn the foreground – form, indeed, a picture that may well bear repetition, and yet be, in many respects, new.

---

* Rienzi: Cola di Rienzi (c.1313–54), tribune of the Roman people, subject of a novel by Edward Bulwer-Lytton (1835) and an opera by Richard Wagner (1838).

from

Illustrated Excursions in Italy,

Volumes I and II (1846)

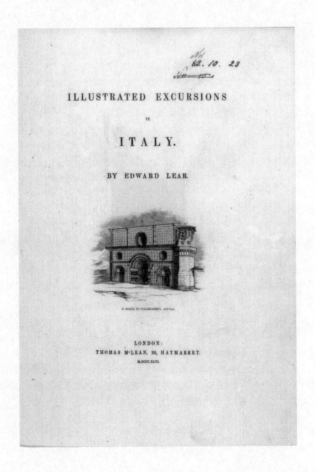

ILLUSTRATED EXCURSIONS

IN

I T A L Y.

BY EDWARD LEAR.

S. MARIA DI COLLEMAGGIO. AQUILA.

LONDON:
THOMAS M'LEAN, 26, HAYMARKET.
M.DCCC.XLVI.

The Three
Abruzzi

from Illustrated Excursions in Italy, Volumes I and II *(1846)*

This two-volume work is the first of the four illustrated books for which Lear's text was taken from his own travel journals. It has not been reprinted since its first publication (by subscription) in 1846. Moreover, it did not feature in the 1952 selection from Lear's journals edited by Herbert Von Thal, so it has been almost inaccessible. This is a pity, as it is one of Lear's most attractive and enjoyable travel books, full of high spirits, comedy, incident, and memorable evocations of people and places. Queen Victoria liked it enough to employ the author as her drawing-master after reading it.

The book may have been neglected until now because of its sometimes uneasy marriage of solid scholarship and personal reminiscence. Lear always researched his travels in a professional spirit, reading up on the history and culture of the regions he was visiting; and the *Illustrated Excursions* include lengthy excerpts from authorities on the Abruzzi region, with meticulous footnoting of some thirty sources. But the passages of history and social geography are not integrated into the journals, and the book gains much in liveliness and readability by omitting most of them, as I have done in the selections below. Lear seems to have come to a similar conclusion himself, because his next two volumes of Journals wear their background learning relatively lightly; but he returned to a more scholarly presentation, with long excerpts, in his book on Corsica.

The first volume was successful enough for Lear to follow it speedily with a second; but for this he reverted to something much closer to the *Views in Rome*, confining himself to brief historical and geographical notes on the lithographed views.

Lear's travelling companion in the early parts of these excursions was Charles Knight, a young friend from Rome, with whom he had already toured the Alban hills in 1842. We join them, after the Preface, as they are leaving Mentorella for Subiaco. Lear is riding Knight's Arab horse, Gridiron.

Preface to Volume I

In offering this Volume to the Public, it is almost necessary to state, that its object is the illustration of a part of Italy which, though nowise inferior in interest to those portions of that country so commonly visited, has hitherto attracted but little attention. With the exception of the Tours by Sir R. COLT HOARE, Bart., and the Honourable KEPPEL CRAVEN,* I am not aware of any published account of the Abruzzi provinces in English; and the drawings with which the following pages are illustrated are, I believe, the first hitherto given of a part of Central Italy as romantic as it is unfrequented.

I would beg the indulgence of the Public towards the literary portion of the Work, which I have thought it right to print with little alteration from my own journals written during my rambles, adding only such historical and other information concerning the places visited, as I have sought for in various Authors. Much yet remains to be explored and illustrated throughout the northern provinces of the Kingdom of Naples, and so far from this Volume containing a full account of that interesting country, I should wish it to be regarded as a suggestion for the more careful observation of future and abler Tourists.

I have executed the whole of the Lithographic drawings from my own sketches, and have endeavoured to preserve a close fidelity to the Originals. The Vignettes are also by my own hand, excepting the Architectural subjects, which were transferred to wood by Mr R. BRANSTON.

---

* Sir Richard Colt Hoare, *A Classical Tour through Sicily and Italy* (1819), and the Hon. R. Keppel Craven, *Excursion in the Abruzzi and Northern Provinces of Naples* (1837).

To those Ladies, to whose kindness I owe the arrangement of the Airs given at the end of the Volume, my best thanks are due; but I regret, that owing to the difficulty of writing correctly such music as is only retained by ear, the Appendix is less perfect than I could have wished.

The Lithographic Drawings have been printed at the establishment of Messrs HULLMANDEL and WALTON. To those Gentlemen, and to the various Artists by whom my drawings on wood have been engraved, as well as to Messrs. BENTLEY and Co., Printers, I am desirous of expressing my thanks for the care bestowed on their several departments.

During a long residence in Italy, I have had opportunities of collecting numerous illustrations of scenery little known in England, especially of that in the near neighbourhood of Rome; and should the present Volume meet with the approbation of the Public, a second series of Excursions may be anticipated at some future period.*

EDWARD LEAR.

27, DUKE STREET, ST JAMES'S
April, 1846.

---

* Volume II was published at the end of the year, but – reverting to the mode of *Views in Rome and Its Environs* – it consisted only of twenty-five views with brief descriptions (see below, pp. 164–5).

The Abruzzi Provinces

July 26, 1843. La Mentorella
Having sufficiently rested and fed Gridiron, Iron-grey, and ourselves, we proceeded downward on our way to Subiaco; but, about a quarter of a mile below the town, the remarkable Hermitage and Church of La Mentorella caused us some delay. These are built on the edge of an isolated precipice, jutting out from the mountain side over the valley of Girano, and possess interest from their antiquity and the legends attached to them, as well as from the wild character of the scenery in which they are placed.

Here, in a cave at the foot of the rock, San Benedetto is believed to have lived in the sixth century, previous to his going to Subiaco; and a tradition of far earlier date (during the reign of the Emperor Trajan) represents the crag of La Mentorella as that where a vision of the deer with a crucifix between his horns led to the conversion of St Eustace to Christianity. A flight of stairs outside the chapel, leads to the Campanile, which is surmounted by a pair of antlers, commemorating the event; and these steps are diligently ascended by kneeling pilgrims on the *fête*-day of September 29.

It is certain that a church existed here as early as the year AD 594, since it was then bestowed by Gregory I on the Abbot of Subiaco. In AD 958, the mountain of Guadagnolo, (then known by the names Wultvilla or Vulturella, whence Mentorella,) together with its church, dedicated to Sta Maria, was possessed by the monastery of San Gregorio in Rome; but the building appears to have been abandoned after the fourteenth century, though it was restored by the Emperor Leopold I in 1660. The Gothic chapel now standing is of the tenth century.

I have often been present at an annual *festa* held here on the 29th of September, and I remember at my first visit to have been particularly struck with all I saw. As I climbed the sides of Guadagnolo, on one of those cloudy afternoons of an Italian autumn before the rain clears the sky for a bright October, numerous parties of peasants were slowly following the winding track, chaunting litanies, or saying prayers in an under-tone. Many carried large stones from the summit to a spot not far below the town, where they were added to an enormous heap, the result of centuries of such annual visits. Lower down, on a platform of rock in front of the Mentorella Chapel, were gathered many hundred people (for a fair is held during all the night, and part of the day following); and the confusion of men, women, horses, asses, and goods of all kinds, was strikingly picturesque, seen, for it was now dark, by the broken light of many scattered fires. The Chapel itself on its solitary crag, backed by the high line of sombre mountains which divide the Roman from the Neapolitan dominions, and hang over the dim valley of Girano and Siciliano far below, was crowded with peasants, kneeling or sleeping under its dark arches; forming altogether so wild a scene, that, unable to tear myself away, I remained wandering from fire to fire, among the groups of people, nearly the whole night through.

From La Mentorella, there is a sort of path of steps cut in the rock, leading to the valley of Girano; a steep descent and narrow, choked by overgrowing brambles, and crossed by roots of chestnut trees, streams, etc. This we adopted by way of a short road to Subiaco, and were soon sufficiently embarrassed by losing the track, or by getting among high beech-woods, whence we saw nothing: our steeds, too, decidedly objected to being led down such ugly rocks and steep corners; so we drove them before us, which was scarcely a better plan, since they bothered us sadly, by striking into private short cuts of their own imagining, or by falling in their attempts to make quicker way. By reason of all such delays, it was late ere we reached the valley of Girano; fully owning the justice of Signor Nibbi's remark on the situation of Guadagnolo, '*incommoda oltremodo è la sua situazione*'.*

Glad to be at the bottom of the mountain, we crossed the little plain, passed Girano, and wound through beautiful chestnut woods, till we reached the hills overlooking the valley below Civitella, just as heavy purple clouds shut out the last red line of sun-set. Thenceforth we journeyed on in utter darkness, over paths by no means pleasant, to Subiaco, where we slept.

July 27, 1843. Near Cavaliere
To me the whole picture** is one of pastoral and cheerful industry, and the life of the Abruzzese Pecoraro is the *beau idéal* of a shepherd's existence. On his native mountains his amusement is playing on the bagpipes or samboni, whose long-drawn notes you

---

* 'its location is extremely inconvenient'.
** The picture of the annual march to Apulia of the Abruzzo shepherds with their flocks.

APPENDIX.

No. 1. (see Excursion 1. page 10)

The following air is generally known as that of the Pifferari, because at Christmas time it is played on the Bagpipes before the shrines of the Madonna in Rome. The shepherds who perform it in that city are most frequently from the neighbourhood of Sora, in the Province of Terra di Lavoro, but it is in common use throughout all the mountains of the Abruzzi, where I have learned it from many shepherds. The first part is usually repeated 4 or 5 times; the last is played but once. The music of this air is said to be of great antiquity.

Music of the Pifferari

may hear hour after hour in the summer days, an accompaniment of indescribable romance to those poetical scenes. In the plains of the Campagna you will observe him knitting stockings, or reading some book of a devotional character. Altogether a more inoffensive and contented race of beings I never met with, though they certainly are more sedate in their deportment than the noisy denizens of Naples.

One or two more general remarks regarding the provinces of the Abruzzi may be allowed. The great valleys in the heart of the Apennines are subject to the scourge of earthquakes, and that most frequently and fatally. And the inhabitants, for courtesy, simplicity, and hospitality, are a proverb among Italians as well as strangers.

A short boundary question ensued on reaching the Neapolitan frontier at Cavaliere, where, however, we were scarcely detained by some very civil officials, so on we cantered, fording a stream below Poggio Cinolfo, and soon arriving at Carsoli, hidden from the plain in a little nook of its own. A ruined bridge below, and a shattered castle above, give a more picturesque than comfortable air to the modern town, which contains eight or nine thousand inhabitants, and is successor to, though not on the same site as, the ancient Carseoli: within, dirty narrow streets, only-redeemed here and there by a bit of Gothic door or window, raise no favourable idea of the present condition of this once respectable abode of the Equi, where they sacrificed foxes to Ceres, and where the Romans imprisoned Bituitus, king of Thrace.

It was nearly noon: so we put up our horses, and having satisfied the authorities as to our passports and *permessi*[1] for our steeds, we adjourned to a wretched *Locanda*, where the *Oste** flattered us with hopes of something to eat, bidding us wait in a closet, very nearly filled up by a large bed, a cracked spinette, and an inclined table with uncertain legs: but when the repast was brought, both eatables and drinkables were such that, though pretty well used to uncommon food, we were compelled to be content with bread and water: and, leaving our dinner in the charming chamber, where 'cold and unhonoured, its relics were laid',** we strolled by the

---

1 A permission is necessary from the Neapolitan minister resident in Rome for introducing horses from the Papal states into the Neapolitan dominions.

---

* *Locanda*: inn. *Oste*: landlord.
** James McHenry (1785-1845), *O'Halloran; or The Insurgent Chief* (1824), vol. 2, ch. 12.

willow-edged Turano, a stream which rises near Carsoli, till our horses were ready to start. This was the first place where we encountered that horrible beverage, called *vino cotto*, which is wine boiled when new to make it keep; and, spite of its nastiness, is drunk all over the Abruzzi by the common people. I have tasted some, kept for many years, that was little inferior to good Marsala, but when new, it is filthy beyond imagination.

About two, we set off again, by a pathway through a rising valley. Beyond Carsoli, there is no road for carriages into the Abruzzi: bare rocks were on our left, and on our right high hills, covered, as far as eye could reach, with forests of oak, looking black and untrodden enough to shelter a world of bears and wolves. Patience, and endurance of heat, bore us to Colli, an uninteresting village, which offered us nothing to remark beyond the courtesy and simple good-breeding of its peasant inhabitants.

Beyond this, we toiled onward through this long stony pass, and all our hopes were fixed on Rocca di Cerri, a village at the top of the hill; on arriving at which, we confessed to being well repaid for our labour, by the view over the sublime Marsica. On our left, the snowy peaks of Velino, more than 7,000 feet in height, were gloomy beneath threatening clouds, and a wild confusion of misty mountains closed that side of the scene. Far below, in bright sunshine, lay a long streak of the blue Lake of Fucino, with its beautiful plain, dotted and spangled with woods and villages; and beyond the Lake uprose the strangely-formed mountain of Celano, with many a high range of faint, blue hills, while the dark-castled rocks and formidable pass of Tagliacozzo were at our feet. Having admired all this, we descended by a steep serpentine path, and were soon at the level of the Castle of Tagliacozzo, which guards the entrance to the plain below.

I have never seen anything more majestic than the approach to Tagliacozzo. It is a precipitous ravine, almost artificial in appearance, and, by some, indeed, considered as having been partly formed by the Romans, for the transit of the Via Valeria. A monastery, with a *Calvario*, or range of shrines, stands at the entrance of this extraordinary gorge, the portals of which are, on one hand, huge crags, crested with a ruined castle; on the other, perpendicular precipices: between them is placed the town, receding step by step to the plain below, while the picture is completed by the three peaks of the towering Monte Velino, entirely filling up the opening of the ravine.

* * * *

An indescribable quiet, a feeling of distance from the busy world, pervades this sequestered district.* No road connects the Marsica, (or district where the ancient Marsi resided,) with either Rome or Naples. The old Via Valeria passed through it from Rome, and its vestiges are still visible near the Castle of Tagliacozzo; but now the only roads for carriages in the whole territory are from Tagliacozzo to Avezzano, Celano, and Magliano: and one from Capistrello to Sora, not yet completed. Shut up in its own circle of high mountains, the Marsica has no communication (beyond that afforded by mule-tracks) with any great city; and it possesses, besides the delight of its unfrequented tranquillity, more attractions among its inhabitants, its scenery, and antiquities, than any place it has been ever my fortune to visit.

Passing on through the village of Capelle and leaving Alba on our left, to be visited in my second journey, we were soon in sight of Avezzano, standing on the low ground near the Lake of Fucino, which lay behind it, a narrow blue line, bounded by beautiful mountains, purple in the light of evening. The wish to explore its rocky sides and glittering towns was strong within us as we advanced towards Avezzano, hoping much for our morrow.

All was bustle of harvest; treading out of corn, and bearing away of sheaves on the common before the gate of Avezzano, whose fine castle, built by the Colonna in the fifteenth century, stands well at the entrance of the town, and is a good specimen of a baronial residence. We asked for some inn or *Locanda,* but these are desiderata in Abruzzo; and unluckily we had to seek our night's quarters in a place to which we had not brought a letter of introduction. One house, a *casa Corradini*, was indicated as likely to receive us, and so we entered the town in search of it.

Though a Capo di Distretto,** Avezzano is not a promising town in appearance; there are some few good palaces and convents, but the general effect of its streets is mean and uninteresting. It is not, I believe, the successor of any ancient city, yet Corsignani*** and

---

*   Near Scurcola.
** District capital.
*** Pietro Antonio Corsignani, author of *De Viris Illustribus Marsorum* (*Of the Famous Men of the Marsica,* 1712) and *Reggia Marsicana* (*The Marsican Kingdom,* 1727).

others seek to derive its name from a temple of Janus – Ara Jani. Be this as it may, the decay of such important places of antiquity as Alba, Marrubium, Angizia, etc., may well have given rise to the more modern towns in their neigbourhood. Avezzano was probably no inconsiderable town in the middle ages, since we read of it as the temporary abode of the emperor Frederic, in 1242. Of the people here, as of all we had met since our entering the Abruzzi, the prevailing character was politeness and good nature. The town contains about 2,500 inhabitants.

We sate sometime on our horses, waiting for the Padrone of our lodgings, that were to be, and meanwhile, were highly amused by one of those torrents of pigs, common to Italian country towns, when the sable tribe, for black they are all, return at night to supper. Most of these towns being upon hills, the swine are obliged to go *up*, and therefore arrive in a state of placid expectation; but at Avezzano, they all have to come *down* hill, and so rush into the piazza in an uncontrollable frenzy. How we did laugh, to the diversion of half the rabble of the town, who had come to gaze on us, as the immense current of grunters burst from the long street into the market-place, with a wonderful hubbub, and ran shrieking away through all the lanes of the place.

When the pig-storm was over, and we had seen to our steeds, we made the most of the short remaining light and hurried to our lodgings, where three ineffably polite females shewed us into a large, raftered room, of bewildering aspect, with much furniture, and a great assortment of old clothes, and strewed with articles of female dress, intermixed rather oddly with fowls of all sizes, fluttering about in every direction, over and under two very misshapen beds. All this, added to the walls having a speckly appearance, which to the initiated, denotes the presence of certain flat entomological visitors, did not promise much repose; nor did the pensive chirping of an afflicted one-winged chicken, upon whom one of our landladies lavished the most touching caresses, at all strengthen our admiration of the dormitory we had selected.

Meantime, while one of our hostesses reduced our chamber to order, we assisted the other two (one of whom was very handsome, but alarmingly fierce), to pluck and roast some pigeons, which eventually produced us no bad supper: – for wine, alas! the horrible *vino cotto* was a most unsatisfactory substitute. As for our horses, fortunately for them, they were far better lodged than their masters.

Still there was daylight left for a stroll; so we set off on foot to the Lake, (hardly a mile distant,) through the quietest green lanes of turf, bordered by poplars, and enclosing plantations of low vines. How fresh the air! How deliciously calm the shallow, transparent waters! How grateful the placid beauty of that lovely prospect, after all the heat of the day! Numbers of horses and flocks of sheep were scattered over the low meadows, near the water's edge: herds of goats were slowly and sedately winding their homeward way. It was not easy to quit the enjoyment of so tranquil a scene; and we wandered till it was dark, by the still mirror, – an enjoyment ill exchanged for a return to our strange abode, to which, notwithstanding, the pigeons, boiled and roast, together with some good macaroni, partly reconciled us.

There was no lock to our door. All night long, two or three frantic hens kept tearing round the room, and would by no means be expelled: the afflicted chicken with a broken wing scrambled about the floor without intermission: vermin of two species, (politely called B flats and F sharps,) worried us beyond endurance: a perpetual chorus of pigeons thrilled over our heads, and an accompaniment of pigs resounded from below. So we were very glad when morning appeared.

Thus ended our first day and night in the Abruzzi.

July 28, 1843. Lake Fucino
By the pleasant lanes we traversed last evening, we arrived at the Lake, but soon changed our road for a wofully stony one, under the mountain on its south side; this soon brought us to the celebrated Emissario,* the position of which vast work is easily traced at a distance by mounds of earth at intervals, between the hill through which it is carried, and the Lake. There is no very great degree of the picturesque in its crumbling walls of red brick-work; but the view from the hill-side, above the higher part of this gigantic witness of Roman grandeur, fully atones for the want of outward magnificence in its ruins. Here my companion left me, to explore and measure the Emissario; while I, unapt to make

---

* Elsewhere in the book Lear glosses 'the great Emissario' as 'a passage or tunnel, about nineteen feet in height, nine broad, and nearly three miles in length, constructed by the Emperor Claudius, for the purpose of carrying off the waters of the Lake (which frequently inundated the surrounding country) into the river Liris'.

researches in the bowels of the damp earth, greatly preferred reclining in the bright sunshine, untired with the solemn prospect below me.

The plain of Avezzano; the clear blue lake; Alba; and Velino, with its fine peaks, alternately in bright light, or shaded by passing clouds; the far snow-covered mountains beyond Solmona; the bare pass of Forca Carusa; the precipitous crag of Celano, – all these at once, brilliant with the splendour of Italian morning, formed a scene not to be slightly gazed at or lightly forgotten – the utter quiet of all around! the character of undisturbed beauty which threw a spell of enchantment over the whole!

A herd of white goats blinking and sneezing lazily in the early sun; their goatherd piping on a little reed; two or three large falcons soaring above the Lake, the watchful cormorant sitting motionless on its shining surface; and a host of merry flies sporting in the fragrant air, – these were the only signs of life in the very spot where the thrones of Claudius and his Empress were placed on the crowd-blackened hill: a few distant fishing-boats dotted the Lake where, eighteen centuries ago, the cries of combat rent the air, and the glitter of contending galleys delighted the Roman multitude.

The solitary character of the place is most striking; no link between the gay populous past and the lonely present, no work of any intermediate century breaks its desolate and poetical feeling. I could willingly have lingered there for hours, for I can recall no scene at once so impressive and beautiful.

* * * *

Trasacco, the Transaqua of old records, now a small town of 750 inhabitants, seems to have no claim to antiquity of origin, beyond its having been built on the site of a palace of Claudius, afterwards inhabited by Trajan. On the ruins of this palace San Rufino is said to have erected the church which now bears his name: he was the first Bishop of the Marsi, about AD 237, and suffered martyrdom under the Emperor Maximinian, together with San Cesidio, whose relics are great objects of veneration to the Marsi of the present day. Whatever may have been the former state of Trasacco, its present condition is sufficiently forlorn; though its church, and several bits of Gothic architecture about the town, are well worth some attention, which I regret I did not give to them.

On asking for a *Locanda*, we were directed to the first family of the town, the De' Gasparis, who had resided there for several centuries; to whose house we went, and asked boldly for aid for ourselves and horses. This was cheerfully given, though we were strangers, and without any letter of recommendation: Don Serafino – (everybody is called Don throughout the Neapolitan states, a remnant of old Spanish customs) – doing the honours of his establishment, a small but decent dwelling, with great friendliness.

After a dull and hungry hour of converse with some younger sons of our host, mostly on the subjects of hunting, etc., we were taken, with many apologies for its being fast-day, into another room, where a repast was already on the table. The father De' Gasparis did not appear, but his six sons supplied his place; and, to say truth, the hospitality of this worthy family was rather oppressive, for there was no end of dinner, and the way in which they continually loaded our plates seriously threatened apoplexy. The macaroni, a word used in the Abruzzi to express long slices of paste (usually in summer dressed with *Pomi d'oro* or Tomatas) was what we could least fight off; and, since Benjamin's days, nothing was ever seen like the supplies we groaned under. *'Bisogna mangiare!' 'è un piatto nazionale!'* exclaimed the six brothers if we paused in the work set before us. *'Non possiamo più!'* said we. *'Mangiate! mangiate! sempre mangiate!'** said they.

Fruit and excellent coffee having closed our refreshment, and rather relieved us from the terror we felt at the continual exhortation *'mangiare,'* K. and I, spite of our friends' earnest entreaties not to brave the sun, wandered forth to explore the land. It was indeed too hot for any exertion, and we got little for our pains, sheer rock and deep water soon ending our research; and all we could do was to gaze at the grey Lake, for many a cloud was rising westward, as we stood at the end of a fearfully hot slip of white pebbles, bordered by a fringe of meditative green frogs, which went pop into the classic wave on the approach of our disturbing footsteps.

On our return to the town, Don Serafino, who is arch-priest of the Church of S. Cesidio, lionized us all over it; and shewed us some of the Gothic windows, etc. I have alluded to above. But what most pleased me at Trasacco was a view near a curious but picturesque old tower, square at its base, and round at top, over-looking all the wide Lake, with the distant Velino beyond. Oderisius, Count of the

---

* 'You must eat!'; 'It's a national speciality!'; 'We can't manage any more!'; 'Eat! Eat! Keep eating!'

Marsi, is said to have resided in '*la torre anticha di Trasacco*'* in the year 1050; but whether this were the building, I know not.

Our horses were brought forth, though we were much pressed to remain until to-morrow: this, however, could not be. So, wishing a hearty farewell to our friendly hosts, and promising to revisit them if possible, we set off towards Avezzano with a very pleasant store of feelings called forth by such unaffected courtesy.

It was waxing late, and fast the clouds were gathering. Back we galloped, by the low vineyards, and past the fish-getting and harvest-collecting Luco; but in vain. The storm spread dark and wide over mountain and water, and burst fearfully on us as we reached the Emissario; whence, in drenching torrents, we went at full speed down the long green lanes, the scenery but half visible through a driving mist of hail and rain. Pretty well soaked we were as we entered Avezzano, driving before us an immense troop of unhappy donkeys, who had lost all command of their intellects at our first rapid approach, and rushed wildly before us all the way home.

We found our landladies in a state of distress at the death of the before-mentioned invalid chicken, who had committed suicide in a tub of water. This did not, however, disturb our peace so much as the summons of an inspector of police to his office, on the ground of our passports not being in order: but, as we considered them to be quite right, (setting aside the fact of our being wet through, and that our supper was waiting,) we politely requested him to come to us instead; which eventually he did, and signed our passports on looking at some of our introductory letters. A distinct '*Carta di Passo*' is, however, requisite for every separate province of the kingdom of Naples for those who travel out of the high-road, – a circumstance they had not informed us of at Carsoli; and, although we were not to blame for our involuntary ignorance, the inspector was no less in the right.**

After these events we retired to bed, and were charmed for another night by the sportive proceedings of fowls, fleas, bugs, pigeons, and pigs, as before.

---

*   'the ancient tower of Trasacco'.
*   Later, in Città di Penne, the police declare Lear and Knight's passports out of order, and they are detained for two nights.

August 3, 1843. Above Montebello, crossing the ridge separating the provinces of Teramo and Aquila
After a great toil to the summit, we struck into dark paths through wide beech forests broken by grey rocks, whence, at intervals, the view of the Gran Sasso, rising above an unbroken distance of wood, was infinitely grand. At length, long after the great prospect towards the Adriatic had been fairly shut out, we opened on a broad green valley encircled by rocky hills, and full of cattle of all kinds. It was near sunset; and yet two peasants, whom we met, declared that Villa Santa Lucia was *'lontano assai'*,* and there was not any habitation nearer.

There was no remedy: we passed over the lonely, quiet *Pianura*,** and proceeded to scale its boundary, a high and weary ridge of rock, – sore work for poor old Gridiron. At its summit, how different a view surprised us! that to the north had appeared as a vast plain, but tangled and cut up into a thousand gutter-like divisions: here, we came on a wild chaos of mountain-tops, ridge above ridge, peak above peak: the high line of the Marsic mountains, the noble Velino, an interminable perspective of Apennines – all seemed below our feet; a dark purple world, still and solemn, outlined with the utmost delicacy against the clear sky, where the daylight yet lingered along an horizon of golden red. These unexpected effects of beauty constitute one of the chief charms of such methodless rambles as ours.

Immensely below us was the deep valley to which our course was to be directed; and there, about the second hour of the night,[2] we arrived well tired with our long day's journey. Villa Santa Lucia, a poor village, but our home for the night, did not look especially inviting; neither did the house of Don Domenico Nunzio, to whose care we had been recommended by our anonymous friend at Città di Penna.

Yet this, though dark and small, was not nearly so unpleasant an abode as our first at Città di Penna, inasmuch as the poor people who received us here offered all they had with the greatest cheerfulness; nor were the rooms so irretrievably filthy. But what a

2   Ave Maria, or the termination of the day, is always one half-hour after sunset throughout Italy; and the succeeding hours are called one, two, three, etc. of the night.

*   'quite far away'.
** Plain.

stable! How often, on opening the door, did startled hens dash wildly against the candle and leave us in darkness! How often, when we had effected an entrance, did misguided calves, and eccentric goats, pigs, and asses, rush against us to our utter discomfort! And, having settled our steeds, how queer a place was shewn us for our supper and sleeping-room! a sort of granary, holding one diminutive bed, and a table to match; all the rest of the space being choked up with sacks, barrels, baskets, hams, etc. etc. But the apologies made for all these inconveniences were profuse, and attention was shewn us far more than could have been expected: so we congratulated ourselves on being once more in the province of Aquila, whose bounds are defined by the mountain-wall we had so recently climbed.

Having tossed up who should have the bed, it fell *to* me, and directly afterwards fell *under* me, because it had but three legs, and one of those but feeble. As for K., he took up his quarters upon the small table, and we talked and slept as much as we might, till day broke; when a sound of Choc! choc! choc! pervaded the room, and forthwith numbers of little chanticleers rushed from all corners, and, mounting the table, were astonished to find their accustomed crowing-place already occupied.

In the Kingdom of Naples, 1843

August 11, 1843. Rieti

Having no longer a companion to share the ups and downs of a rambling life, I could not look forward to my second series of explorings with great pleasure. To be sure, it is better to be alone than in company with a grumbler, or a caviller about farthings, or one who is upset by little difficulties, or – what is worse, perhaps, than all – one who regards all things with total apathy; but as my late co-mate had none of these ill conditions, and was moreover, of an imperturbably good temper, and fully capable of enjoying every variety of wandering, come in what shape it might, I confess to having been somewhat dreary at first starting. However, – *non v'era rimedio*,* – and it was necessary to make sketches.

The good-natured Signor Filippo Carocci drove me very early to Civita Ducale, – and so far, the pleasant valley of the Velino and its wooded hills were cheerful enough: not so the mournful pseudo-convent** we had dined in a week ago, whose cloisters and corridors, with the royal arms in every possible corner, seemed more deadly dull than ever. Dulness and Civita Ducale are, indeed, synonymous.

Until dinner, having amused myself by sketching the Piazza before the shadows had all changed, I explored the place; though I found little to draw, either at a thriving convent on a hill above the town, or about the old walls, crumbling among broken rocks well mantled by the luxuriant wild-fig. The natural politeness of the Abruzzesi gave me one or two traits to muse on: a peasant standing for a quarter of an hour on the rocks, to see that I did not miss my way to the river, continued to call out, and make signs as to the short cuts with laudable anxiety; and near the stream, all gay with many-coloured washerwomen, a polite swineherd chastised one of his pigs for conveying his mud-covered body too near my steps. '*Volete buttarvi in faccia al Signore?*'*** – quoth he, as he enforced his remonstrances with a resounding thump.

The worst of taking up one's abode in these Government places,

---

* There was no remedy.
** Lear and Knight had dined with Don Francesco Console, the Sub-Governor, on August 6 at his 'Palazzo, once a convent, but now the Sottintendenza, or Sub-Governor's official residence'.
*** 'Do you want to throw yourself in the gentleman's face?'

however desirable in other respects, is the uncertainty of the official hours of eating. It was two o'clock ere dinner was announced, and that is long to wait, from 4 a.m., on a mere cup of coffee. In the meantime the Sub-Governor's servant was highly anxious to shave me and cut my hair, which operations he impressively assured me would be so well performed that I should ever more bitterly repent the neglecting of his offer, – 'E poi in questi Abruzzi, non ci sarà mai meglior' occasione.'* Don Francesco Console, the Sottintendente, is an amiable and gentlemanlike man in his way, though our tête-à-tête repast was not over-brilliant, from the lack of any common ground for conversation; nor, perhaps, did the fact of the dinner consisting wholly and solely of eggs add to the liveliness of the discourse, which, by-the-bye, was chiefly about the Thames Tunnel** – an object of immense interest to foreigners, but which I had never seen, and should have been little able to describe if I had.

I drew again till evening, and then waited for Don Francesco, who had gone to Antrodoco, until I was heartily tired of pacing those silent corridors, whose stillness was only broken by the stealthy steps of clandestine cats. Thought I, – two months of the Abruzzi after this fashion will be more than enough. – My host, on his arrival, reported that Prince Giardinelli would come here on the 13th, on his way (by Rome) to an immense festa, which takes place at Tagliacozzo once a century.

Eggs again for supper!

August 13, 1843
The cool valley of Antrodoco is in deep shade till late in the morning. I was sauntering by the brawling river, when a little boy passed me carrying a dead fox. 'It is delightful food (*cibo squisito*),' said he, 'either boiled or roast'; – said I, 'I wish you joy.' The odd parties rushing about to and from the *Bagni* diverted me extremely. The Baron Caccianini, Segretario-Generale of the province, and acting as Vice-Intendente during the Prince's absence, sent to ask me to dine at one o'clock – an invitation I was glad to accept; and

---

* 'What's more, there won't be a better opportunity here in the Abruzzi.'
** The Thames tunnel between Rotherhithe and Wapping, designed by Marc Isambard Brunel, opened in 1843. It was the first sub-aqueous tunnel built for public use.

I excused myself to the amiable *Bagnanti** of yesterday evening, whom I joined in an odd luncheon of beans and wine, to make amends for leaving them at dinner. Our party at the Baron's consisted only of himself, the Guidice, and his Secretary, – an agreeable, well-bred set of persons, though not over well informed about Europe generally, or England especially, except the Thames Tunnel. – *'Siete Cristiani da voi?'* said the Baron's Secretary. *'Si, Signore,'* said I. *'Mi piace davvero,'* was the reply; *'aveva un non so che d'idea vi ci fossero de' Protestanti.'* *'Quanto sei sciocco!'*** said the Baron. – Supper with the *Bagnanti*, at D.B. Todeschini's: a light-hearted, simple set of people.

August 14–15, 1843
These two days I spent in sketching the town, and the pass up to the picturesque Madonna delle Grotte. The only chance for drawing is by rising before the sun, and making use of every moment of time until the heat (which in this valley is very great) obliges one to return to shelter. After the mid-day meal, which was a cheerful one enough, at the Casa Todeschini, sleep and music divided the hours until it was time to recommence drawing. The stillness of an Italian town during this period of the day is striking. Three or four children are playing with a tame sheep under my window, making a hundred pretty groups and pictures; the two widows are humming faintly to the guitar; all the rest of Antrodoco seems fast asleep.

The magnificence of the pass just above the town towards evening is extreme: except in the creations of Titian or Giorgione, one seldom sees such hues of purple and blue and gold as those with which those lofty hills are clothed with in an Italian sunset.

I decided to go with the Intendente's suite to-morrow to Tagliacozzo (though my first intention had been to return to Aquila), as I thought I might see more of the people by this arrangement. So I took leave of the Baron Caccianini, and, paying for my *Bagnante* lodging, retired to rest, being awoke every quarter of an hour afterwards for half the night by the question, *'Eccellenza, a che ora vuol alzarsi?'* from a boring old servant of the Segretario, whose

---

* The *'Bagnanti'*, Lear explains, were 'the bathers, or invalids, who resort to the mineral waters of Antrodoco, and fill the town for a short Summer-season'.

** 'Are you Christians over there?' 'Yes, Sir.' 'Indeed I'm glad to hear it, I had some sort of idea that they were all Protestants there.' 'How stupid you are!'

obsequious attentions had been overpowering during my stay. *'Permettete!' 'Scusate!' 'Eccellenza!'** were perpetually in his mouth; but he never did any earthly thing of service.

August 16, 1843
An hour before daylight being the time named for our starting, we assembled in the market-place, although two hours after the sun was fully risen we were still unprepared to set off. Great was the tumult in the narrow street where the Intendente had lodged: the arrangement of his luggage – the soothing and menacing of eccentric mules and perverse horses – the collecting together all his Excellency's suite of domestics – the simultaneous drinking of coffee at the last moment – and the noisy adieux of the Antrodochesi spectators. How many saddles were found to be inverted, just as they should have been on their bearers' backs! How much string was required to tie on irregular articles of baggage! And how many times all the horses, mules, asses, luggage, grooms, guides, and spectators were involved in the wildest confusion, by some sudden freak of one or two ungovernable quadrupeds! These are matters only to be guessed at by those who have sojourned in Italy.

At length we were in order: the Secretary and the Judge on very forlorn-looking mules; the cook and all the male household, with most elaborate accompaniments of food and utensils, on creatures of every description; and the *Maestro di Cavalleria*,** with a mounted groom leading Prince Giardinelli's grey horse, and two others on little animals as ugly as vicious, (with no tails, and eyes a long way out of their heads,) dignified by the title of Pomeranian ponies, and intended for the use of Donna Caterina. As for me, I had a very decent black horse, with a most uneasy saddle, the stirrups appertaining to which gave way in about a quarter of an hour, and rolled hopelessly down the ravine. Behind came the *gend'armes,* with guides and baggage-mules; and a highly-picturesque cavalcade we were, however our appointments might want the full dignity to be looked for in a Governor's establishment.

Slowly we wound up the pass as far as Rocca di Corno, where we halted for about an hour (though to what purpose I have not

---

*   'Your Excellency, what time would you like to get up?' 'Permit me!' 'Excuse me!' 'Your Excellency!'
** Master of Horses.

the faintest idea), and then, having proceeded two or three miles further on the Aquila road, we struck into a mule-track leading to the right. For the last part of our route we had varied the sleepy monotony of our progress by a trot or canter along the good highway; but, as we began to ascend a wild and steep mountain, we gradually resumed our sedate single line, except the wretched little Pomeranians, who were particularly alert in climbing up the rocky paths, and aimed kicks profusely at everybody they passed. It occupied a weary while in the glaring heat of the day to conquer this mountain; and when we did so (except a short glimpse of the wall-like range of the Gran Sasso), there was nothing to repay us for our trouble: a long and tiresome plain of undulating ground, with no one spot prettier or more remarkable than another. At noon we halted for repose and repast in a ruined *tenuta*, or cattle-shed.

There is always much fun in the wild roughing character of this kind of expedition; and the excellent cold mutton, bread, and onions, were by no means the worse for being eaten off the top of a barrel, our seats being the trunk of a tree. Our wine, alas! was that wretched *vino cotto* – equally unpalatable and unwholesome; for, little as I drank of it, there being no water, I paid a dear penalty in the shape of a headache. In the afternoon we again set off, most of the party complaining bitterly of fatigue, and not the least sympathising with my admiration of the beauty of the views, which, as we descended, opened into yellow plains fringed with fine oak-woods, stretching away on all sides at the foot of the magnificent Marsic mountains, for we had now entered the old territory of the Marsi.

Our road wound through one of these forests, and below the picturesque town of Corbara del Conte; whence, leaving on our right the distant Turano, whose towers were glowing in the setting sun, we made for Sant' Anatolia, a neat-looking little village, where we were to pass the night. All this part of the Abruzzi abounds with very ancient remains, and the sites of several cities of the Aborigines of Italy are fixed by antiquaries in these valleys. Martelli's *History of the Sicoli* also gives much information on the subject, if one dare to sift it from his two volumes of laborious trifling.

Part of our company, myself among them, rode on to proclaim our arrival, and bestir our unexpecting hosts in our favour; but as all the Dons and Donnas Placidi (the principal people of the place) were out walking, we got nothing by our move, and had to wait in the street for a considerable time. As for me, I fell into a comfortable sleep; and when I awoke, the rest of our cavalcade had arrived in a state of great fatigue, and were employed in drinking cold water with spirit of aniseed, administered to them by a variety of hospitable old women without shoes or stockings.

Soon after the Placidi family appeared – a very striking group, composed of a most venerable old lady, 98 years of age, whose long white hair fell on her shoulders, and two sons, both upwards of 70, and in appearance as old as their mother, who called them 'fanciulli miei' and 'figliuolini.'* By these good people we were taken to the Palazzo Placidi – a huge, rambling old house, with gloomy, dirty state-rooms, full of ancient furniture arranged round the walls, damask sofas and leather chairs, and tables with gilded legs, none of them apparently having been in use since the days of the early Sicoli Kings, of whose names D.F. Martelli** obligingly gives a list from Shem downwards. The emptiness of rooms in these Palazzi, the absence of books, needle-work, or any of the little signs of mental occupation so constant in our own homes, is always observable, and to an English feeling gives an air of chill and discomfort far from agreeable.

Nothing could be more hospitable or well supplied than the supper-table, which we were glad to join. Donna Serafina de' Placidi was a wondrous old lady, in full possession of all her faculties, and conversing while she knitted with great assiduity. A chaotic-looking chamber was shown me as mine for the night, containing a vast bed, with crimson velvet about it enough for three such; on which I was glad to repose in my cloak, seeing that its comfort and propriety were wholly external.

August 19, 20, 21, 1843
To those who have no idea of an Italian *fête*, a description of that I witnessed here*** may be amusing; and the details of one will suffice for the whole three days of its duration. Suppose yourself, therefore, in the Casa Mastroddi at sun-rise; a cup of coffee is brought to you in your own room (a biscuit also if you ask for it, though the natives do not indulge in anything so like a breakfast),

---

* 'my lads'; 'little sons'.
** Felice Martelli, in *Le Antichità de Sicoli* (*The Antiquities of Sicoli*, 1835).
*** 'Here' is Tagliacozzo, greatly changed in appearance since Lear's visit in July, in preparation for the '*festa* de la Madonna dell'Oriente', a *fête* held only once a century, and named after a painting supposed to be of Eastern workmanship.

or you go to seek your *café* in the room of Donna Caterina, the step-mother of the two brothers Mastroddi, who continually labours to fill little cups, which are dispersed by her domestics all over the mansion. Then you wander into the large room, and into the great Loggia, where you find the ladies and officers walking about in parties, or listening to the bands of music incessantly performing below the window. The Piazza is like a scene in a theatre, all hung with crimson and gold draperies and tapestry from window and door, and crowded with people, the constant hum of the multitude filling up the pauses between the music. About eleven, a stir takes place among the magnates of the house; everybody comes forth full-dressed and the Intendente, (with his staff in full uniform,) and all the company following, walk through lines of military to the temporary chapel, where the Bishop of Solmona officiates at High Mass. A friar having preached a Latin sermon of most painful duration, the Prince and the Mastroddi party return to the palace in the same order and state; the gay colours, and the brilliant light of summer over the whole procession making it a very sparkling scene. Nor should I omit, that the dress of a Neapolitan Bishop (a bright-green satin hat, amethyst-coloured silk robes lined with scarlet, gold chain and cross, with lilac stockings,) is in itself a world of glitter. Then, between the *'fonzioni'* and *'pranzo'*,* we all went, – one day, to make a call of ceremony on some grandees of the town; – or, on another, we attended the Bishop and the Prince to the foundation school, where we earnestly inspected samplers and artificial flowers, made by the prettiest set of little girls possible, the Bishop noticing all with a kindness of manner that shewed the old gentleman's heart was full of good feelings. In all these visitings, as we passed along the streets, the military saluted the Prince, and the people kneeled, without intermission, for the Bishop's benediction.

To one whose greatest horror is noise, this sort of life was not a little wearying; but having been informed that to leave the house during the *festa* would be considered as the greatest insult to the family, I felt obliged to remain, and resigned me to my *fête* accordingly.

Next came the dinner: the company in the Palazzo Mastroddi now amounted to above sixty persons, (not including servants,) and I confess to being somewhat amazed, much as I had heard of Abruzzo

---

* *fonzioni*: functions, *pranzo*: lunch.

hospitality, at the scale on which these entertainments were conducted. A gay scene it was; and I always had the pleasure of getting a place by some one of the ladies of the company; a piece of good fortune I owed to my being the only foreigner present, for a dark mass of my superiors in rank – Generals, Judges, etc., were obliged to sit together, unilluminated by any of the lights of Creation.

Immediately after dinner, the suite of rooms and Loggia were thronged by conversing groups, and coffee was handed amongst them. A novel picture was that festive Piazza, alive with thousands of loiterers (there were said to be more than ten thousand visitors at this *fête*, besides the towns-people), listening to the Chieti and Tagliacozzo bands playing alternately.

By this time the sun was sinking, and everybody sallied forth to the promenade outside the town, where platforms were erected to observe the horse-races, which shortly took place, and about which great interest was shown. The winning horse was taken up to the chapel of the Madonna dell' Oriente, and led to the steps of the altar, by way, I suppose, of expressing that a spirit of thankfulness may be graceful and proper upon all occasions.

And after the race, a fire-balloon should have ascended; but somehow or other there was a reigning destiny adverse to balloons, for the first caught fire, and blazed away before it left earth; the second stuck in a tree, where it shared the same fate; and the largest ran erroneously among chimney-pots, and was consumed on the house-tops, to the great disgust of the Tagliacozzesi.

Now followed an invitation from Madame Mancini, or some one-else who possessed a house in the Piazza, in order to see the girandola or fireworks; so away we went, (the Intendente leading the way,) and ate ices in the draped galleries overlooking the square. This was about *Ave Maria*, or later, and I can never forget the scene it displayed; the dense crowd of people, some four or five thousand, were at once on their knees, and burst forth as if one voice were singing the evening chant to the Virgin, the echoes of which rang back from the black rocks of the Pass with a solemnity of deep melody, the more soothingly beautiful after the past hours of hubbub.

Crack – bounce – whizz! the scene was changed in a twinkling by the flash and explosion of all kinds of fireworks; rockets flying hither and thither, serpents rushing and fizzing all round the colonnades and that which should have been the fountain blazing away in streams of fire.

Again a movement, and the point of interest is changed: a long line of people is bending towards the theatre, and threading with difficulty the groups of peasants already composing themselves to sleep. As soon as our party arrived the performance began, and great fun we had between the acts of the Opera, in laughing at the strange dresses of some of the personages from neighbouring towns, who displayed fashions unchanged, said the Tagliacozzesi, since the last century's *festa*. One charming old lady, with a rose-coloured satin bonnet, at least four feet in diameter, and a blue and yellow fan to match, was the delight of the whole audience.

It was past midnight ere we returned, by bright moonlight, through the quiet Piazza, thronged with the same multitude of peasants, who had been unable to find shelter in the over-filled accommodation of the town *Locande* and *Osterie,* and now lay buried in sleep. Many of the groups of mothers and families, with the broken silver rays falling on them through the gothic arches of the little temple, were picturesque and touching beyond description.

To all these events add a very merry supper, and a late going to repose, and such was the routine of three days, the varieties of processions, visits to adjacent villas, etc., excepted. Annoyed, as I had been, at the prospect of such waste of time, I confess to having been pretty well reconciled to it by the kindness and amiable disposition of every one with whom I was brought in contact, and the unbroken cheerfulness with which every moment was filled up.

The concluding events of the last days of the *fête* must, however, yet be related; which, though only occasioning great confusion, might have had very sad results. During the last act of '*Il Barbiere*',* a breathless indivdual rushed into the theatre, and yelled out the fatal word – '*Incendio!* ——' Great was the confusion, and on gaining the narrow street, the scene was terrible: an immense body of flame was rising behind the old Ducal Palace, and dense volumes of smoke obscured the moon. The fire had not yet reached the building, but must inevitably do so unless speedily checked, as the offices of the Institution immediately communicated with an extensive magazine (or *fenile)* of straw, whose contents had been burning internally for some time before the flames burst forth, and led to the alarm being given.

To rescue the children was the first object, and great good feeling and promptitude were manifested on all sides. As soon as the terrified females – most of them carried straight from their beds to

---

* Rossini's *The Barber of Seville* (1816). *Incendio*: 'Fire!'

various adjacent houses, were out of danger, and the furniture moved to the street, every one did his best towards the extinction of the fire, – no easy matter, since no water was within reach; and the only method adopted was, to unroof that part of the *fenile*, nearest the Palazzo, and smother the flames as far as possible with continual baskets of earth, until the rooms joining the premises to the burning barn could be destroyed, to prevent the further spread of the conflagration. This was a long operation, though many men were immediately pressed into the service, and commenced the work of demolition with rapidity. Meanwhile we were all marshalled into companies, and set to work in a garden to fill tubs and baskets with earth, which were handed, when full, to the top of the wall of the unroofed *fenile*, where lines of men threw their contents out on the burning fuel.

The exact amount of good resulting to the common cause from my individual exertions was small: for having grubbed and clawed away at the ground till I had filled a very handsome tub, I turned round hastily to carry it to its destination, – but not being aware that the ladies' garden was formed terrace-wise, and being too blind to perceive it, I fell down a height of about six feet, into the centre of a bed of broccoli, where all my carefully-filled tub was *bouleversé* on to my own respectable person.

Happily, after the burning barn was isolated, by all communication between it and the surrounding buildings being destroyed, the danger to the town was diminished, though the showers of falling sparks throughout the night gave great cause for uneasiness. I could hardly help thinking, that the origin of all this might be sought for in the fireworks of the evening; but I found that the Tagliacozzesi were rather scandalized at such an idea. And thus ended the great *festa* of Tagliaccozzo in 1843.

August 22, 1843. Magliano
My next destination was to Magliano, to the house of Don Giambattista (or, called for shortness, Don Tita), Masciarelli, one of the richest persons in the Abruzzi, to whom I had a letter of recommendation from M. le Chevalier Kestner.[3] Thither, accordingly, I went in his carriage, which had been sent to Tagliacozzo to bring back the youngest of his two sons, Don Gregorio, who had

3 The Hanoverian Minister in Rome. It would be difficult to mention the name of this excellent person without acknowledging the frequent kindnesses received from him during a long residence in the Roman States.

been present at the *festa*. Poor Don Gregorio Masciarelli is an intelligent young man, about twenty years of age, although so diminutive as to appear a boy of ten or twelve. Unable to move a step, having become lame from a fall during his infancy, he is always cheerful; and though outwardly deprived of pleasure, the balance of happiness may be in his favour in a capacity for self-improvement, and a variety of resources known to few of the more healthy: his days pass in reading, or quiet games, or in studying the flute, violin, and piano; and he is no contemptible performer in drawing. In the early mornings, or in the bright evenings of summer, he is seated on the bench before his wealthy father's Palazzo, conversing with the passing villagers: or he is carried hither and thither by an old domestic. Poor little fellow! with what glee he reverted to all the gaieties and fun of the past *fête*, and how he dwelt on all the best scraps of the Prima Donna's performances!

August 28, 29, 1843. Avezzano
I decided on a short visit to Civita D'Antino and the valley of the Liris, and taking all I required in the ample pockets of a shooting-jacket and a large portfolio, I set off without any introductory letters, determined on trying my fortune for a night's lodging. By sunrise I had reached the town of Luco, where some people who had heard of our visit to Trasacco insisted on my taking coffee with them. After this hospitable interlude, I began to scale the great wall of mountain which confines the Val di Roveto down to Balzorano and Sora; and this was no light undertaking towards nine o'clock on an August morning. At the commencement of the ascent I passed several peasants slowly toiling up the path, all of whom affectionately conjured me not to attempt to proceed, as the exploit was not fit for '*gente di città*'.* In spite, however, of their prophetic warnings, I got to the summit, to their great amusement, before them all. With the marked friendliness of these people, they made me eat some pears and drink wine – luckily, not *vino cotto*; three of them also offered me clean shirts – '*é pericoloso lo stare sudato in cima di queste montagne alte.*'** One cannot but be struck with these little incidents.

Far below my feet, though yet high above the valley of Roveto, through which the Liris glides, lay the town of Civita D'Antino;

---

* 'city folk'.
** 'It's dangerous to stay sweaty on top of these high mountains.'

and a long descent through splendid forests of beech brought me to its level. A feeling of dreariness, of which I can give no idea, pervades the surrounding scenery.

Opposite were the savage crests of Serra di Sant Antonio, (whose deep recesses shelter a considerable waterfall,) and, as far as eye can reach, the Vale of the Liris is closed on each side by long lines of solemn mountains, of an indescribably stern and gloomy character, clad to their summits with thick forests, which, until within the last quarter of a century, bears were not uncommonly known to inhabit.

Civita D'Antino, a wild and scattered place, has a poetical and sullen grandeur in its aspect, as if it were altogether out of the world of life: no other dwellings are in sight, and its own bear the stamp of desolate and melancholy antiquity.

The present town, containing about twelve hundred inhabitants, occupies but a small portion of the extensive site of the ancient city, the capital of the Antinates, the remains of which are here and there to be traced by fragments of cyclopean architecture.

August 29, 1843
I passed the morning in drawing, though the magnitude of the mountain lines prevents Civita D'Antino from being easily transferred to paper; and some time was devoted to the ancient Cyclopean remains round the town. After our noon-day dinner I set off, (though much entreated to stay by these good people,) Don Manfredi* accompanying me for two or three miles. A curious change of life had occurred to this young man: he had been educated at Naples, and was well accustomed to the gaieties of the metropolis: a short time since he had been called from (what was in his case) the livelier position of a younger son to fulfil graver duties, as representative of his father, his elder brother having suddenly renounced all claim to his family property by becoming a Jesuit. I could not help thinking, from the remarks of Don Manfredi, that this prospect of riches and dignity seemed a poor compensation for loss of liberty; for the Abruzzese proprietor seldom quits his paternal estate: *'Siamo come i lupi, chiusi in queste montagne'*; – said he, *'non vado più in città.'***

---

*   Don Manfredi Ferrante, his host in Civita D'Antino.
**   'We're like the wolves, closed in by these mountains', 'I don't go to the city any more'.

I wandered down to the river Liris, through a beautiful oak wood; dwelling much on the memory of such frequent hospitalities; such warm-hearted people; such primitive mountain homes.

September 1, 2, 3, 1843. Celano
Another morning I allotted to the Bocca di Castelluccio, a narrow and formidable pass behind the mountain, at whose foot Celano stands. The entrance to this lonely ravine, ever unvisited by the sun, is between terrific rocks, which in parts of the pass are so close together as barely to admit the passage of a loaded mule. Throughout the winter, torrents, or snow, prevent any communication by this untoward road; but during summer it is visited by a few poor people, who gather the wood left in it by the winter's ravages. '*Che fai solo solo solo in queste aspre montagne?*' said an old creature laden with sticks, in amazement at my unknown employment. '*Statevi buono – ma, che cosa fai?*' said one or two woodmen. '*Badate vi del caldo quando uscite,*'* said others with a good-natured consideration. After these rare interruptions, the scream, or rushing flight of a hawk, or the fall of a stone from the lofty sides of this mountain *foce*, as these chasms are called, were the only sounds that broke its deadly stillness, and I was glad to return to the '*caldo*', and the merry family at Celano.

On fast days these good but homely people were sadly distressed at my having no meat, though I assured them I did not care about it; which was not strictly true, for I hate crabs, bream, barbel, and frogs. And then the novelty of pear-soup, and the potatoes, which were dressed in fifty fashions! – '*E vero che campono loro di Patate?*' – '*Buono lei pel addatarsene.*'** – I shall always remember each division of the twenty-four hours as passed at Celano with peculiar pleasure; the mornings in the fresh meadows at the foot of the town, straying among the tall poplars wreathed with vines, till the sun came over the vast crag, and forced one to retreat to cooler haunts; the cloudless mid-day when all was still; the calm evenings, so full of beautiful incidents; the return at sunset to the town with groups of peasants carrying up their corn, or large parties of girls bearing each her *conca*, or vessel of water from the

---

* 'What are you doing all all alone in these harsh mountains?' 'Be sensible – but what are you doing?' 'Be careful of the heat when you leave.'
** 'Is it true that you lot live on potatoes there?' 'Well done for putting up with it.'

pure spring at the foot of the rock. And at night, how calm and bright was the lake, like a line of silver, below the palace windows in the light of the full moon, the old castle flinging long shadows over the silent town!

September 4, 1843. Lake Fucino

Don Angelo Felici Ottavi, to whom Don Pamfilo Tabassi had recommended me, was a hearty good sort of a man, who offered to take charge of my luggage, while I crossed the Lake of Fucino to Trasacco, (of which I wanted to make a drawing,) provided I would dine at his house on my return.

I was placed in a flat-bottomed boat or punt, and two men soon carried me over the quiet lake, whose glassy surface reflected every cloud in the loveliest colours. Distant Alba and Velino were diminished to faint horizon objects, but the mountains on the eastern and southern side of the water were very grand. Numbers of cormorants hover over the Lake, or sit watching on poles placed for fishing in the shallowest parts of it.

At Trasacco, where I arrived before noon, I found old Don Bernardo de' Gasparis, with his six sons, Dons Serafino, Cesidio, Loreto, Filippo, Giacomo, and Odoardo, who all received me with the same cordiality as on our first visit,* and treated me with every kindness. All Trasacco was in agitation at the horrible news just arrived, that Don Tita Masciarelli's coachman had murdered the housekeeper at Paterno; that the murderer, who had been committed to the prison of Celano, had strangled himself almost immediately on being left alone, so that no further light could be thrown on the tragedy, which created a great sensation throughout the Marsica, where murders are exceedingly unfrequent.

September 9, 1843. Lake Scanno

Drawing the beautiful Lake and the costumes of the servants in the house occupied me all day. But it was in vain to hope for a smile from these very obliging, but too sedate people, who were unlike the families I had hitherto seen. I thought, why *do* you build such rooms and a new palace, with nothing to fill it but this dulness? And how *can* you live day after day on tench and barbel, barbel and tench ?

It was my last evening at Scanno. The dark-eyed sister was hope-

---

* On July 28; see pp. 134–6 above.

lessly mute, *'E stata in Solmona?'* – *'Non Signore,'* – *'In Aquila?'* – *'Nemmeno'* – *' Va qualche volta a spasso ? '* – *'Signor no.* – *' 'Si occupano le donne di Scanno dalle affari di casa,'* said Don ——.

So I gave it up. – *'Prosit.'**

September 13, 1843. Pass of Anversa
Drew much at the mouth of the pass; a scene so majestic that much time might be spent in doing it justice. As I sat below a huge rock, on which a little goat-herd was piping to his scattered charge, the sound of a chorus of many voices gradually roused the echoes of the mighty walls: a most simple and oft-repeated air, slowly chanted by long files of pilgrims, mostly women of Castel di Sangro (perhaps fifty in number); they were on their way to the shrine of S. Domenico, in Cocullo, and came in succession down the winding path, carrying large bales of different coloured cloths on their heads, and walking with long sticks.

Such little incidents are sought for in vain by the high-road traveller. Long after the last of the pilgrims had disappeared, the notes rang at intervals through the hollow, and then all was left to its own gloomy silence.

September 28, 1843. Città di Penna
*'Volete veder certi ritratti dei Re Inglesi?'*** said some persons to me, as I was loitering in the Piazza awhile before *Ave Maria*; so I followed my friend to the Casa Forcella, where the Marchese or his brother, (one of them is in exile,) fairly astonished me by the display of a collection of original portraits, all of the Stuart Family; Charles I and II; James II; the Pretender, Charles Edward; Duchess of Albany; and Cardinal York, the four last in all stages of their lives; most of these were miniatures and well executed, though carelessly preserved. There was also an old harpsichord which had belonged to the late Cardinal, – *'sommamente armonioso'*** according to Gentile, (a statement which, seeing it had no chords, I cannot confirm,) and against the wall hung a long pedigree of the Nortons of Grantley, one of whom, said my friend, *'è una zia mia, e*

---

* 'Have you been to Solmona?' 'No sir'. 'Or Aquila?' 'Not there either.' 'Do you sometimes go out walking?' 'Sir, no.' 'The women of Scanno take care of domestic matters.' 'Goodbye.'

** 'Would you like to see some portraits of the English kings?'

*** 'supremely harmonious'.

The Pass of Anversa

sta presentamente (vecchia però), vicinissimo a Northampton ossia Nottinghamshire.'

These reliques of our Monarchs (the last curiosities one would have searched for in the town of Città di Penna,) had passed from the late Cardinal York, Bishop of Frascati, by bequest to the Forcella, a female of that family having been about the person of the Countess of Albany.

September 30, 1843. Città di Penna
The clouds still hung heavily on the mountains, but I decided on starting for Isola, a little town at the foot of the Gran Sasso, the monarch of the Abruzzi, with which I longed to have a closer acquaintance. I left Città di Penna early. The whole of my day's journey was close to the high mountain-range, dividing the provinces of the Abruzzi 1° and 2° Ulteriori, and did not present any particular point of interest; nor, excepting Bacucco and Colle d' Oro, were there any towns or villages in our day's route, which lay among low wooded hills, overlooked by the dark-topped mountains beyond, or crossing the bed of streams which in winter musk be formidable torrents. Towards evening, by paths winding through beautifully wooded landscapes we reached Isola, which stands on a peninsula formed by two rivers that nearly surround it. It is an exceedingly pretty place, and immediately above it rises the single pyramid of Monte Corno, the Gran Sasso, a most noble back-ground.

Don Lionardo Madonna, to whom I had a letter, was extremely shy and uneasy, and seemed to think I might be a Bolognese rebel escaped over the frontier, until I relieved him by proposing to go at once over the Gran Sasso to Aquila, rather than await the risk of another fall of snow, which would block up the pass, and oblige me to return to the coast. This pass immediately over the shoulder of the mountain, is closed, except during the hot summer months, when it is used by the people of Teramo as the most direct road to transport the produce of their province (wine and oil), to Aquila.

Don Lionardo having illness in his own house, found me a lodging in a very unhappy-looking building, within whose forlorn walls I was nevertheless, after drawing the town, most glad to take shelter by a good wood-fire, for the evening was bitterly cold.

---

* 'She is an aunt of mine, and she's now living (but she's very old) very close to Northampton, which is to say Nottinghamshire.'

An old woman, Donna Lionora (who like many I had observed in the course of the day, was a *gôitreuse**) cooked me some beans and a roast fowl; – but the habitation was so dirty and wretched that one had need have had a long journey to provoke any appetite. While I was sitting near the chimney (it had the additional charm of being a very smoky one), I was startled by the entrance of several large pigs, who passed very much at their ease through the kitchen – if so it were called – and walked into the apartment beyond, destined for my sleeping room. *'Sapete, – che ci sono entrati i porchi?'* said I to the amiable Lionora. *'Ci vanno a dormire'*** quoth she, nowise moved by the intelligence. They shan't sleep there while I'm in the house, thought I; so I routed them out with small ceremony, and thereby gave great cause for amazement to the whole of the family.' *E matto,'* suggested some of the villagers *sotto voce. 'Lo sono tutti, tutti, tutti,'* responded an old man, with an air of wisdom, *'tutti gl' Inglesi sono matti,'*** an assertion he clearly proved on the ground that the only Englishman who had ever been known to visit Isola (several years previously), had committed four frightful extravagancies, any one of which was sufficient to deprive him of all claim to rationality, viz.; he frequently drank water instead of wine; he more than once paid more money for an article than it was worth; he persisted in walking even when he had hired a horse; and he always washed himself *'si, – anche due volte la giornata!**** the relation of which climax of absurdity was received with looks of incredulity or pity by his audience.

October 17, 1843. Tufo
The weather had become cold and gloomy at best, and although I should have liked to have made drawings throughout the Cicolano, and in the neighbourhood of Carsoli; yet the season was becoming too far advanced, and, to tell truth, I was rather tired of wandering alone; so I took leave of my kind friends the Coletti, with much regret, and set out towards Rome.

A short walk of four or five miles brought me to Carsoli, by which town we had entered the Abruzzi three months before, and thence my path lay across the Pianura di Cavaliere, and up to the

---

* A sufferer from goitre.
** 'Did you know that the pigs have come in here?' 'They come in to sleep.'
*** 'He's mad'. 'They're all mad, every single Englishman is mad.'
**** 'Yes, twice a day even!'

picturesque little town of Riofreddo, the outpost of the Roman States, whence, passports and luggage being examined, I went on by La Spiaggia and Vico Varo to Tivoli, and the following morning to Frascati.

The romance of three months' wandering was finished. To the classic or antiquarian the ground I had gone over is rich in interest. To the landscape painter certain portions possess great beauty; but the greater part of the scenery is on too large a scale, and of too barren a character to be available for the pencil, while much can boast of only cheerfulness of cultivation as a compensation for downright ugliness. But apart from the agreeable variety of impressions so many new scenes had left on my mind, the number of really hospitable and kind people with whom I had become acquainted will ever be remembered by me with great pleasure; and should I never revisit this part of Italy, I shall not cease to cherish the memories of my stay in the three provinces of Abruzzo.

In the Kingdom of Naples, 1844

September 26, 1844. Rome
I set out again for the Abruzzi, intending, during a stay of two months, to glean much from parts I had neglected, or had been unable to reach in former visits, – particularly several churches and convents in the three Provinces, and the country north of Monte Corno towards Teramo and Ascoli. There is a newly-established Diligence to Rieti, leaving Rome at 5 p.m., and making the journey in ten hours: not a bad conveyance.

A sultry night, but a bright moon made it pleasant till I fell asleep among the tiresome hills of Poggio S. Lorenzo; – at 3 after midnight we reached Rieti.

September 28, 1844
By day-break I was above the Castle of Antrodoco, and on my way to the pass of Sigillo, the most interesting part of which was to be sketched before returning to Rieti, and that most easily from this side, since the last few miles from La Posta are far less fine.

All through the sullen valley of San Quirico, the few remains of whose ancient Abbey are turned into a *Vignarola's* dwelling; the vines are thickly bespattered with patches of lime. This is also the practice all through the vale of Borghetto, etc., where the grapes when nearly ripe are sprinkled with lime to prevent their being plucked by passers by.

The morning was grey and cloudy; bye and bye it became black and grisly, and torrents of rain began to pour; but being determined on my object, I walked or ran through the frowning pass as far as Sigillo, where I remained till the rain ceased, and then sketched my way back again.

Sigillo, the ancient Sigillum, six miles from Antrodoco, is a frightful place: why it was ever built one cannot guess; or why, being built, anybody lives there. It stands in one of the wildest parts of the pass, (the whole of which is of the grandest character,) at the foot of crag and precipice, and is wholly uncomfortable to look at. A few vineyards by the side of the Velino, goats climbing among the toppling rocks, announce your approach to habitations – a nest of high-roofed melancholy abodes, in jeopardy from the mountain above, and the torrent below.

The ancient Via Salaria* runs here through the very heart of the mountains, close to the Velino, which rises in the district of C. Ducale, about thirty miles above Rieti, receiving twelve streams in its passage from Fano and Borbona to Antrodoco.

It is hardly possible to conceive anything more extraordinary than this portion of that great work, the Via Salaria; one while supported by massy stones rising from the river's edge, then carried by the most formidable rocks along the brink of precipices cut into sheer walls to admit its passage, it zigzags across the torrent, (the foundations of the Roman bridge alone remain,) runs giddily at a great height above it, or compels the angry waters into a narrow channel, by walls yet partly existing after 2,000 years of wear and tear from earthquake and inundation. In some places the course of the old road is quite obliterated by loose stones which have rolled from the mountains above, in others, the great blocks which formed its substructions, are tossed about as if they had been pebbles. Here you follow a narrow mule track over fragments shivered by the fall of some vast mass from an overhanging rock; there you cross a little opening, where, through a narrow valley you catch a glimpse of the lofty Terminillo, or his surrounding heights, already tipped with snow or folded in rolling clouds; from his sides of many channels in spring and autumn descend furious streams, blotting out all work of man as they spread downwards to the rapid Velino, and recording their passage by a desolate broad tract of bare white stones.

Of the several cuts in the rock to allow of the formation of the old road, that about five miles from San Quirico is the most remarkable, being a perpendicular height of one hundred *palmi*.** About five feet from the bottom is a space where, until lately, a tablet remained, with an inscription of the time of Trajan.*** 'This,' says

---

* An ancient highroad of Italy, which ran 151 miles from Rome to the Adriatic coast.
** *palmi*: a *palmo* is eight and three-quarter inches.
*** The Roman inscription reads: IMP.CAES.DIVI / NERVAE F. NER / VA. TRAIANUS / AUG. GERMAN. / DACICUS PONTIF / MAXIMUS. TRIB / POTEST. XV. IMP. / VI. COS. VII. SUB / STRUCTIONEM. CON / TRA TABEM. MONTIS / FECIT. Modern scholars translate the tablet (reading 'labem' for 'tabem') as: 'The Imperator Caesar Nerva Trajan Augustus Germanicus Dacicus, son of the deified Nerva, pontifex maximus (chief priest), holding the tribunician power for the fifteenth time, (saluted) Imperator for the sixth time, consul for the seventh time, built this substructure to prevent the subsidence of the mountain.'

Galetti, 'was carried to Antrodoco,' but I could not hear of it there.

This gigantic remnant of man's work in so wild a solitude, has a strange effect: nor is it wonderful that the peasantry attribute all these stupendous monuments to diabolical agency: one Cecco di Ascoli, a learned doctor and engineer, who repaired the road under Carlo, Duke of Calabria, is the luckless mortal charged by popular opinion with having availed himself of such unhallowed means.

So much for this part of the Via Salaria: it is certainly one of the most impressive of the Roman roads, from the grand scenery through which it has been constructed by that wonderful people. Yet I cannot say I was sorry to be out of it, nor, indeed, to be fairly away from Antrodoco, for there is something constrained and mournful in the never-get-out-again feeling those gloomy passes invariably beget; so after an early dinner with the Mozetti, off once more to Rieti.

Before starting I visited the judge, Dei Pasquinis, whom I had known last year; he had become a cripple, poor fellow, from constant rheumatism, a complaint he attributed to the damp of Antrodoco, which, to say truth, looks as if it never had been, or could be, very dry: putting aside its low situation, and the want of free circulation of air, the danger to which it is exposed from the frequent and sudden inundations of the Velino, makes it by no means a desirable residence.

'Mi spinge la curiosita,' said Signora Pasquinis, *'di sapere per chi porta lutto?'** These people always *will* know who you are in mourning for.

Nothing particular happened in the walk back, except being wet through by storms of rain; but at Civita Ducale a three-parts drunken *carabinière* prevented my entering, insisting on knowing my name, which I not only told him, but politely showed him my passport, which was one from the Foreign Office in 1837, with 'Viscount Palmerston' printed thereon in large letters, 'Lear' being small, and written. *'Niente vero,'* said the man of war, who seemed happy to be able to cavil, *'voi non siete Lear! siete Palmerstoni!'* 'No I am not,' said I, ' my name's Lear.' But the irascible official was not to be so easily checked, though, knowing the power of these worthies, I took care to mollify his anger as much as might be. *'Quel ch' è scritto, scritto è: dunque, ecco qua scritto Palmerstoni: – dunque*

---

*   'I'm curious to know for whom you are wearing mourning.' Lear's mother had died in May 1844.

siete Palmerstoni voi.' You great fool! I thought; but I made two
bows, and said placidly, 'take me to the Sott' Intendente, my dear
sir, as he knows me very well.' *'Peggio,'* said the angry man, *'Tu!
incommodare l' eccellente Signor Sott' Intendente? vien, vien subito: ti
tiro in carcere.'**

Some have greatness thrust upon them. In spite of all expostu-
lations, Viscount Palmerston it was settled I should be. There was
nothing to be done, so I was trotted ignominiously all down the
High-street, the *carabinière* shouting out to everybody at door and
window, *'Ho preso Palmerstoni!'*

Luckily, Don Francesco Console was taking a walk and met us,
whereon followed a scene of apologies to me, and snubbing for the
military, who retreated discomfited.

So I reached Rieti by dark, instead of going to prison.

October 2, 1844. Monte Leonessa
Great forests stretch away all over the huge sides of this beautiful
mountain, and shelter numbers of wolves and roe-deer. Bears have
not been known there of late years.

What a walk! Such rocks and velvet turf! Such green hills,
crested with tall white-trunked woods, like those in Stothard's**
paintings! Such hanging oaks, fringing the chasms deep below
your path! Such endless flocks of sheep in the open glades!

At a turn of the mule-path, through a sombre vale, we met a
single capuchin – the only creature throughout the day – with a
silver white beard below his girdle: a most merry old monk, who
laughed till the tears ran down his face, because I would make a
sketch of him. *'Morrò, morrò, chiuso in un saccoccio! Vado in
Inghilterra dentro un libro!'**** Long after I walked on, the old man's
noisy merriment showed that his perception of the fun was
undiminished.

Hour after hour followed of park-like wood: the red fallen leaves
and the greystone reminding me of many a spot in old England.

---

* 'That's not true, you aren't Lear! You're Palmerstoni!' 'What's written is written:
and so Palmerstoni is written here: so you're Palmerstoni!' 'You! Disturb his
excellency the sub-governor? Come, come quickly. I'm taking you to prison.'
'I've got Palmerstoni!' Palmerston was known in Italy for championing liberal
ideas, and was disliked by the monarchists.
** Thomas Stothard (1755–1834), best known to Lear as the illustrator of *Robinson
Crusoe*.
*** 'I'll die, I'll die, shut up in a satchel! I'm going to England inside a book!'

(*Mem*. One advantage of having a man with a slow donkey – more time for writing notes.) Towards the back of the mountain, a northern aspect – shadows and cold wind prevailed, and dreary barren slopes of rock succeeded to the merry woods: a long descent brought me at last to the plain of Leonessa, and soon after to the city itself, than which, at the foot of its finely-formed wall of mountain, few objects are more striking.

* * * *

The supper would have been agreeable if it had not been for the old lady of the house,* whose conversation was of the oppressive order, being strictly confined to a detailed description of the dislocation of her hip during the preceding Autumn, on which unpromising subject she was peculiarly fluent. The whole account she gave about five times in the course of the evening, and every time she came to the resetting by an unskilful surgeon, by whom she was *'rovinata'*, and *'sagrificata'*, she performed what she was pleased to call the ' *strilli e convulsioni*',** with so alarmingly natural an effect, that a huge house-dog rushed wildly into the room in a paroxysm of sympathy at every repetition, and joined in the chorus, just as, no doubt, he had thought it his duty to do on the original occasion. As for me I sat grinding my teeth in patience.

October 5, 1844. Ametrice
Returning to the Casadel Guidice, I found a most admirable dinner awaiting at which were present all his family,*** and very nice people they were. The wines of Capestrano are beyond praise.

All my afternoon went in hard work, interrupted only by being obliged to visit a miraculous image of great sanctity, which, though only shewn once a year, they did me the honour, as a stranger, to exhibit to me. My daylight I wound up by a ramble about the walls and ravine, a joyless wild sort of scenery, frowned at from a purple cloud, which capped the lofty Sibilla as the sun went angrily down.

Played till supper time with my host's merry little children, and the evening would have ended pleasantly but for rumours of suspected persons having made their way over the frontier, and

---

*   Sister of the 'vicar of Spoleto'.
**   'ruined… sacrificed… screams and convulsions'.
*** The family of Don L. Ameliorati.

having been seen near the town.

A report of two or three frantic Dragons casually supping in the vicinity could not be half so horrible as that of passportless persons moving about the Kingdom of Naples, especially when supposed to have escaped from trouble-brewing Bologna. So the town was alarmed, the rural guard mounted round it all night, the Judge foreboded, and Signora Ameliorati, having already lost some relations in the last disturbances of one of these unquiet petty places, wept amain during great part of the night.

October 10, 1844. Aquila
These days I passed in Aquila, hoping for finer weather, now and then tantalized by a day of sunshine, though the morrow was surely wet, so that after several disappointments, I finally decided to return to Rome, leaving the Teramana unexplored, my churches undrawn, and my good Marsican friends unrevisited.

October 24, 1844. Aquila
Once more I essayed to go from Aquila to Teramo, and had arranged with a guide to sleep at Pizzoli the first, and at Montorio the second night, but lo! when morning came, pouring torrents once more forbade the attempt: a sad disappointment after spending so much time and money. So not to be again deluded, I hired a coach at once to Rieti, and proceeded thence immediately to Rome.

Preface to Volume II

The Twenty-five Views comprised in the present Volume, are all of places in the States of the Church – most of them within the easy reach of visitors to Rome; yet, with the exception of Isola Farnese, Castel Fusano, and Caprarola, but seldom seen by Tourists. The greater number of these Illustrations derive at least as much interest from their classical and historical associations, as from the extreme beauty of the scenery represented.

I have confined the descriptive letter-press attached to each subject to a short notice of its early history, etc.

As in my first volume of Illustrated Excursions, the whole of the present Drawings are Lithographed by my own hand from my sketches; and the Vignettes, excepting three, are also of my own drawing.

To Messrs Hullmandel and Walton, to Messrs Bentley and Co., and to the Artists who have engraved my vignettes on wood, my thanks are again due for the care bestowed on every part of this volume.

Edward Lear.

27, Duke Street, St James's,
August, 1846.

PLATE 1. CIVITA LAVINIA

Civita Lavinia is distant twenty miles from Rome, and two from Genzano. It is clearly identified by inscriptions, etc., with the ancient Lanuvium (said to owe its foundation to Diomed); though, on account of its present name, it has been sometimes confounded with Lavinium, the modern Pratica. During the reign of Antoninus Pius, who was born in Lanuvium, the city greatly increased in importance and splendour; as well as in the time of Marcus Aurelius and Commodus. After the extinction of paganism, and the consequent fall of its celebrated temple of Juno Sospita, Lanuvium fell into decay, which was completed by the devastations of Goths, Saracens, etc. through succeeding centuries, nor, until about AD 1300, does it appear to have revived as a town. During the fifteenth century it was frequently besieged by the Colonna, Orsini, etc.; and its history presents a long narrative of vicissitude, until, in 1564, the town and territory were sold by Marc-Antonio Colonna to the Cesarini family, in whose possession they still remain.

Civita Lavinia stands to the right of the road from Rome to Naples, on the slope of the Alban Hill: it possesses a charm for the landscape painter in its picturesque outline, and from the noble view it commands over the whole of the Volscian Plains nearly to Terracina. Portions of the ancient walls yet remain; and many traces of roads leading towards the towns on the coast, Antium, etc. A fountain, the work of Bernini, ornaments the piazza outside the gates; and there are pretty walks by lanes and vineyards far and near.

from Journals of a
Landscape Painter in Albania, Etc.
(1851)

from Journals of a Landscape Painter in Albania, Etc. *(1851)*

This was the first of Lear's travel books to be published in a smaller format and not by subscription, and it was a great success, with a second edition in 1852. It included twenty lithographic plates and a map (see p. 167), not easy to decipher even in the original, but a very good record of his movements. 'I receive *heaps* and *loads* of compliments and congratulations about the book,' wrote Lear, not a boastful man (letter to Henry Catt, April 1851). In her excellent edition *Edward Lear in the Levant*, to which my notes are indebted, Susan Hyman suggests it is 'the most extensive artistic survey ever attempted of Albania', and one of Lear's biographers calls it 'one of the best travel books ever written'. He gave a copy of the book to Alfred and Emily Tennyson as a wedding present, for which Tennyson thanked him with the poem 'To E.L. on his Travels in Greece'.

The title of the book is a little disputable ('Albania, Etc.' on the title-page, 'Albania and Illyria' on the spine), and so was the region he toured. It had once been part of Greece, and it was now part of 'Turkey in Europe', fiercely policed by the declining Ottoman empire after the eventual subjugation of the despotic governor of Yannina, Ali Pasha, assassinated in 1822. By the time Lear returned to Albania in 1856 after the Crimean war, the country was quieter, and there was a greater British presence. But in 1848 it was a remote place for a British traveller. For one thing, it was an Islamic country, which meant that Lear tended to be stoned and shouted at if he sketched in the open air without some kind of police protection. In the highlight and centerpiece of the book, he engages a local guide to take him to Khimára , the former Acroceraunia, and home to the court of Alí Pashá. Lear believed his to be the first English account of this region of 'savage, yet classic, picturesqueness', where he encounters tales of murder and reprisal, and figures of secret exile. But the wildness makes it an idyllic place too, and unlike a number of British Philhellenes of the time, Lear does not express anti-Turkish views.

In September 1848 he started out from Constantinople (now Istanbul), where he had been convalescing for six weeks from what was probably an attack of malaria. He had spent June and July in and around Athens with Charles Church, the nephew of Sir Richard Church, who had commanded the Greek forces during the War of Independence. The plan was to meet up with him again at Mount Athos, but – as he recounts below – a cholera alarm and quarantine regulations made this impossible, and with great resource he set out on a more ambitious trip without his companion. He travelled light – very light in comparison to the lordly train of Byron a generation earlier – and his advice about what to pack was quoted by Murray in his guide.

He planned for many years to publish 'a more general Topography of Greece to be one day printed with my journals', but this was never completed.

Introduction

The following Notes were written during two journeys through part of Turkey in Europe: – the first from Saloníki in a north-western direction through ancient Macedonia, to Illyrian Albania, and by the western coast through Epirus to the northern boundary of modern Greece at the Gulf of Arta: – the second, in Epirus and Thessaly.

* * * *

Geographer, antiquarian, classic, and politician, having done all in their power for a region demanding great efforts of health and energy to examine it, there is but little opportunity left for the gleanings of the landscape painter. Yet of parts of Acroceraunia – of Króia (the city of Scanderbeg), and of scenes in the neighbourhood of Akhridha – the Lake Lychnitis, the Author believes himself to be the only Englishman who has published any account; and scanty and slight as his may be, it is something in these days to be able to add the smallest mite of novelty to the travellers' world of information and interest.

The general and most striking character of Albanian landscape is its display of objects, in themselves beautiful and interesting – rarely to be met with in combination. You have the simple and exquisite mountain-forms of Greece, so perfect in outline and proportion – the lake, the river, and the wide plain; and withal you have the charm of architecture, the picturesque mosque, the minaret, the fort, and the *serai* – which you have not in modern Greece, for war and change have deprived her of them; you have that which is found neither in Greece nor in Italy, a profusion everywhere of the most magnificent foliage recalling the greenness of our own island – clustering plane and chestnut, growth abundant of forest oak and beech, and dark tracts of pine. You have majestic cliff-girt shores; castle-crowned heights, and gloomy fortresses; palaces glittering with gilding and paint; mountain-passes such as you encounter in the snowy regions of Switzerland; deep bays, and blue seas with bright, calm isles resting on the horizon; meadows and grassy knolls; convents and villages; olive-clothed slopes and snow-capped mountain peaks; – and with all this a crowded variety of costume and pictorial incident such as bewilders and delights an artist at each step he takes.

Let us add besides that Olympus, Pindus, Pharsalia, Actium, etc., are no common names and that every scene has its own link with some historic or poetic association, and we cannot but perceive that these parts of Turkey in Europe are singularly rich in a combination of qualities, hardly to be found in any other land.

* * * *

Previously to starting, a certain supply of cooking utensils, tin plates, knives and forks, a basin, etc., must absolutely be purchased, the stronger and plainer the better; for you go into lands where pots and pans are unknown, and all culinary processes are to be performed in strange localities, innocent of artificial means. A light mattress, some sheets and blankets, and a good supply of capotes and plaids should not be neglected; two or three books; some rice, curry-powder, and cayenne; a world of drawing materials – if you be a hard sketcher; as little dress as possible, though you must have two sets of outer clothing – one for visiting consuls, Pashás, and dignitaries, the other for rough, everyday work; some quinine made into pills (rather leave all behind than this); a *boyourldí*, or general order of introduction to governors or Pashás; and your *teskeré*, or provincial passport for yourself and guide. All these are absolutely indispensable, and beyond these, the less you augment your impedimenta by luxuries the better; though a long strap with a pair of ordinary stirrups, to throw over the Turkish saddles, may be recommended to save you the cramp caused by the awkward shovel stirrups of the country. Arms and ammunition, fine raiment, presents for natives, are all nonsense; simplicity should be your aim. When all these things, so generically termed *Roba* by Italians, are in order, stow them into two Brobdignagian saddle-bags, united by a cord (if you can get leather bags so much the better, if not, goats'-hair sacks); and by these hanging on each side of the baggage-horse's saddle, no trouble will ever be given from seceding bits of luggage escaping at unexpected intervals. Until you adopt this plan (the simplest of any) you will lose much time daily by the constant necessity of putting the baggage in order.

Journeys in Albania vary in length according to your will, for there are usually roadside *khans* at from two to four hours' distance. Ten hours' riding is as much as you can manage, if any sketching is to be secured; but I generally found eight sufficient.

A *khan* is a species of public-house rented by the keeper or *Khanjí* from the Government, and is open to all comers. You find food in it sometimes – sometimes not, when you fall back on your own rice and curry powder. In large towns, the *khan* is a three-sided building enclosed in a courtyard, and consisting of two floors, the lower a stable, the upper divided into chambers, opening into a wooden gallery which runs all round the building, and to which you ascend outside by stairs. In unfrequented districts the *khan* is a single room, or barn, with a raised floor at one end for humanity, and all the rest devoted to cattle – sometimes quadrupeds and bipeds are all mixed up together. First come, first served, is the rule in these establishments; and as any person who can pay the trifle required by the *Khanjí* for lodging may sleep in them, your company is oftentimes not select; but of this, as of the kind of *khan* you stop at, you must take your chance.

The best way of taking money is by procuring letters on consular agents, or merchants from town to town, so as to carry as little coin as possible with you; and your bag of piastres you pack in your carpet bag by day, and use as a pillow by night.

Part I

9 September to 12 November 1848

September 9, 1848. Constantinople

3 p.m. – Came on board the *Ferdinando,* an Austrian steamer running between Constantinople and Saloníki; and a pretty place does it seem to pass two or three days in! Every point of the lower deck – all of it – is crammed with Turks, Jews, Greeks, Bulgarians, wedged together with a density, compared to which a crowded Gravesend steamer is emptiness: a section of a fig-drum, or of a herring-barrel is the only apt simile for this extraordinary crowd of recumbent human beings, who are all going to Saloníki, as a starting-point for Thessaly, Bosnia, Wallachia, or any part of Northern Turkey. This motley cargo is not of ordinary occurrence; but the second Saloníki steamer, which should have started today, has fallen indisposed in its wheels or boiler; so we have a double load for our share.

Walking carefully over my fellow-passengers, I reached the first-class part of the deck – a small, raised triangle, railed off from the throng below, half of which is allotted to Christians (the Austrian Consul at Saloníki and his family being the only Christians besides myself), and the other half tabooed for the use of a harem of Turkish females, who entirely cover the floor with a diversity of robes, pink, blue, chocolate, and amber; pea, sea, olive, bottle, pale, and dark green; above which parterre of colours are numerous heads, all wrapped in white muslin, excepting as many pairs of eyes undistinguishably similar. There is a good cabin below; but owing to a row of obstructive Mussulmen who choose to cover up the grated opening with shutters, that they may sit quietly upon them to smoke, it is quite dark, so I remain on deck. We are a silent community: the smoking Turks are silent, and so is the strange harem. The Consul and his wife, and their two pretty daughters, are silent, because they fear cholera at Saloníki – which the young ladies declare is *'un pessimo esilio'*[1] – and because they are regretting northern friends. I am silent, from much thought and some weakness consequent on long illness: and the extra cargo in the lower deck are silent also – perhaps because they have not room to talk. At four, the anchor is weighed and we begin to paddle

---

1   An odious banishment.

away from the many domed mosques and bright minarets of Constantinople and the gay sides of the Golden Horn, with its caïques and its cypresses towering against the deepening blue sky, when lo! we do not turn towards the sea, but proceed ignominiously to tow a great coal-ship all the way to Buyúkdere, so there is a moving panorama of all the Bosphorus bestowed on us gratis – Kandilí, Baltalimán, Bebék, Yenikoi, Therapia, with its well-known walks and pines and planes, and lastly Buyúkdere, where we leave our dingy charge and return, evening darkening over the Giant's Hill, Unkiar Skelessi, and Anatóli Hissár, till we sail forth into the broad Sea of Marmora, leaving Scútari and the towers of wonderful Stamboul first pale and distinct in the light of the rising moon, and then glittering and lessening on the calm horizon, till they, and the memory that I have been among them for seven weeks, seem alike part of the world of dreams.

September 11. On board ship
There were wearily long flat points of land to pass (all, however, full of interest as parts of the once flourishing Chalcidice), ere Saloníki was visible, a triangle enclosed in a border of white walls on the hill at the head of the gulf; and it was nearly six p.m. before we reached the harbour and anchored.

Instantly the wildest confusion seized all the passive human freight. The polychromatic harem arose and moved like a bed of tulips in a breeze; the packed Wallachians, and Bosniacs, and Jews started crampfully from the deck and disentangled themselves into numerous boats; the Consular Esiliati departed; and lastly, I and my dragoman* prepared to go, and were soon at shore, though it was not so easy to be upon it. Saloníki is inhabited by a very great proportion of Jews; nearly all the porters in the city are of that nation, and now that the cholera had rendered employment scarce there were literally crowds of black-turbaned Hebrews at the water's edge, speculating on the possible share of each in the conveyance of luggage from the steamer. The enthusiastic Israelites rushed into the water and seizing my arms and legs, tore me out of the boat and up a narrow board with the most unsatisfactory zeal; immediately after which they fell upon my enraged dragoman in the same mode, and finally throwing themselves on my luggage, each portion of it was claimed by ten or twelve

---

* Giorgio Coggachio, Lear's Smyrniote guide.

frenzied agitators who pulled this way and that way, till I who stood apart, resigned to whatever might happen, confidently awaited the total destruction of my *roba*. From yells and pullings to and fro, the scene changed in a few minutes to a real fight, and the whole community fell to the most furious hair-pulling, turban-clenching, and robe-tearing, till the luggage was forgotten and all the party was involved in one terrific combat. How this exhibition would have ended I cannot tell, for in the heat of the conflict my man came running with a half-score of Government *Kawási*, or police; and the way in which they fell to belabouring the enraged Hebrews was a thing never to be forgotten. These took a deal of severe beating from sticks and whips before they gave way, and eventually some six or eight were selected to carry the packages of the Ingliz, which I followed into the city, not unvexed at being the indirect cause of so much strife.[2]

* * * *

Presently in came Giorgio with the dreariest of faces, and the bearer of what to me were, in truth, seriously vexatious news.

The cholera, contrary to the intelligence received in Stamboul, which represented the disease as on the decline, had indeed broken out afresh and was spreading, or – what is the same thing as to results, if a panic be once rife – was supposed to be spreading on all sides. The surrounding villages had taken alarm and had drawn a strict *cordon sanitaire* between themselves and the enemy; and, worse than all, the monks of Mount Athos had utterly prohibited all communication between their peninsula and the infected city; so that any attempt on my part to join C.M.C.* would be useless, no person being allowed to proceed beyond a few miles outside the eastern gate of Saloníki. No one could tell how long this state of things would last; for, although the epidemic was perhaps actually decreasing in violence, yet the fear of contagion was by no

2   The Jews in Saloníki are descended from those expelled from Spain in the fifteenth century: they are said to amount in number to four thousand.

*   Charles Church, a Greek scholar and linguist, had planned to set off with Lear from Saloníki but had been delayed. Church and Lear had toured in Attica and Boetia in June and July 1848, until Lear was struck with fever; this was the planned continuation of their travels together.

means so. Multitudes of the inhabitants of the suburbs and adjacent villages had fled to the plains, and to pass them would be an impossibility. On the south-western road to Greece or Epirus, the difficulty was the same: even at Katerína, or Platamona, the peasants would allow no one to land.[3]

Here was a dilemma! – a pleasant fix! yet it was one that required the remedy of resolve, rather than of patience. To remain in a city full of epidemic disease (and those only who have seen an Oriental provincial town under such circumstances can estimate their horror), myself but convalescent, was literally to court the risk of renewed illness, or at best compulsory detention by quarantine. Therefore, after weighing the matter well, I decided that my first step must be to leave Saloníki at the very earliest opportunity. But whither to go? Mount Athos was shut; the west coast of the gulf was tabooed. There were but two plans open – the first was to return by the next steamer to Constantinople; but this involved a fortnight's waiting, at least, in the place of pestilence, with the chance of being disabled before the time of departure came; and even could I adopt such means of escape, the expense and mortification of going back was, if possible, to be shunned.

The second *modus operandi* was to set off directly, by the north-west road, through Macedonia to Illyrian Albania, by the ancient Via Egnatia, and so rejoin C.M.C. at Yannina. This plan, though not without weighty objection – of which the being compelled to go alone, and the great distance of the journey were prominent – appeared to me the only safe and feasible one; and after much reflection I finally determined to adopt it. After all, looking at things on their brightest side, when once they were discovered to be inevitable – though I was unable to meet my friend, I had a good servant accustomed to travel with Englishmen: health would certainly improve in the air of the mountain country, and professional objects, long in view, would not be sacrificed. As for the risk run by thus rushing into strange places and among unknown people, when a man has walked all over the wildest parts of Italy he does not prognosticate danger. Possibly one may get only as far as Monastír – the capital of Macedonia – and then make southward, having seen Yenidjé and Edéssa – places all full of beauty and

---

3   Such were the representations made to me at the time, and which naturally deterred me from attempting to reach Mount Athos; but I have since had reason to believe that the state of alarm and panic was greatly exaggerated.

interest; or, beyond Monastír, lies Akhridha and its lake, and farther yet Elbassán, or even Skódra – highest in the wilds of Ghéghe Albania. Make, thought I to myself, no definite arrangement beyond that of escape from Saloníki; put yourself, as a predestinarian might say, calmly into the dice-box of small events, and be shaken out whenever circumstances may ordain: only go, and as soon as you can. So, Giorgio, have horses and all minor matters in complete readiness at sunrise the day after tomorrow.

September 12. Saloníki
Whatever the past of Saloníki, its present seems gloomy enough. The woe, the dolefulness of this city! – its narrow, ill-paved streets (evil awaits the man who tries to walk with nailed boots on the rounded, slippery stones of a Turkish pavement!); the very few people I met in them, carefully avoiding contact; the closed houses; the ominous silence; the sultry, oppressive heat of the day; all contributed to impress the mind with a feeling of heavy melancholy. A few Jews in dark dresses and turbans; Jewesses, their hair tied up in long, caterpillar-like green-silk bags, three feet in length; Greek porters, aged blacks, of whom – freed slaves from Stamboul – there are many in Saloníki; these were the only human beings I encountered in threading a labyrinth of lanes in the lower town, ascending towards the upper part of this formerly extensive city. Once, a bier with a corpse on it, borne by some six or eight of the most wretched creatures, crossed my path; and when I arrived at the beautiful ruin called the Incantada two women, I was told, had just expired within the courtyard, and, said the ghastly-looking Greek on the threshold, 'You may come in and examine what you please, and welcome; but once in you are in quarantine, and may not go out', an invitation I declined as politely as I could, and passed onward. From the convent at the summit of the town, just within its white walls, the view should be most glorious, as one ought to see the whole of the gulf and all the range of Olympus; but, alas! beyond the silvery minarets relieving the monotonous surface of roofs below and the delicately indented shore and the blue gulf, all else was blotted out, as it were, by a curtain of hot purple haze, telling tales to my fancy of miasma and cholera, fever and death.

September 13. Yenidjé
Curious to know how one would be off for lodgings in Macedonia, I found Giorgio at the postmaster's house, where, in one of the above-noticed wooden galleries (six or eight silent Turks sat puffing around), I was glad of a basin of tea. But it is most difficult to adopt the Oriental mode of sitting; cross-leggism, from first to last, was insupportable to me and, as chairs exist not, everything must needs be done at full length. Yet it is a great charm of Turkish character that they never stare or wonder at anything; you are not bored by any questions, and I am satisfied that if you chose to take your tea while suspended by your feet from the ceiling not a word would be said or a sign of amazement betrayed; in consequence you soon lose the sense of the absurd so nearly akin to shame, on which you are forced to dwell if constantly reminded of your awkwardness by observation or interrogation.

September 14. Yenidjé
While taking a parting cup of coffee with the postmaster I unluckily set my foot on a handsome pipe-bowl (pipe-bowls are always snares to near-sighted people moving over Turkish floors, as they are scattered in places quite remote from the smokers, who live at the farther end of prodigiously long pipe-sticks) – crash; but nobody moved; only on apologising through Giorgio, the polite Mohammedan said: 'The breaking such a pipe-bowl would indeed, under ordinary circumstances, be disagreeable; but in a friend every action has its charm!' – a speech which recalled the injunction of the Italian to his son on leaving home, 'Whenever anybody treads upon your foot in company, and says, "*Scusatemi,*" only reply: "*Anzi – mi ha fatto un piacere!*"'[4]

* * * *

Of Giorgio, dragoman, cook, valet, interpreter, and guide, I have had as yet nothing to complain; he is at home in all kinds of tongues, speaking ten fluently, an accomplishment common to many of the travelling Oriental Greeks, for he is a Smyrniote by birth. In countenance my attendant is somewhat like one of those strange faces, lion or griffin, which we see on door-knockers or urn-

4   'I beg pardon.' 'On the contrary, you have done me a pleasure.'

handles, and a grim twist of his under-jaw gives an idea that it would not be safe to try his temper too much. In the morning he is diffuse, and dilates on past journeys; after noon his remarks become short, and sententious – not to say surly. Any appearance of indecision evidently moves him to anger speedily. It is necessary to watch the disposition of a servant on whom so much of one's personal comfort depends, and it is equally necessary to give as little trouble as possible, for a good dragoman has always enough to do without extra whims or worryings from his employer.

September 15. Ostrovo
At Ostrovo I decided to remain,[5] too fearful of returning fever to hazard the seven hours' journey between it and the next village – Tilbelí; and on descending a steep path to the lake, the little town and mosque shone out brightly against the lead-coloured waters and cloud-swept mountains, a scene of grandeur reminding me in its hues of Wastwater and Keswick, while the snow peaks, dark cypresses, and gay white minarets stamped the whole as truly Moslem-Macedonian. But, notwithstanding all these ecstasies, what a place is Ostrovo for a night's abode! This most wretched little village contains but one small *khan*, with two tiny rooms on the ground floor, in one of which, half suffocated by the smoke of a wood fire, I was too glad to change dripping garments and don dry ones; let the traveller in these countries be never forgetful of so wrapping up his *roba* that he may have dry changes of raiment when needful. Happily the weather cleared after the storm, and I drew till dusk, none the worse for the morning's wetting, and feeling hourly the benefit of the elastic mountain air.

September 19. Monastír
Sunrise: and I am drawing the plain and hills from the *'Piazza de' Cani'*; lines of convicts are passing from the Barracks, carrying offal in tubs to the ghouly burying-grounds and followed by some hundreds of dogs, who every now and then give way to their feelings and indulge in a general battle among themselves. It is no easy matter to pursue the fine arts in Monastír, and I cannot but think – will matters grow worse as I advance into Albania? For all the passers-by having inspected my sketching, frown or look ugly,

---

5   Counted as four hours from Vodhená.

and many say, *'Shaitán'*, which means, Devil; at length one quietly wrenches my book away and shutting it up returns it to me, saying, *'Yok, Yok!'*[6] – so as numbers are against me, I bow and retire. Next, I essay to draw on one of the bridges, but a gloomy sentinel comes and bullies me off directly, indicating by signs that my profane occupation is by no manner of means to be tolerated; and farther on, when I thought I had escaped all observation behind a friendly buttress, out rush legions of odious hounds (all bare-hided and very like jackals), and raise such a din that, although by means of a pocket full of stones I keep them at bay, yet they fairly beat me at last, and give me chase open-mouthed, augmenting their detestable pack by fresh recruits at each street corner. So I gave up this pursuit of knowledge under difficulties and returned to the *khan*.

Giorgio was waiting to take me to the Pashá; so dressing in my 'best', thither I went, to pay my first visit to an Oriental dignitary. All one's gathered and hoarded memories, from books or personal relations, came so clearly to my mind as I was shown into the great palace or serai of the Governor that I seemed somehow to have seen it all before; the ante-room full of attendants, the second state-room with secretaries and officers, and, finally, the large square hall, where – in a corner and smoking the longest *nargilleh*,* the serpentine foldings of which formed all the furniture of the chamber save the carpets and sofas – sat the Seraskíer Pashá himself – one of the highest grandees of the Ottoman empire. Emím Seraskíer Pashá was educated at Cambridge, and speaks English fluently. He conversed for some time agreeably and intelligently, and after having promised me a *Kawás*, the interview was over, and I returned to the *khan*, impatient to attack the street scenery of Monastír forthwith under the auspices of my guard. These availed me much, and I sketched in the dry part of the river-bed with impunity – ay, and even in the Jews' quarter, though immense crowds collected to witness the strange Frank and his doings; and the word, *'Scroo, Scroo'*,** resounded from hundreds of voices above and around. But a clear space was kept around me by the formidable baton of the *Kawás*, and I contrived thus to carry off

---

6   No, no!

---

*   A hookah.
** 'He writes, he writes.' Frank: a general name for any Westerner.

some of the best views of the town ere it grew dark. How pictur-esque are those parts of the crowded city in the Jews' quarter, where the elaborately detailed wooden houses overhang the torrent, shaded by grand plane, cypress, and poplar! How the sunset lights up the fire-tinged clouds – floating over the snow-capped eastern hills! How striking are the stately groups of armed guards clearing the road through the thronged streets of the bazaars for some glittering Bey, or mounted Pashá! Interest and beauty in profusion, O ye artists! are to be found in the city of Monastír.

September 20. Akhridha
In this, the first town I had seen in Northern Albania, the novelty of the costumes is striking; for, rich as is the clothing of all these people, the tribes of Ghegheria (a district comprising all the territory north of the River Apsus, generally termed Illyrian Albania, and of which Skódra may be said to be the capital and Akhridha the most western limit) surpass all their neighbours in gorgeousness of raiment, by adding to their ordinary vestments a long surtout of purple, crimson, or scarlet, trimmed with fur, or bordered with gold thread, or braiding. Their jackets and waist-coats are usually black, and their whole outer man contrasts strongly with that of their white neighbours of Berát, or many-hued brethren of Epirus. Other proofs were not wanting of my being in a new land; for as we advanced slowly through the geese-frequented kennels (a running stream with *trottoirs* on each side, and crossed by stepping-stones, is a characteristic of this place) my head was continually saluted by small stones and bits of dirt, the infidel air of my white hat courting the notice and condemnation of the orthodox Akhridhani; 'and,' quoth Giorgio, 'unless you take to a Fez, Vossignoria will have no peace and possibly lose an eye in a day or two.'

September 21. Akhridha
An early walk in the town, which is full of exquisite street scenes (the castle-hill, or the mountains always forming a background), would have been more agreeable had I not been pelted most unsparingly by women and children from unexpected corners. Escaping to the outskirts, I sketched the town and castle from a rising ground, when a shepherd ventured to approach and look at my doings; but no sooner did he discover the form of the castle on

the paper than shrieking out *'Shaitán!'* he fled rapidly from me, as from a profane magician. A mizzling rain began to fall, and when – avoiding herds of buffali, and flocks of sheep, with large dogs on the look-out – I made for the lake through some by-lanes, several of these wild and shy people espied me afar off, and rushed screaming into their houses, drawing bolts and banging doors with the most emphatic resolve against the wandering apparition. Returning to the *khan*, I prepared to visit Sheréeff Bey, the Governor and principal grandee of Akhridha, to whom the Seraskíer Pashá's letter was addressed.

* * * *

The room in which Sheréef Bey was sitting – a square chamber (so well described in Urquhart's *Spirit of the East*) – was full enough of characters and costumes to set up a dozen painters for life. The Bey[7] himself, in a snuff-coloured robe trimmed with fur, the white-turbaned Cogia,[8] the scarlet-vested Gheghes, the purple-and-gold-brocaded Greek secretary, the troops of long-haired, full-skirted, glittering Albanian domestics, armed and belted – one and all looking at me with an imperturbable fixed glare (for your nonchalant Turkish good breeding is not known here) – all this formed a picture I greatly wished I could have had on paper. The Bey, after the ceremonies of pipes and coffee, offered a letter to Tyrana, a town on the road to Skódra, and expressed his willingness to send guards with me to the end of the world, if I pleased, declaring at the same time that the roads, however unfrequented, were perfectly safe. Mindful also of missiles, I begged for a *Kawás* to protect me while drawing in the town of Akhridha, and then returned to the *khan* to dine, and afterwards passed the afternoon in sketching about the town with my Mohammedan guard, unannoyed by any sticks or stones from the hands of true believers.

23 September. Akhridha
The *khan* was swarming with magnificence when I returned to it, the Bey of Tyrana and all his train having arrived. Simplicity is the rule of life with Albanian grandees; they sit silently on a mat and

---

7 Bey, a person of superior rank, frequently governor of a town.
8 Cogia, a priest.

smoke, but their retinue bounce and tear about with a perfectly fearful energy, and after supper indulge in music according to their fashion until a late hour, then throwing themselves down to sleep in their capotes, and at early morning going through the slightest possible form of facial ablution – for cleanliness is not the most shining national virtue. These at Akhridha seem a wild and savage set, and are not easy to catch by drawing. Yet tomorrow I enter the wildest parts of Ghegheria and must expect to see 'a rugged set of men'* indeed. In preparation, the Frangistán 'wide-awakes' are packed up, as having a peculiar attraction for missiles, on account of their typically infidel appearance. Henceforth I adopt the Fez, for with that Mohammedan sign on the head it matters not how you adorn the rest of your person.

September 25. Kukues
In spite of the apparent discomforts of the place, I slept well enough. The lively race of 'F sharps' do not abound in these solitary *khans* half as much as in an Italian *Locanda*. The Albanians never stirred; and as the fire burned more or less all night their feet must have been handsomely grilled. Once only I was awakened suddenly by something falling on me – flomp – miaw – fizz! – an accidental cat had tumbled from some unexplored height, and testified great surprise at having alighted on a movable body. Would that her disturbance of my slumbers had been her only fault, and that she had not carried off a whole fowl and some slices of cold mutton – the little all I had to rely on for dinner through tomorrow's journey! Our Albanian co-tenants of the *khan* would assuredly have been blamed for this *mancanza*,[9] had not a fierce quarrel over the fowl, between the invading robber and an original cat belonging to the establishment, betrayed the cause of evil – the bigger cat conquering and escaping from the roof with the booty.

At half past five a.m. we were off; the red morning sky and the calm shade of that broad valley were very striking; and the line of country we were to pursue promised a hard day's work. Continuing to ascend, on the left bank of the Skumbi, towards those gigantic rocks I had drawn yesterday evening, and once or

9 Loss.

* 'Land of Albania, […] thou rugged nurse of savage men' (Byron, *Childe Harold's Pilgrimage*, Canto II, stanza 38).

twice pausing to make hasty memoranda sketches, we advanced by perilous paths along the mountain-sides towards a village at a great height above the river. It is very difficult, on such days of travel as this, to secure anything like a finished drawing. Even let the landscape be ever so tempting, the uncertainty of meeting with any place of repose or shelter obliges the most enthusiastic artist to pass hastily through scenes equal or superior to any it may be again his lot to see. Our progress here, too, is of the very slowest: either along sharp narrow paths cut in the rock, at the very edge of formidable precipices, or by still narrower tracks running on the bare side of a perpendicular clay ravine, – or winding among huge trunks of forest trees, between which the baggage-mule at one time, is wedged – at another loses her load, or her own equilibrium, by some untimely concussion; such was the order of the day for travelling ease and accommodation; so that Dragoman Giorgio, greatly desirous of reaching Elbassán ere nightfall, strongly besought me not to linger. Nevertheless, after diving by a tortuous path into the depths of an abyss – (the home of a lateral stream which descended from the mountains to the Skumbi) – and after mounting a zigzag staircase out of it to the village above-mentioned, I could not resist sitting down to draw when I gazed on the extraordinary scene I had passed; it combined Greek outline – Italian colour – English luxuriance of foliage – while the village, with its ivory minarets peeping from huge walnut and chestnut groves, was hanging, as it were, down the stupendous precipices to the stream below; – all these formed one of the wildest and grandest of pictures.

September 26. Elbassán
A grey, calm, pleasant morning, the air seeming doubly warm, from the contrast between the low plains and the high mountains of the last two days' journey.

I set off early, to make the most of a whole day at Elbassán – a town singularly picturesque, both in itself and as to its site. A high and massive wall, with a deep outer moat, surrounds a large quadrangle of dilapidated houses, and at the four corners are towers, as well as two at each of the four gates: all of these fortifications appear of Venetian structure. Few places can offer a greater picture of desolation than Elbassán; albeit the views from the broad ramparts extending round the town are perfectly exquisite: weeds, brambles, and luxuriant wild fig overrun and cluster about the grey heaps of ruin, and whichever way you turn you have a middle distance of mosques and foliage, with a background of purple hills, or southward, the remarkable mountain of Tomóhrit, the giant Soracte of the plains of Berát.

No sooner had I settled to draw – forgetful of Bekír the guard – than forth came the populace of Elbassán; one by one, and two by two, to a mighty host they grew, and there were soon from eighty to a hundred spectators collected, with earnest curiosity in every look; and when I had sketched such of the principal buildings as they could recognize, a universal shout of '*Shaitán!*' burst from the crowd; and, strange to relate, the greater part of the mob put their fingers into their mouths and whistled furiously, after the manner of butcher-boys in England. Whether this was a sort of spell against my magic I do not know; but the absurdity of sitting still on a rampart to make a drawing, while a great crowd of people whistled at me with all their might, struck me so forcibly that come what might of it, I could not resist going off into convulsions of laughter, an impulse the Gheghes seemed to sympathize with, as one and all shrieked with delight, and the ramparts resounded with hilarious merriment. Alas! this was of no long duration, for one of those tiresome Dervíshes – in whom, with their green turbans, Elbassán is rich – soon came up, and yelled, '*Shaitán scroo! – Shaitán!*'[10] in my ears with all his force; seizing my book also, with an awful frown, shutting it, and pointing to the sky, as intimating that heaven would not allow such impiety. It was in vain after this to attempt more; the '*Shaitán*' cry was raised in one wild chorus – and I took the consequences of having laid by my Fez for comfort's sake – in the shape of a horrible shower of stones which pursued me to the covered streets, where, finding Bekír with his whip, I went to work again more successfully about the walls of the old city.

Knots of the Elbassániotes nevertheless gathered about Bekír, and pointed with angry gestures to me and my 'scroo'. 'We will not be written down,' said they. 'The Frank is a Russian, and he is sent by the Sultan to write us all down before he sells us to the Russian Emperor.' This they told also to Giorgio, and murmured bitterly at their fate, though the inexorable Bekír told them they should not only be scroo'd, but bastinadoed, if they were not silent and obedient. Alas! it is not a wonder that Elbassán is no cheerful

---

10 'The Devil draws! – the Devil.'

spot, nor that the inhabitants are gloomy. Within the last two years one of the most serious rebellions has broken out in Albania, and has been sternly put down by the Porte.* Under an adventurer named Zulíki, this restless people rose in great numbers throughout the north-western districts; but they were defeated in an engagement with the late Seraskíer Pashá. Their Beys, innocent or accomplices, were exiled to Koniah or Monastír, the population was either drafted off into the Sultan's armies, slain, or condemned to the galleys at Constantinople, while the remaining miserables were and are more heavily taxed than before. Such, at least, is the general account of the present state of these provinces; and certainly their appearance speaks of ill-fortune, whether merited or unmerited.

Beautiful as is the melancholy Elbassán – with its exquisite bits of mosques close to the walls – the air is most oppressive after the pure mountain atmosphere. How strange are the dark covered streets, with their old mat roofings hanging down in tattered shreds, dry leaves, long boughs, straw or thatch reeds; one phosphorus match would ignite the whole town! Each street is allotted to a separate bazaar, or particular trade, and that portion which is the dwelling of the tanners and butchers is rather revolting, – dogs, blood, and carcasses filling up the whole street and sickening one's very heart.

At three p.m. I rode out with the scarlet-and-gold-clad Bekír to find a general view of the town. But the long walled suburbs, and endless olive gardens are most tiresome, and nothing of Elbassán is seen till one reaches the Skumbi, spanned by an immensely long bridge, full of ups and downs and irregular arches. On a little brow beyond the river I drew till nearly sunset; for the exquisitely graceful lines of hill to the north present really a delightful scene, – the broad, many-channelled stream washing interminable slopes of rich olives, from the midst of which peep the silver minarets of Elbasán.

The dark *khan* cell at tea-time was enlivened by the singing of some Gheghes in the street. These northern, or Sclavonic Albanians are greatly superior in musical taste to their Berát or Epirote neighbours, all of whom either make a feeble buzzing or humming over their tinkling guitars, like dejected flies in a window-pane, or yell

---

* The Ottoman court at Constantinople.

forth endless stanzas of a whining, motonous song, somewhat resembling a bad imitation of Swiss *jödeling*. But here there is a better idea of music. The guardian Bekír indulged me throughout yesterday with divers airs, little varied, but possessing considerable charm of plaintive wild melody. The Soorudgí,* also, made the passes of the Skumbi resound with more than one pretty song.

September 27. Between Elbassán and Tyrana
How glorious, in spite of the dimming sirocco haze, was the view from the summit, as my eyes wandered over the perspective of winding valley and stream to the farthest edge of the horizon – a scene realising the fondest fancies of artist imagination! The wide branching oak, firmly riveted in crevices, all tangled over with fern and creepers, hung halfway down the precipices of the giant crag, while silver-white goats (which chime so picturesquely in with such landscapes as this) stood motionless as statues on the highest pinnacle, sharply defined against the clear blue sky. Here and there the broken foreground of rocks piled on rocks, was enlivened by some Albanians who toiled upwards, now shadowed by spreading beeches, now glittering in the bright sun on slopes of the greenest lawn, studded over with tufted trees, which recalled Stothard's graceful forms,** so knit with my earliest ideas of landscape. These and countless well-loved passages of auld lang syne, crowded back on my memory as I rested, while the steeds and attendants reposed under the cool plane-tree shade, and drank from the sparkling stream which bubbled from a stone fountain. It was difficult to turn away from this magnificent mountain view – from these chosen nooks and corners of a beautiful world – from sights of which no painter-soul can ever weary: even now, that fold beyond fold of wood, swelling far as the eye can reach – that vale ever parted by its serpentine river – that calm blue plain, with Tomóhr in the midst, like an azure island in a boundless sea, haunt my mind's eye, and vary the present with visions of the past. With regret I turned northwards to descend to the new district of Tyrana; the town (and it is now past eleven) being still some hours distant.

* * * *

---

*   Lear's driver, 'a wild gipsy Soorudgi'.
** Lear again recalls Stothard's illustrations to *Robinson Crusoe*, in the edition he had read as a boy (see p. 161, above).

A snake crossing the road gave Giorgio an occasion, as is his afternoon's wont, to illustrate the fact with a story.

'In Egitto,' said he, 'are lots of serpents; and once there were many Hebrews there. These Hebrews wished to become Christians, but the King Pharaoh – of whom you may have heard – would not allow any such thing. On which Moses (who was the prince of the Jews) wrote to the Patriarch of Constantinople and to the Archbishop of Jerusalem, and also to San Carlo Borromeo, all three of whom went straight to King Pharaoh and entreated him to do them this favour; to which he only replied, "No, signori."

'But one fine morning these three saints proved too strong for the King, and changed him and all his people into snakes; which,' said the learned dragoman, 'is the real reason why there are so many serpents in Egypt to this day.'

* * * *

Tyrana
Two *khans*, each abominable, did we try. No person would undertake to guide us to the palace of the Bey (at some distance from the town), nor at that hour would it have been to much purpose to have gone there. The sky was lowering; the crowds of gazers increasing – Albanian the only tongue; so, all these things considered, I finally fixed on a third-rate *khan*, reported to be the Clarendon of Tyrana, and certainly better than the other two, though its horrors are not easy to describe nor imagine. Horrors I had made up my mind to bear in Albania, and here, truly, they were in earnest.

Is it necessary, says the reader, so to suffer? And when you had a Sultan's *bouyourldí* could you not have commanded Beys' houses? True; but had I done so, numberless arrangements become part of that mode of life, which, desirous as I was of sketching as much as possible, would have rendered the whole motives of my journey of no avail. If you lodge with Beys or Pashás, you must eat with them at hours incompatible with artistic pursuits, and you must lose much time in ceremony. Were you so magnificent as to claim a home in the name of the Sultan, they must needs prevent your stirring without a suitable retinue, nor could you in propriety prevent such attention; thus, travelling in Albania has, to a landscape painter, two alternatives; luxury and inconvenience on the one hand, liberty, hard living, and filth on the other; and of these two I chose the latter, as the most professionally useful, though not the most agreeable.

O the *khan* of Tyrana! with its immense stables full of uproarious horses; its broken ladders, by which one climbed distrustfully up to the most uneven and dirtiest of corridors, in which a loft some twenty feet square by six in height was the best I could pick out as a home for the night. Its walls, falling in masses of mud from its osier-woven sides (leaving great holes exposed to your neighbour's view, or, worse still, to the cold night air); – its thinly raftered roof, anything but proof to the cadent amenities resulting from the location of an Albanian family above it; its floor of shaking boards, so disunited that it seemed unsafe to move incautiously across it, and through the great chasms of which the horses below were open to contemplation, while the suffocating atmosphere produced thence are not to be described!

O *khan* of Tyrana! when the Gheghe Khanjí strode across the most rotten of garrets, how certainly did each step seem to foretell the downfall of the entire building; and when he whirled great bits of lighted pitch-torch hither and thither, how did the whole horrid tenement seem about to flare up suddenly and irretrievably!

O *khan* of Tyrana! rats, mice, cockroaches, and all lesser vermin were there. Huge flimsy cobwebs, hanging in festoons above my head; big frizzly moths, bustling into my eyes and face, for the holes representing windows I could close but imperfectly with sacks and baggage: yet here I prepared to sleep, thankful that a clean mat was a partial preventive to some of this list of woes, and finding some consolation in the low crooning singing of the Gheghes above me, who, with that capacity for melody which those Northern-Albanians seem to possess so essentially, were murmuring their wild airs in choral harmony.

September 28. Tyrana
But even with a guard it was a work of trouble to sketch in Tyrana; for it was market, or bazaar day, and when I was tempted to open my book in the large space before the two principal mosques, (one wild scene of confusion, in which oxen, buffaloes, sheep, goats, geese, asses, dogs, and children, were all running about in disorder) – a great part of the natives, impelled by curiosity, pressed closely to watch my operations, in spite of the *Kawás*, who kept as clear a space as he could for me; the women alone, in dark *feringhís*, and ghostly white muslin masks, sitting unmoved by

their wares. Fain would I have drawn the exquisitely pretty arabesque-covered mosques, but the crowds at last stifled my enthusiasm. Not the least annoyance was that given me by the persevering attentions of a mad or fanatic Dervísh, of most singular appearance as well as conduct. His note of '*Shaitán*' was frequently sounded; and as he twirled about, and performed many curious antics, he frequently advanced to me, shaking a long hooked stick, covered with jingling ornaments, in my very face, pointing to the *Kawás* with menacing looks, as though he would say, 'Were it not for this protector you should be annihilated, you infidel!' The crowd looked on with awe at the holy man's proceedings, for Tyrana is evidently a place of great attention to religion. In no part of Albania are there such beautiful mosques and nowhere are collected so many green-vested Dervíshes. But however a wandering artist may fret at the impossibility of comfortably exercising his vocation, he ought not to complain of the effects of a curiosity which is but natural, or even of some irritation at the open display of arts which, to their untutored apprehension, must seem at the very least diabolical.

* * * *

No sooner, after retiring to my pig-stye dormitory, had I put out my candle and was preparing to sleep, than the sound of a key turning in the lock of the next door to that of my garret disturbed me, and lo! broad rays of light illumined my detestable lodging from a large hole a foot in diameter, besides from two or three others, just above my bed; at the same time a whirring, humming sound, followed by strange whizzings and mumblings, began to pervade the apartment. Desirous to know what was going on, I crawled to the smallest chink, without encountering the rays from the great hiatus, and what did I see? My friend of the morning – the maniac Dervísh – performing the most wonderful evolutions and gyrations; spinning round and round for his own private diversion, first on his legs, and then pivot-wise, *sur son séant*,* and indulging in numerous other pious gymnastic feats. Not quite easy at my vicinity to this very eccentric neighbour, and half anticipating a twitch from his brass-hooked stick, I sat watching the event, whatever it might be. It was simple. The old creature pulled

---

* On his behind.

forth some grapes and ate them, after which he gradually relaxed in his twirlings, and finally fell asleep.

September 29. *Tyrana*

It was as late as half-past nine a.m. when I left Tyrana, and one consolation there was in quitting its horrible *khan*, that travel all the world over a worse could not be met with. Various delays prevented an early start; the postmaster was in the bath, and until he came out no horses could be procured (meanwhile I contrived to finish my arabesque mosques); then a dispute with the *Khanjí*, who, like many of these provincial people, insisted on counting the Spanish dollar as twenty-three instead of twenty-four Turkish piastres. Next followed a row with Bekír of Akhridha, who vowed he would be paid and indemnified for the loss of an imaginary amber pipe, which he declared he had lost in a fabulous ditch, while holding my horse at Elbassán; and lastly, and not the least of the list, the crowd around the *khan* gave way at the sound of terrific shrieks and howlings, and forth rushed my spinning neighbour, the mad Dervísh, in the most foaming state of indignation. First he seized the bridles of the horses; then, by a frantic and sudden impulse, he began to prance and circulate in the most amazing manner, leaping and bounding and shouting 'Allah!' with all his might, to the sound of a number of little bells, which this morning adorned his brass-hooked weapon. After this he made an harangue for ten minutes, of the most energetic character, myself evidently the subject; at the end of it he advanced towards me with furious gestures, and bringing his hook to within two or three inches of my face, remained stationary, in a Taglioni* attitude. Knowing the danger of interfering with these privileged fanatics, I thought my only and best plan was to remain unmoved, which I did, fixing my eye steadily on the ancient buffoon, but neither stirring nor uttering a word; whereon, after he had screamed and foamed at me for some minutes, the demon of anger seemed to leave him at a moment's warning; for yelling forth discordant cries and brandishing his stick and bells, away he ran, as if he were really possessed. Wild and savage were the looks of many of my friend's excited audience, their long matted black hair and brown visage giving them an air of ferocity which existed perhaps more in the outward than the inner man; moreover, these Gheghes are all

---

*   The Taglioni family were famous Italian dancers and choreographers.

armed, whereas out of Ghegheria no Albanian is allowed to carry so much as a knife.

* * * *

The Bey's palace in Króia
In the arabesqued and carved corridor, to which a broad staircase conducted me, were hosts of Albanian domestics; and on my letter of introduction being sent in to the Bey, I was almost instantly asked into his room of reception – a three-windowed, square chamber (excellent, according to the standard of Turkish ornament, taste, and proportion) – where, in a corner of the raised divan, sat Alí, Bey of Króia – a lad of eighteen or nineteen, dressed in the usual blue frock-coat now adopted by Turkish nobles or officers. A file of kilted and armed retainers were soon ordered to marshal me into a room where I was to sleep, and the little Bey seemed greatly pleased with the fun of doing hospitality to so novel a creature as a Frank. My dormitory was a real Turkish chamber; and the raised cushions on three sides of it – the high, square, carved wooden ceiling – the partition screen of lofty woodwork, with long striped Brusa napkins thrown over it – the guns, horse-gear, etc., which covered the walls – the fireplace – closets – innumerable pigeonholes – green, orange, and blue stained-glass windows – all appeared so much the more in the light of luxuries and splendours when found in so remote a place as Króia. It was not easy to shake off the attentions of ten full-dressed Albanian servants, who stood in much expectation, till, finding I was about to take off my shoes, they made a rush at me as the Jews did at Saloníki, and showed such marks of disappointment at not being allowed to make themselves useful that I was obliged to tell Giorgio to explain that we Franks were not used to assistance every moment of our lives and that I should think it obliging of them if they would leave me in peace. After changing my dress, the Bey sent to say that supper should be served in an hour, he having eaten at sunset, and in the meantime he would be glad of my society; so I took my place on the sofa by the little gentleman's side, and Giorgio, sitting on the ground, acted as interpreter. At first Alí Bey said little, but soon became immensely loquacious, asking numerous questions about Stamboul and a few about Franks in general – the different species of whom he was not very well informed. At length, when the conversation was flagging, he was moved to discourse about ships that went without sails, and

coaches that were impelled without horses; and to please him I drew a steamboat and a railway carriage; on which he asked if they made any noise; and I replied by imitating both the inventions in question in the best manner I could think of – 'Tik-tok, tik-tok, tik-tok, tokka, tokka, tokka, tokka, tokka – tok' (crescendo), and 'Squish-squash, squish-squash, squish-squash, thump-bump' – for the land and sea engines respectively – a noisy novelty, which so intensely delighted Alí Bey, that he fairly threw himself back on the divan, and laughed as I never saw Turk laugh before.

For my sins, this imitation became fearfully popular, and I had to repeat 'squish-squash', 'tik-tok', till I was heartily tired, the only recompense this wonderful little Pashá offered me, being the sight of a small German writing-box (when new it might have cost three or four shillings), containing a lithograph of Fanny Ellsler* and two small looking-glasses in the lid. This was brought in by a secretary, attended by two Palikari,[11] at the Bey's orders, and was evidently considered as something uncommonly interesting. So, when this very intellectual intercourse was over, I withdrew to my wooden room, and was glad of a light supper before sleeping.

September 30. Króia
The routine of dinner was as follows: ten servants, in full Albanian dress, came in at once, for all the world like in an opera ballet. One of them places a little stool on the ground, upside down, as much as to say that it is not to be sat upon; others fix thereon a large flat plate of tin, or some similar metal, with a spoon, or piece of bread, to each diner (there were two guests beside myself); then an ewer with water is handed to each person by one of the domestics, who kneels until you have used it and the Brusa towel. Soup, somewhat like sago and vinegar, was the first dish placed before us; and here my good genius basely forsook me, for endeavouring to sit cross-legged like my entertainers I somehow got my knees too far below the pewter table-top, and an ill-conditioned violent cramp seizing me at the unlucky moment in which the tureen was placed on the table, I hastily endeavoured to withdraw the limb, but unsuccessfully – gracious! – sidelong went the whole table, and all the soup was wasted on the ground! Constantly as a Frank is called on to

---

11 Palikari – Albanian or Greek military.

---

*   A Viennese dancer (1810–84).

observe the unvarying good breeding and polite ease of Turkish manner, this was a most trying proof of the endurance of those qualities. Nobody spoke, or even looked, as if anything had gone amiss; one of the *corps de ballet* wiped up the catastrophe and others soon brought in a new bowlful of soup as if nothing had happened. Nor was my awkwardness alluded to except by Giorgio, who, by my orders, offered a strong apology for the stiffness of Franks' legs in general, and of mine in particular.

October 1. Aléssio
Nearly all the Christians in this part of Northern Albania (that is, on the north-western coast, where the Venetian Republic was once so powerful) are of the Latin Church, and the residents of the Greek persuasion are the minority. From this spot the views are most exquisite. Looking south, they extend towards the high mountains above Króia and Tyrana; and northward they range over a beautiful river which winds down from the heights above Skódra, reflecting trees and hills in the clear water.

The sole tenant of the convent, a Capuchin Friar, came forth to meet me, when, having advanced a few yards, he set up a shout, ejaculating, '*O, possibile! Sì: – è il Signor Odoardo!*' while I on my part recognised him as a monk I had fallen in with some years back when staying with some friends in the Maremma near Corneto, and afterwards had frequently seen at Ara-Coeli in Rome; but the singularity of the circumstance – that we should meet again in this remote corner of Illyria – was one of those events that we should reject if in a novel, as too impossible to happen. Fra Pietro exhibited great glee at seeing a 'Christian', as he called me; and on the other side I was glad enough to hear good Roman speech. 'But,' said I, 'the people of Aléssio are Christians, are they not?' – '*Cristiani sì, lo sono,*' said the monk; '*ma se domani volesse il buon Dio far crescere il fiume per portargli tutti in Paradiso, ci avrei gusto! – Cristiani? Ladri! Cristiani? – porchi! – Cristiani? Lupi, animali, sciocchi, scimie, brutte bestie, Grechi, Turchi, Albanesi – che gli piglia ad uno e tutti un accidente. O che Cristiani! O che rabbia.*'[12] Seeing that a sojourn in the Latin

---

12 'Yes, they are! But if it pleased Heaven tomorrow so to swell the river as that they might be all swept off into Paradise, I should be happy, etc. etc. May they all die of apoplexy!'*

---

* Lear's 'etc. etc.' stands for 'Christians? Thieves! Christians? – pigs! – Christians? – Wolves, animals, idiots, apes, bestial brutes, Greeks, Turks, Albanians.'

bishopric of Lissus had by no means improved my friend Fra Pietro's disposition to suavity (he was never, in the days when I formerly knew him, of the calmest or happiest temper), I hastened to change the conversation, but during the rest of our discourse this victim of exile *in partibus* continued to growl out bitter anathemas at all his Aléssian flock. At sunset I left the angry friar (after all, a solitary life here must be no slight *penitenza)*, and, promising to visit him on my return, I re-crossed the Drin to Signor Giuseppe's house, where I found bed and supper ready in the upper chamber.

October 5. Skódra
Osmán Pashá affects European manners, and (to my great relief) we all sat on chairs round a table; a Bímbashi (or captain on guard) appearing about as much at ease in his new position as I had done when in that of the natives. As for the legion dinner, it is not to be described. I counted up thirty-seven dishes, served, as is the custom in Turkey, one by one in succession, and then I grew tired of reckoning (supposing that perhaps the feast was going on all day) though I think there were twelve or fourteen more. But nothing was so surprising as the strange jumble of irrelevant food offered: lamb, honey, fish, fruit; baked, boiled, stewed, fried; vegetable, animal; fresh, salt, pickled; solid; oil, pepper; fluid; sweet, sour; hot, cold – in strange variety, though the ingredients were often very good. Nor was there any order in the course according to European notions; – the richest pastry came immediately after dressed fish, and was succeeded by beef, honey, and cakes; pears and peaches; crabs, ham, boiled mutton, chocolate cakes, garlic, and fowl; cheese, rice, soup, strawberries, salmon-trout, and cauliflowers – it was the very chaos of a dinner! Of those who did justice to the repast I was not one; and fortunately it is not considered necessary, by the rules of Turkish etiquette, to do more than taste each dish; and although the Pashá twice or thrice helped me himself; it is sufficient to eat the smallest atom, when the attendant servant removes your plate. As for drink, there were marsala, sherry, hock, champagne, Bass's pale ale, bottled porter, rakhí, and brandy – a large show of liquor in a Mohammedan house; nor did the faithful seem to refrain particularly from any fluid; but there was no unbecoming excess, and as is remarkably the case with Turkish manners, quiet and order were observable throughout the festivity. Only the Bímbashi, a heavy, dull man, seemed marked out for practical jokes, and they made him take an

amazing mixture of porter and champagne, assuring him it was a species of Frank soup, which he seemed to like little enough. As the entertainment draws to a close, it is polite to express your sense of the host's hospitality, by intimating a sense of repletion, and, by pointing to your throat, the utter impossibility of eating any more; and perhaps the last delicate act of complimentary acknowledgement, which it is not easy to describe otherwise than as a series of remarkable choral ventriloquism, was the queerest and most alarming trait of the whole *fête*. On the whole, there was much to amuse, though I should not like to dine with Pashás often. Osmán Pashá surprised me by his questions concerning Ireland, Scotland, the game laws, etc., and appeared to have read and understood a good deal about European nations. After dinner, I amused him greatly by drawing one or two of his attendants, and should have obtained the portraits of more, had not the Mufti, or Mollah, or Cadi, in an orthodox green and white turban, been suddenly announced, a visit which put a stop to my unholy pastime. At six we came away. How disagreeable the raised pavement of Skódra is, none but those who have slipped off it into deep mud and water every five minutes can tell.

October 6. Skódra
At four we adjourned to the house of Antonio Súmma – a substantial building in a large courtyard, all the appurtenances about which indicated opulence and comfort. The usual compliments of pipes, coffee, and lemonade were gone through, and I made a drawing of the worthy merchant in his Skódra costume; but on his younger brother coming in (both were men of about 40 years of age), and requesting to be sketched also, I, for want of paper, was obliged to make a small though accurate portrait of him on the same page as that on which I had drawn his eldest brother, on a larger scale.

'*O, santo cielo!*' said the younger, in a fury of indignation, when he saw the drawing; 'why have you done this? It is true I am the youngest, but I am not smaller than my brother; and why should you make me so diminutive? What right have you thus to remind me of my inferior position? Why do you come into our house to act so insultingly?'

I was so amazed by this afflicting view of my innocent mistake that I could hardly apologize when the elder brother took up the tale.

'I, too,' said he, 'am vexed and hurt, O Signore! I thought you meant well; but if you think that you win my esteem by a compliment paid at the expense of the affection of my brother, you are greatly mistaken.'

What could I say? Was there ever such a lesson to unthinking artists in foreign lands? I had made two enemies by one sketch, and was obliged to take a formal *addio*, leaving the injured brothers bowing me out with looks of thunder.

October 7. Caléssio

I found the friar more energetic than ever in abuse of his Albanian flock, '*Maledetti tutti dal cielo*'* being his mildest expression concerning them; the fact of a favourite servant having been that morning found murdered at a short distance from the convent, being no slight excuse for his anger. The tenantless cells and large gloomy refectory of the monastery, joined to the unceasing vituperation of its sole occupant, did not add liveliness to the evening. My own stores set forth a very tolerable supper, and the Monk's acid wine contributed to vary the repast. In the first part of the evening the poor man was diffuse about his own situation '*Vita d'inferno*', etc.; and with that of his co-mates in exile, '*Sparsi siamo noi altri frati della religione vera. Sparsi quà e là ne' boschi come majali spaventati.*'[13] This subject exhausted, he fell upon Pope Pio IX, whose inaptitude to govern, he predicted, was about to bring great miseries on Rome and the Church; then he lashed out against the Turchi of the district, attributing vices by wholesale to their community in a comfortless category of bitter accusation; nor did the Christians escape. A black list of crimes, falsehood, unbelief, immorality of all kinds covered them with blots, and he summed up his maledictions by saying: '*In fine, sono tutti porchi pregiati del gran Diavolone nero.*' Poor Signor Bonatti** came in for his share, too, though poverty seemed to be the only evil condition to be attributed to him; and a slight seasoning of flattery to, '*Quella nazione tanta forte che amabile, quel gran popol d'Inghilterra,*'*** filled

---

13 'We brethren of the true religion are dispersed here and there in these woods like frightened pigs.'

---

* 'All cursed by Heaven'.

** 'To sum up, they are all pigs worshipping the great black Devil.' Signor Bonatti was the British vice-consul in the city of Skódra.

*** 'That nation as strong as it is amiable, that great people of England.'

up his eloquent discourse. After supper, Padre Pietro insisted on giving up his room to me, a favour I firmly resisted as long as it was possible, for I should greatly have preferred the bare corridors to a close dormitory filled with books and furniture; but the monk was inexorable, so I retired for the night to wrap myself in my plaid, and endeavour to think lightly of the gnats, which are very numerous from the vicinity of the river. In the chamber hang engravings of the Piazza del Popolo and San Pietro. How clearly and sharply in this remote place do they bring back the memory of years passed in Rome!

October 8. Between Aléssio and Króia
The Króia range of mountains were magnificently indistinct in a watery haze; and as the sun sank a thousand tints were thrown over all the wide landscape. After this, the beautiful oak wood was reached, and the green oases, with the scattered flocks and the slippery causeway or selciata, winding beneath the fresh, tall trees seemed a perfect paradise after the frightful copse-wilderness on the plain of Aléssio. About five we arrived at the first *khan* in the forest; but as there was a moon, or three quarters of a moon, it was judged feasible to press on to the *khan* at which we lunched on the 1st, making a better division of distance between Aléssio and Tyrana; so on we went. As the moonlight gained strength, nothing could exceed the beauty of those silent groves, where the giant aerial stems of abeles, with their white branches loaded with wild vine grouped together with the majestic oak, and spreading beech – it is long since I have enjoyed so exquisite a forest scene by moonlight. Yet some drawbacks were notable by a short-sighted man; the projecting boughs, against which I came often with great force, had more than once well nigh done a mischief to head and eyes. By seven p.m. furious barking proclaimed the neighbour-hood of the 'roast fowl *khan*', and there we shortly arrived. The raised part of it was already occupied by five very unclean-looking Albanians, but one side of the fire was at liberty and soon swept and arranged for me; and Giorgio ere long prepared tea on the little squat stool-table, after which sleep quickly followed; not, however, before I had leisure to meditate on the fact that I was now actually in the very wildest phase of Albanian life.

Those five wild creatures, blowing the fire, are a scene for a tale of the days of past centuries. When they have sipped their coffee they roll themselves up in capotes, and stretching out their feet to the embers, lie motionless till an hour before daybreak. The large *khan* is now silent (for even the vile little fussy chickens cease to scrabble about in the dead of night), and only the champing of the horses in the farther part of this great stable-chamber is heard; the flickering light falls on these outstretched sleepers, and makes a series of wonderful pictures never to be forgotten, though I fear, also, never to be well imitated by the pencil. That I do not speak the language, and that I had not previously studied figure-drawing, are my two great regrets in Albania.

October 12. Between Kaváya and Tjermí, crossing the River Skumbi
Several times we turned towards the river, but always retreated at the approach of peasants who exclaimed: ' *Yok, yok!*' '*Mir ist!*'[14] said some Albanians, pointing to the sea, so on we went for two hours – the plain becoming more and more beautiful as the sun sank lower in the horizon, and the great monarch Mount Tomóhr, frowned in purple grandeur amid cloud and storm. At last we arrived at the formidable river – one too broad, deep, and rapid, to be forded, while the bridge, a long and narrow structure of a shaking and incoherent nature, presented wide gaps through which you saw the rushing stream between the loose wattles that formed its floor. The transit was really not a little dangerous. I felt relieved when the last man had passed over it, each leading his horse very slowly from end to end before the next put foot on the crazy fabric, which would not have supported two parties at once: – if the river continued to rise, we must assuredly have been the last who ever made use of that bridge as a medium of passage.

October 13. Between Tchúka and Berát
The difficulty of changing all one's wet clothes (and to escape fever this precaution is always most requisite) can only be appreciated by those who have made their toilette under similar circumstances; but this done, a good dinner of rice, pilaf, and kebabs, with coffee and a cigar, are beyond description refreshing; and the wayfarer soon forgets the inconveniences of travel while recording with pen or pencil its excitements and interests. Truly, in such weather as this of the last week, there is little pleasure in travels even where better accommodation exists: so to Yannina, unless times grow better, must be my direct path.

---

14 'No, no!' 'Yonder it is good!'

At three the storm cleared, and then came the pleasing reflec-
tion that had I proceeded I might have reached Berát, though
possibly it was more prudent to stop here. I go on to the bridge –
the river rolls furiously below, and heaps of purple and golden-
edged clouds hang over the shaded base of Tomóhrit.

Midnight – O *khans* of Albania! Alas! the night is not yet worn
through! I lie, barricaded by boxes and bundles from the vicinity
of the stable, and enduring with patience the fierce attacks of
numberless fleas. All the *khan* sleeps, save two cats, which indulge
in festive boundings, and save a sleepless donkey, which rolls too
contiguously to my head. The wood-fire, blazing up, throws red
gleams on discoloured arches within whose far gloom the eye
catches the form of sleeping Albanian groups. Bulky spiders,
allured by the warmth, fall thick and frequent from the raftered
ceiling. All is still, except the horses champing straw within, and
the gurgle of the rapid river chafing without.

October 15. Berát
The mountain Tomóhr is nearly clear; I draw figures from the
window till eight; then putting on 'society dress', I go with Giorgio
and a *Kawás* to make a morning call on Hussein, Pashá of Berát. A
most picturesque palace is his residence; galleries and courtyard
full of the pomp of attendant guards as usual, and in the reception-
room is no lack of secretaries and officials, among whom a Cadi,*
in white turban, and long brown gold-embroidered robes, shone
resplendent. The visit was much like other Turkish visits. The
Pashá was agreeable in manner, and conversation, by the aid of
continual pipes and coffee, dragged its slow length along. The
cholera at Saloníki being touched upon, Hussein Pashá asked
Giorgio to inquire if I had known in that city (where he, the Pashá
was educated) an English Bey called 'Jim', who resided there and
used to take the Pashá out hunting, with *'cani magnifici'* and *'fucili
stupendi'*;[15] but I, never having heard of 'Jim', could give no infor-
mation. I made a point of asking for good horses for the journey
from hence to Avlóna, remembering what I had suffered by those
of the Kaváya priest;** and his Highness ordered the matter to be

15 Magnificent dogs, and stupendous guns.

---

*   An Islamic judge.
** The baggage-horses had been decrepit, and one had failed to complete the
    journey.

looked to instantly, for he said: 'It is a pleasure, as well as a duty, to assist an Englishman; Inghilterra, and his master the Sultan, loved each other, and so should all the subjects of both countries.' After this visit I employed two hours by sketching from the door of the *khan*, supported by the *Kawás*, the crowds gazing at a respectful distance; not that this self-restraint on their parts saved them from disgrace and evil, for a huge *Bolubáshi* (or head of the police), casually passing, and being seized with an extemporaneous conviction of some impropriety requiring castigation, thereupon he rushed wildly into the midst of the spectators, with the energy of a Samson, dashing his stick at their legs, heads, and backs, and finally dispersed the unresisting crowd. After this, the enraged guardian of public manners gave my *Kawás* a blowing up for allowing the slightest symptom of interruption, and finally committed two large staves to some lively juveniles, with a stern charge that they should use them well and frequently. This unnecessary harshness grieved me, and on finding my remonstrances were unheeded, I gave up my sketch. Of all the numerous Beratíni so unceremoniously struck, I observed but one who did not exhibit great signs of fear and dismay; this man remained steadily till he was twice hit, when he picked up a stone and walked away scowlingly and muttering suppressed anger. A pleasant land to live in!

October 17. Tchúka

At half past two we reached Khan Tchúka, recrossed the Beratíno, and following its right bank quitted the road by which we had come from Kaváya and Leustri on the right hand. The priest and his friend advise me to go for the night to the Greek convent of Ardhénitza, which, say they, is but three or four hours from Apollónia, and stands on a high hill commanding a view of all the world. Meanwhile he tells me a marvellous story of his having travelled here with a party of six friends some years back in a violent thunderstorm. The horses took sudden fright at the lightning while passing along the narrow path we are now upon, and one and all fell into the river; swimming over to the other bank with the seven riders holding fast, when all of them landed safely and undamaged, excepting that one of the party became entirely deaf, and has ever since remained so. The history, if true, is uncomfortable to hear just now, because the path is so slippery and narrow that I contemplate the ducking, if not the deafness, as extremely probable occurrences. At half past three we came in sight of a long, low, isolated hill, a dark spot on the highest part of which is pointed out to me as the convent trees; but though another hour was passed in wading through mud in uncultivated places, where now and then, remote from every other sign of life, a tranquil young buffalo peered calmly out of a pool of black water, yet still Ardhénitza on its hill seemed 'never the nearer'.

October 19. Between Apollónia and Avlóna
The great flocks on these beautiful quiet tracts would inspire the stranger with a complete idea of peace, were they not always attended by huge guardian dogs, who rush out like enraged demons at the horses, and threaten the riders' legs. One company of these angry brutes was particularly outrageous; and although the *Kawás* repeatedly shouted to the wild shepherd, as he lay on his shaggy cloak, he merely looked up, and neither checked his hounds by voice or gesture. The neglect cost him dear; for as the horse on which the *Kawás* rode became unruly, from the persevering attacks of some eight or ten of the dogs (who gather, at the sound of battle, from all parts of the plain), the man of arms lost patience, and galloping straight to the peasant, thundered over his shoulders with his *kourbatch*[16] till he yelled. This, however, did not mend the matter; for the beaten man showed signs of fight, by setting on all the dogs at once, and threatening the *Kawás* with an immense club, so that I momentarily expected to see my Berát escort suffer the end of Actaeon; when suddenly he changed weapons, and pointing his gun at the enemy, reduced him to terms. The dogs were called off and the club thrown away: and the shepherd was left to reflect that resistance to armed Turks and setting dogs upon travellers is an unprofitable pastime.

* * * *

Passing through the town [Avlóna], I made my way to the residence of a merchant, Herr J——, who, with Herr S——, a doctor of quarantine in these coasts, lives in a two-storied wooden house overlooking town, plain, and sea; and by means of a walled courtyard, a broad verandah, a gallery, and some inner rooms, has made himself a very comfortable place for such an out-of-the-way part of the world. I was received, on presenting a letter from Signor

---

16 Whip.

Bonatti of Skódra, with courtesy, though with an eternity of fuss and compliment I would have dispensed with. A good room, used as an office, was given me to abide in, but the difficulty of attaining the usual degree of travelling cleanliness was greater here than at the houses of either Greeks or Turks, seeing that the masters of this continually came in and out, and scrutinized with infantine curiosity all their guests' acts and property. Having read with avidity some German papers conveying the latest intelligence of the past six weeks (news of the most extraordinary events occurring throughout all Europe),* I sat with my hosts till their supper-time, conversing about parts of Albania, especially Acroceraunia or Khimára, with which the doctor is well acquainted. They advise me to visit that coast and its unknown villages, and offer their servant [Anastasio] as guide – a trustworthy Khimáriote, who speaks Italian well, and is known throughout his native territory. At supper-time Herr S—— held forth on German and European politics with alarming enthusiasm. Prophecy succeeded prophecy, as to all the royal and noble heads to be cut off; and the plates and salt-cellars jingled to the thumps which accompanied each denunciation of tyrants, and each appeal to liberty. Not thinking it well-bred to expostulate with my host on the length of his monologue, and not quite agreeing with all his sentiments, I wished he was a silent Turk, and entreated to retire to sleep.

October 20. Avlóna
In the afternoon we are to ride somewhere – Herr S—— being well acquainted with all the ins and outs of the neighbouring landscape; and in the meantime I draw the portraits of two Mohammedan Gheghes of Elbassán, who come to visit my hosts. No sooner were these good people squatted in the little wooden gallery, with their garments, faces, and pipes in complete arrangement for my drawing, than a bit of india-rubber fell from my book, and making two small hops upon the ground, as is the wont with that useful vegetable substance when dropped accidentally, caused

---

* Lear refers to the European revolutionary uprisings of 1848. The National Assembly in Germany spent the summer attempting to draw up a national constitution and create a centralized government. On September 21, radical democrats proclaimed the 'German Social Republic', which may have been what especially enthused Lear's hosts.

indescribable alarm to the two orthodox Gheghes, who jumped up and hissed at it, saying, *'Shaitán! Shaitán!'* and trembling with horror as the little imp remained close to their feet. Nor did my taking it up calm their fears; and when I put it in my pocket their disgust was increased at such ostentatious buckling to the comforts of a familiar demon. So as I found they could not be again induced to remain tranquil enough to be sketched, I seized a moment when they were not looking at me, and bounced the offending caoutchouc on the planked floor, when up it flew to such a degree that the unhappy and tormented Mohammedans screamed aloud, and shrieking out *'Shaitán! Shaitán!'* jumped off the accursed platform and fled away.

October 21. Kánina
At eleven we went down to the town, and therein to the gallery of a Dervish's house, where two Cogias* brought us coffee and pipes, after which our sitting broke up, and my late hosts returned to Avlóna, leaving me in charge of the Khimáriote, who, with a pietone,** sent with me by the Turkish police, formed my whole retinue. Down the opposite side of the hill of Kánina we rode. A small knapsack contained all my property (the fewest articles of toilet ever known to have been taken by a Milordos Ingliz) – a plaid and great coat (for there are snowy mountains to cross), and a large stock of drawing materials. I had arranged about payment of expenses by giving Anastásio, who is a trustworthy servant of the Casa J——, a sum of money, from which he is to defray all the outlay and account to me for the same, though I anticipate no great prodigality, as I am to live at the houses of the natives and go from village to village experiencing the full measure of Khimáriote hospitality.

Before one p.m., we reached the shore, and made for a little cove (there are many like it on the coast east of Plymouth), where a spring of pure and icy fresh water gushes from the foot of a rock into the sea, and offers a natural halting-place for all who travel between Khimára and Avlóna. Kría Néra is the name of this seaside station; and it was pleasant to rest on a carpet thrown down on the smooth sand beneath the high rocks which shut in this little nook. Several peasants with their horses are resting here, and

---

*   A Moslem elder.
*   A police escort: literally, a pedestrian.

Anastásio and the policeman join them in a lunch of bread and cheese; beyond them are grey cliffs and green dun heights – a strip of white sand and the long promontory of Linguetta stretching out into the gulf; the clear splashing sea at my feet, and above all the bright streaked sky. A quiet half-hour in such a scene crowds many a reflection into the tablets of thought, but such can have no place in journals.

Of the peasants halting at this natural *khan* with my own party, most are Khimáriots, going to Berát or other mid-districts of Albania; others are Beratíni. These wild and rugged men have in general a forlorn and anxious look, and are clad in blanket-like capotes, their caps mostly white. 'Some,' saith Anastásio, 'two years ago, were *"roba fina de' ladri"*,'[17] but now Albania is purged of danger and romance, thieves and rebellion, from end to end.

But it is past one, and time to set off once more, for there are four long hours to Draghiádhes, the first Khimáriot village. The pathway is ever along the side of the gulf, and rises far above the blue, blue water. Anything more frightful than these (so-called) paths, along the iron rocks of Acroceraunia, it is not easy to imagine: as if to baffle invaders, the ledges along which one went slowly, now wound inward, skirting ravines full of lentisk and arbutus, now projected over the bald sides of precipices, so that, at certain unexpected angles, the rider's outer leg hung sheer over the deep sea below. To the first of these surprising bits of horror-samples of the highways of Khimára I had come all unknowingly, my horse turning round a sharp rocky point, and proceeding leisurely thence down a kind of bad staircase without balustrades; I declined, however, trying a second similar pass on his back, and at the first spot where there was safe footing, dismounted. Meanwhile the Khimáriote, who ever and anon kept shouting, '*Kakos dromos, Signore*,'[18] fired off his pistol at intervals, partly, as he said, from '*allegria*'[19] and partly to prevent anyone meeting us in this dire and narrow way. When we had overcome the last of the Kakos dromos – lo! a beautiful scene opened at the narrow end of the gulf, which lay like a still and dark lake below the high wall of Khimára territory. Draghiádhes, the door, as it were, of Acroceraunia, stands on a height immediately in front, while the

---

17 'The cleverest of robbers.'
18 'A bad road, Sir.'
19 Mirth.

majestic snowy peak of Tchíka (the lofty point so conspicuous from Corfú, and on the southern side of which stand the real Khimáriot villages), towers over all the scene, than which one more sublime, or more shut out from the world, I do not recollect often to have noticed. At the sea-side I stole time for a short sketch, and then remounting, our party rode on over the sands to nearly the end of the gulf, whence we turned off to the left, and gradually ascended to Draghiádhes.

* * * *

Presently we came to the oak-clad hills immediately below the town, where narrow winding paths led upwards among great rocks and spreading trees worthy of Salvator Rosa* and not unlike the beautiful serpentára of Olévano. I have never seen more impressively savage scenery since I was in Calabria. Evening, or early morn, are the times to study these wild southern places to advantage; they are then alive with the inhabitants of the town or village gathering to, or issuing from it; here were sheep crowding up the narrow rock-stairs – now lost in the shade of the foliage – now bounding in light through the short lentisk – huge morose dogs, like wolves, walking sullenly behind – shepherds carrying lambs or sick sheep, and a crowd of figures clad in thick large trousers and short jackets, and bearing immense burdens of sticks or other rustic materials. These last are the women of Draghiádhes, for here, and at the next village (Dukádhes), the fair sex adopt male attire, and are assuredly about the oddest-looking creatures I ever beheld. Worn and brown by hard labour in the sun, they have yet something pensive and pleasing in the expression of the eye, but all the rest is unfeminine and disagreeable. They are, as far as I can learn, the only Mohammedan women in these regions who do not conceal their faces – whether it be that their ancestors were Christians, and turning to the faith of the Prophet, did not think it worth while in so remote a place as Khimára to adopt articles of such extra expense as veils, I know not – but such is the fact, and they are the only females of their creed whose faces I ever saw. 'But,' said Anastásio, 'when we have passed Tchika, and are in true Khimára, out of the way of these Turks, then you will see women like women and not like pigs. Ah, Signor mio! these are not women!

---

*   Italian painter (1615–73).

– these are pigs, pigs – Turks – pigs, I say! For all that, they are very good people, and all of them my intimate friends. But, Signore, you could not travel here alone.' And, although Anastásio certainly made the most patronizing use of his position as interpreter, guide, and guard, I am inclined to believe that he was, in this, pretty near the truth, for I doubt if a stranger could safely venture through Acroceraunia unattended. Assuredly also all the world hereabouts seemed his friends, as he boasted, for the remotest and almost invisible people on far-away rocks shouted out *'Capitagno'* as we passed, proving to me that I was in company with a widely known individual.

At length we reached Draghiádhes, the houses of which were by no means pretty, being one and all like the figures of 'H was a House' in a child's spelling-book. Alas! for the baronial castle or the palazzo of Italy! the whole place had the appearance of a gigantic heap of dominoes just thrown down by the Titans. Sunset had given place to shadowy dusk as we passed below two of the very largest plane trees I ever beheld, where, in the centre of the village, the trouser-wearing damsels of Draghiádhes were drawing water at a fountain – a strange, wild scene. Many came out to greet Anastásio, and all saluted me in a friendly manner, nor was there the least ill-bred annoyance, though I was evidently an object of great curiosity. Sending on the horses to the house we were to sleep at, we first went to one of Anastásio's friends, who would take it as a *'dispetto'** if he did not visit him. I sat on the steps outside and sketched: the rocks of Calabria, with figures such as are to be seen only in Albania, gathered all around – how did I lament my little skill in figure drawing and regret having so much neglected it! The long matted hair and moustache – the unstudied and free attitude – the simple folds of drapery – the expression of the individual – the grouping of the masses all heighten the inconceivable originality of these scenes. Let a painter visit Acroceraunia – until he does so he will not be aware of the grandest phases of savage, yet classic, picturesqueness – whether Illyrian or Epirote – men or mountains; but let him go with a good guide or he may not come back again. Acroceraunia is untravelled ground and might not be satisfactory to a solitary tourist.

---

* 'rudeness' (slight).

October 22. Draghiádhes

Before daylight all were on foot, and Anastásio had made a capital basin of coffee and toast, an accomplishment he had learned of Giorgio. Anxious to see the bright sun after the night's penance, I ran to the door; but hardly had I gone three steps from it when I felt myself violently pulled by the collar and dragged backwards before I had time to resist; a friendly assault on the part of Achmét* and Anastásio, the motion of which was adequately explained by a simultaneous charge of some thirty immense dogs, who bounced out from the most secluded corners and would straightway have breakfasted on me had I not been so aptly rescued; certainly the dogs of Khimára are the most formidable brutes I have yet seen, and every wall and lane here seems alive with them.

'*O Signore!*' said Anastásio, in a tone between anger and vexation, '*tanto sciocco vuoi essere! Ti dico – sarai mangiato – amazzato – e se non vuoi far a modo mio, e tutto cio che ti dico di far quì in Khimára, sei morto; non voglio andar più in avante così; non andrai mai più fuor di vista mia!*'[20] So I promised I would in future be obedient, for after all it was plain that the Khimáriote was in the right.

* * * *

Between Draghiádhes and Dukhádhes

At the highest part of the pass a most singular scene opens. The spectator seems on the edge of a high wall, from the brink of which giddy elevation he looks down into a fearfully profound basin at the roots of the mountain. Above its eastern and southern enclosures rises the giant snow-clad Tchíka in all its immensity, while at his very feet, in a deep, dark green pit of wood and garden, lies the town or village of Dukádhes, its houses scattered like milk-white dice along the banks of a wide torrent, which finds its way to the gulf between the hill he stands on and the high western ridge dividing the valley from the sea.

To this strange place, perhaps one of the most secluded in Europe, I began to descend, and as we slowly proceeded, halted more than once to sketch and contemplate. Shut out as it stood by

---

20 'O, Sir, why will you be such a fool? I tell you you will be eaten, murdered, and if you won't do as I bid you, you are a dead man. I will not go farther with you in this manner; henceforth you shall not stir out of my sight.'

---

*　Achmét Zinani, their host in Draghiádhes.

iron walls of mountain, surrounded by sternest features of savage scenery, rock and chasm, precipice and torrent, a more fearful prospect, and more chilling to the very blood I never beheld – so gloomy and severe – so unredeemed by any beauty or cheerfulness. After a weary ride over rugged places in the bottom of this hollow land of gloom, we stopped at length at one of the houses of the village – standing, like every dwelling of Dukádhes, in the midst of a little garden or courtyard. Its general appearance was very like my last night's abode, only that we had to climb up a very odious ladder to the family 'reception-room' – which, besides being several shades dirtier than that of Achmét Zinani, had not the advantage of being on the first floor. Most of these houses consist of two stories, the upper floor, divided into two or three chambers, being allotted to the women of the family, the lower being a single large room serving for general purposes. It was half past one when we arrived, and before I go out to sketch Anastásio cooks a lunch of eggs roasted and fried in butter, of which he partakes with the Pietone. This last accomplished person does not indulge in shoes, and I observe that when his hands are occupied, he holds his pipe in his toes, and does any other little office with those, to us, useless members. Throughout the whole of the day's journey I have seen numbers of women carrying burdens of incredible size and weight; – from 150 to 180 pounds, I am assured, is no unusual loading. These poor creatures are indeed little like women in appearance, for their faces are worn into lines and furrows of masculine hardness by excessive and early toil; and as they labour pitifully up the rocky paths, steadying their steps with a staff, or cross the stony torrent beds, bent nearly double beneath their loads, they seem less like human beings than quadrupeds. A man's blood boils to see them accompanied by a beast of a husband or brother, generally on horseback, carrying – what? – nothing but a pipe! And when he is tired of smoking, or finds himself overclad, he gives the women his pipe to hold, or throws his capote over her load! The ponderous packages of wool, grain, sticks, etc., borne by these hard-worked creatures are hung to their neck by two strong straps; their dress is dark blue, with a blue handkerchief on the head – dark full trousers – no petticoat or apron – and red worked woollen gaiters. They are short and strongly made in person, with very light hair; their eyes are almost universally soft grey, and very pretty, but the rest of the face, apart from the worn and ground-down expression, is too broad and square in form to be prepossessing.

* * * *

Presently [after supper in Dukádhes] the company came, and queer enough it was! The two Messieurs Zingari, or gipsies, are blacksmiths by profession and are clad in dark-coloured garments, once white, now grey-brown; the contrast between them and the Albanians round them, all of whom have light hair and florid complexions, is very striking. The gipsy, all grin and sharpness, who plays second fiddle, is continually bowing and ducking to me ere he squats down; but the elder, or first performer, is absolutely one of the most remarkable-looking creatures I ever beheld; his great black eyes peering below immensely thick arched brows, have the most singular expression of cunning and ferocity, and his black moustache and beard enclose a mouth which, when shut, argues all sorts of tragic obstinacies, but, on opening, discloses a grin of brilliant ivory from ear to ear. Take him for all in all, anything so like a diabolical South Sea idol I never yet saw living.

At first the entertainment was rather slow. The gipsies had two guitars, but they only tinkled them with a preparatory coquettishness; till another friend dropping in with a third mandolino, a pleasing discord was by degrees created, and increased to a pitch of excitement that seemed to promise brilliant things for the evening's festivities. Anastásio, also, catching the melodious infection, led the performers by his own everlasting Greek refrain – sung at the full power of a tremendous voice, and joined in by all present in the first circle – for now, many more than the chorus had entered the room, remaining seated or standing behind, and the whole formed, in the flickering light of the wood torches, one of the most strange scenes imaginable. Among the auditors were the *padrona* of the house (a large lady in extensive trousers), her daughter (a nice-looking woman), and two pretty little girls, her grandchildren – all unveiled, as is the mode in Dukádhes. As the musical excitement increased, so did the audience begin to keep time with their bodies, which this people, even when squatted, move with the most curious flexibility. An Albanian, in sitting on the ground, goes plump down on his knees, and then bending back crosses his legs in a manner wholly impracticable to us who sit on chairs from infancy. While thus seated he can turn his body half round on each side as if on a pivot, the knees remaining immovable; and of all the gifted people in this way that I ever saw, the gipsy guitarist was pre-eminently endowed with gyratory powers equal almost to the American owl, which, it is said, continues to look round and round at the fowler as he circles about him till his head twists off.

Presently, the fun grew fast and furious, and at length the father of song – the hideous idol-gipsy – became animated in the grandest degree; he sang and shrieked the strangest minor airs with incredible accompaniments, tearing and twangling the guitar with great skill, and energy enough to break it into bits. Everything he sang seemed to delight his audience, which at times was moved to shouts of laughter, at others almost to tears. He bowed backwards and forwards till his head nearly touched the ground and waved from side to side like a poplar in a gale. He screamed – he howled – he went through long recitatives, and spoke prose with inconceivable rapidity; and all the while his auditors bowed and rocked to and fro as if participating in every idea and expression. I never saw a more decided instance of enthusiastic appreciation of song, if song it could be called, where the only melody was a wild repetition of a minor chorus – except at intervals, when one or two of the Toskidhes' characteristic airs varied the musical treat.

The last performance I can remember to have attended to, appeared to be received as a *capo d'opera:* each verse ended by spinning itself out into a chain of rapid little Bos, ending in chorus thus: 'Bo, bo-bo-bo, BO! – bo, bobobo, BO!' – and every verse was more loudly joined in than its predecessor, till at the conclusion of the last verse, when the unearthly idol-gipsy snatched off and waved his cap in the air – his shining head was closely shaved, except one glossy raven tress at least three feet in length, the very rafters rang again to the frantic harmony; – 'Bo, bo-bo-bo, bo-bo-bo, bo-bo-bo, bobobo, BO!' – the last ' BO!' uttered like a pistol-shot, and followed by a unanimous yell.

Fatigue is so good a preparation for rest, that after this savage mirth had gone on for two or three hours, I fell fast asleep, and heard no more that night.

October 23. Dukhádhes

I am awaked an hour before daylight by the most piercing screams. Hark! – they are the loud cries of a woman's voice, and they come nearer – nearer – close to the house. For a moment, the remembrance of last night's orgies, the strange place I was lying in, and the horrid sound by which I was so suddenly awakened, made a confusion of ideas in my mind which I could hardly disentangle, till, lighting a phosphorus match and candle, I saw all the Albanians in the room, sitting bolt upright, and listening with ugly countenances to the terrible cries below. In vain I ask the cause of them; no one replies; but one by one, and Anastásio the last, all descend the ladder, leaving me in a mystery which does not make the state of things more agreeable; for though I have not 'supped full of horror' like Macbeth, yet my senses are nevertheless 'cooled to hear so dismal a night shriek'.

I do not remember ever to have heard so horrid and deadly a sound as that long shriek, perpetually repeated with a force and sharpness not to be recalled without pain; and what made it more horrible was, the distinct echo to each cry from the lonely rocks around this hideous place. The cries, too, were exactly similar, and studiedly monotonous in measured wild grief. After a short time, Anastásio and the others returned, but at first I could elicit no cause for this startling the night from its propriety. At length I suppose they thought that, as I was now irretrievably afloat in Khimára life, I might as well know the worst as not; so they informed me that the wailings proceeded from a woman of the place, whose husband had just been murdered. He had had some feud with an inhabitant of a neighbouring village (near Kúdhesi) nor had he returned to his house as was expected last night; and just now, by means of the Khimáriot dogs, whose uproar is unimaginable, the head of the slain man was found on one side of the ravine, immediately below the house I am in, his murderers having tossed it over from the opposite bank, where the body still lay. This horrid intelligence had been taken (with her husband's head) to his wife, and she instantly began the public shrieking and wailing usual with all people in this singular region on the death of relatives. They tell me this screaming tragedy is universal throughout Khimára, and is continued during nine days, commonly in the house of mourning, or when the performers are engaged in their domestic affairs. In the present instance, however, the distressed woman, unable to control her feelings to the regular routine of grief, is walking all over the town, tearing her hair, and abandoning herself to the most frantic wretchedness. These news, added to the information that it is raining, and that the weather may probably prevent my leaving this delightful abode throughout this or who knows how many more days, are no cheerful beginning for the morning, for one may be fixed here for some time, since the Tchíka pass is impracticable in stormy weather.

* * * *

Lower down in the descent [from the Tchíka pass] a migration of Khimáriotes – the most restless of people – met us; some eighty or one hundred women laden as never women were elsewhere – their male relations taking it easy up the mountain – the ladies carrying the capotes as well as babies and packages.

'Heavens!' said I, surprised out of my wonted philosophy of travel, which ought not to exclaim at anything, 'how can you make your women such slaves?' 'O Signore,' said Anastásio, 'to you, as a stranger, it must seem extraordinary; but the fact is we have no mules in Khimára – that is the reason why we employ a creature so inferior in strength as a woman is *(un animale tanto poco capace);* but there is no remedy, for mules there are none and women are next best to mules. *Vi assicuro, Signòre,** although certainly far inferior to mules, they are really better than asses, or even horses.' That was all I got for my interference.

* * * *

Palása
A few Khimáriotes were idling below the shady trees, and Anastásio was soon surrounded and welcomed back to his native haunts, though I perceived that some bad news was communicated to him, as he changed colour during the recital of the intelligence, and clasping his hands exclaimed aloud with every appearance of real sorrow. The cause of this grief was, he presently informed me, the tidings of the death of one of his cousins at Vunó, his native place, a girl of 18 whose extreme beauty and good qualities had made her a sort of queen of the village, which, said Anastásio, I shall find a changed place owing to her decease. 'I loved her,' said he, 'with all my heart, and had we been married, as we ought to have been, our lives might have been most thoroughly happy.' Having said thus much, and begging me to excuse his grief, he sat down with his head on his hand, in a mood of woe befitting such a bereavement. Meanwhile I reposed till the moment came for a fresh move onwards, when lo! with the quickness of light the afflicted Anastásio arose and ran to a group of women advancing towards the olive trees, among whom one seemed to interest him

---

* 'I assure you, Sir.'

not a little, and as she drew nearer I perceived that she was equally affected by the chance meeting; – finally, they sat down together and conversed with an earnestness which convinced me that the newcomer was a friend, at least, if not a sister, to the departed and lamented cousin of Vunó. It was now time to start, and as the mules were loading, the Khimáriote girl lingered, and I never saw a more exquisitely handsome face than hers: each feature was perfectly faultless in form; but the general expression of the countenance had a tinge of sternness, with somewhat of traces of suffering; her raven tresses fell loose over her beautiful shoulders and neck, and her form from head to foot, was majestic and graceful to perfection; her dress, too, the short, open Greek jacket or spencer, ornamented with red patterns, the many-folded petticoat and the scarlet embroidered apron, admirably became her. She was a perfect model of beauty, as she stood knitting, hardly bending beneath the burden she was carrying – her fine face half in shade from a snowy handkerchief thrown negligently over her head. She vanished when we were leaving Palása, but reappeared below the village, and accompanied Anastásio for a mile or more through the surrounding olive grounds, and leaving him at last with a bitter expression of melancholy which it was impossible not to sympathise with. 'Ah, Signore,' said Anastásio, 'she was to have been my wife, but now she is married to a horrid old man of Avlóna, who hates her, and she hates him, and so they will be wretched all their lives.' 'Corpo di Bacco! Anastásio, why you told me just now you were to be married to the girl who has just died at Vunó!' 'So I was, Signore; but her parents would not let me marry her, so I have not thought about her any more – only now that she is dead I cannot help being very sorry; but Fortína, the girl who has just gone back, was the woman I loved better than anybody.' 'Then why didn't you marry her?' 'Perchè, perchè,' said the afflicted Anastásio, 'perchè, I have a wife already, Signore, in Vunó, and a little girl 6 years old. Si signor, si.'

* * * *

Between Lliáttes and Vunó
The bright orb went down like a globe of red crystal into the pale sea and the fiery hued wall of jagged Acroceraunian mountains above us on our left grew purple and lead-coloured, yet there was still half an hour's hard walking to be accomplished; and before I

turned the angle of the little ravine of Vunó, there was only light enough to allow of a vague impression of a considerable town filling up the end of the gorge, without being able to discern the numerous excellencies of a place, of which Anastásio was constantly remarking in a triumphant tone, *'Ma, Signore, quando si vede Vunó!'** as if Paris or Stamboul were nothing to it. We passed what seemed a large building, which my guide said was 'Casa di Bábba', the house of his uncle, who was head of the family (his father having been a second son), and soon came to the paternal roof, now the property of his own eldest brother; for Anastásio is a *secondo-genito* and obliged to get his living *à la Khimáriote* as he can: his mother still resides in her deceased husband's house, as do Anastásio's wife and child, besides Kyr Kostantíno Kasnétzi, the eldest brother, with his children, he being a widower. All this domestic crowd, joined to a great variety of nephews and cousins, were waiting to receive us as we entered a courtyard, from whence we ascended to a spacious kitchen, where the females of the family saluted me with an air of timidity natural to persons who live in such Oriental seclusion. The manners of Anastásio towards this part of the community appeared to me to savour a good deal of the relation between master and slave; and now that my guide is at home, he walks about with a dignified and haughty nonchalance very different from the subdued demeanour of the domestic in the Casa J—— at Avlóna.

October 24. Vunó
Since the days of Alí Pashá, the great pullerdown of all high persons and places in Khimára (for up to his time it had existed as a set of little republics, nominally dependent on the Porte, but willing at any time to join its enemies), the villages of the Khimáriote district pay certain taxes to the Turkish Government through the Pashá of Delvino, in whose pashalík their territories are included; but no Turk, or rather, no Mohammedan, resides in any of the towns (I do not include Draghiádhes, Rádima, or Dukádhes, as within Khimára), and they may be said still to enjoy a negative sort of independence, though their power of union in resistance, as a body of Greek Christians, is virtually as much gone as that of Parguinote or Suliote, whose habitations, and almost names, have passed away.

---

*   'But Sir, wait till you see Vuno!'

Anastásio relates that two years back a Turkish Bey, with troops, came on a recruiting tour through this territory, and quartered one hundred men in the house of his father and uncle, during whose stay, the *'spavento'*[21] of the Khimáriote women and the *'rabbia'*[22] of the men was unbounded. For four days the women were shut up under lock and key in closets and cellars, and the Bey nightly intoxicated himself with rakhee, making a horrible row, and amusing himself by firing off pistols all about the room and through the ceiling, the damage done by which facetious diversion is visible enough to this day as proof. One of these pistol-balls nearly killed the wife of Kostantíno Kasnétzi, and he and Anastásio thereupon confronted the Bey, who finding his own men disposed to take part against him, consented to evacuate Vunó on the morrow. But, with the exception of such rare visits, or the passing through of the Pashá of Délvino's guards in search of some criminal, Khimára is a tranquil place, though its inhabitants are forbidden to bear arms; and in consequence of various modes of depopulation – such as wandering abroad, enlisting in the Sultan's armies, etc., – they are now but a thinly scattered and broken people.

While this conversation was proceeding, there arose the wail for the poor girl, the cousin of the Kasnétzi, who died three days ago. It was, as at Dukhádhes, a woman's cry, but more mournful and prolonged, with sobs between nearly each cry; and when the first wail was over, a second female took it up in the same strain. Nothing can be more mournful than this lament for the dead; yet there seems to be a sort of pride in executing the performance well and loudly, for when I spoke of the sadness of the sound – '*Ah, Signore!*' said Anastásio, '*ci sono altre chi piangono assai meglio di quella!*'[23] The death of this cousin led the eldest brother to apologize much for the curtailed hospitality which iron custom compelled them to show to me under the circumstances: – they should have killed a sheep – they would have had a dance, and all sorts of *fêtes*, etc. etc.; but on the decease of near relatives, no allegria is ever permitted for nine days.

There was much animated conversation at dinner-time relating to the domestic affairs of an uncle and aunt of the Kasnétzi: the latter is lately remarried to a Khimáriote, and he is already tired of

21 Terror.
22 Rage.
23 'Ah, Sir, there are others who cry ever so much better!'

his bride, and inclines to leave her. *'E perchè?'* said Anastásio; *'E divenuta sorda! ed eccovi tutto!'*[24] But although the party agree that the *povera donna* has no other fault but a growing deafness, still they are equally of accord that the uncle may purchase a separation from the bishop of the diocese by means of so many dollars, even for no sufficient reason. Anastásio concludes the discourse by saying that if his aunt is forsaken, legally or not, he shall *'amazzare'*[25] the *zio* forthwith. The Khimáriotes appear to have a code of some very severe laws, and all tell me that they know no instance of their ever having been broken through. Those, for instance, for the punishment of conjugal infidelity insist on the death of the woman, and the cutting off ears and nose of the other offending party. Two or three instances have occurred among the various towns in the memory of my informers, and one gentleman whose head is unadorned with ears or proboscis, I have myself seen. Another was pointed out to me today, as a man who made a great disturbance in Vunó by destroying the peace of one of its best families: the wife was instantly put to death, but her paramour escaped and remained abroad for two years, when he returned and is now settled here. 'But,' said I, 'how did he remain unpunished?' 'Because he escaped.' 'But why, since your severity in these cases is so extreme, why was he allowed to return?' 'Because we killed his father instead of him!' *'O, cielo,* but what had his father done?' *'Niente! Ma sempre ci vuol qualcheduno ammazzato in queste circonstanze; e così, abbiam preso il padre.* Somebody must have been killed. *E lo stesso – basta così'*[26] – an obliquity of justice alarming to parents with unruly offspring.

October 25. Khimára
At the foot of this celebrated Acroceraunian stronghold I sat down to sketch, before scaling the height. Several Khimáriotes descended to speak with Anastásio, among others the priest of the town, in a tattered blue robe, flowing black beard and red Fez. There came also two old women, with the hope of selling some fowls, which they incautiously left on a ledge of rock a short way above us, while they discussed the terms of the purchase with Anastásio; but behold! two superb eagles suddenly floated over the abyss – and

---

24 'And why? She has become deaf, that is the only reason.'
25 'Murder'.
26 'Nothing at all; but somebody must be killed under these circumstances, so we killlled the father; it is all one.'

Khimára

– pounce – carried off each his hen, the unlucky gallinaceae screaming vainly as they were transported by unwelcome wings to the inaccessible crags on the far side of the ravine, where young eagles and destiny awaited them. Hereupon the two old ladies set up a screeching wail, almost as loud as that in use for the departed relations, and were only to be quieted by being presented with the price of the hens (about twopence each), which had been carried off so unsatisfactorily to all parties excepting the inmates of the eagles' nests. The sketch done, I began to ascend the rock, which is only easily accessible on the eastern or mountain side, and numbers of the inhabitants came down to salute and examine so novel a creature as a Frank, for by the accounts of the people – how true I know not – I am the second Englishman who has been here. From Avlóna hither, I do not find that any English traveller has yet penetrated; no great wonder, considering the nature of the country.

* * * *

Many of these, both outside and in the house, extended their hands for mine to shake, I supposed from being aware of Frank modes of salutation; but among them, three or four gave me so peculiar a twist or crack of my fingers that I was struck by its singularity; though it was not until my hand had been held firmly for a repetition of this manoeuvre, accompanied by a look of interrogation from the holder, that the thought flashed on my mind, that what I observed was a concerted signal. I shortly became fully aware that I was among people who, from some cause or other, had fled from justice in other lands.

Of these was one who, with his face entirely muffled excepting one eye, kept aloof in the darker part of the chamber, until having thoroughly scrutinised me he came forward, and dropping his capote discovered to my horror and amazement features which, though disguised by an enormous growth of hair, I could not fail to recognize.* 'The world is my city now,' said he; 'I am become a savage like those with whom I dwell. What is life to me?' And covering his face again, he wept with a heart-breaking bitterness only life-exiles can know.

Alas! henceforth this wild Alsatia of the mountains – this strange

---

*   Professor John Whittaker has identified the man as Pierre de Boccheciampe, whose story he reconstructs in Vol. 24 of *Thesaurismata* (1994), pp. 320–418.

and fearful Khimára – wore to my thoughts a tenfold garb of melancholy, when I considered it as the refuge during the remainder of a weary life, of men whose early years had been passed in far other abodes and society.

* * * *

Far up the ravine [between Khimára and Vunó] there is a detached rock, covered with Greek inscriptions; I mean modern names, inscribed in Romaic. *'Tutti scrivono,'* said Anastásio, *'scrivete anche voi!'* [27] so as I defaced nothing by the act, I added my name to the visitors' book of the Pass of Khimára, the only Englishman's there, and it will be long before there are many more. Much time must elapse ere Khimára becomes a fashionable watering-place, and before puffing advertisements of 'salubrious situation, unbroken retirement, select society, and easy access from Italy', meet the eye in the daily papers of England.

October 28. Dukádhes

Long before daylight the wail for the man murdered on the day of my last visit commenced; while crowing cocks and howling dogs added their mites also to the morning melodies of Dukádhes. The 'upper chamber' where I abode on the night of the 22nd was the perfection of repose compared with this usual home of the family, which seemed to abound in every parasitical enemy to humanity. Before sunrise, as they were baking their large flat cakes of bread by the fire, Fortína came in and stood for awhile, with the red light shining on her most beautiful features, saddened with the keenest expression of sorrow. She took leave of Anastásio in a very few words, and turning to me, wished me, with a half-broken voice, 'many happy years of life', and then wrapping her handkerchief closely over her head, went out rapidly, and by the time the sun rose must have been already far on her journey towards Palása.

October 29. Avlóna

At sunrise I went down into the plain with the Black Margiánn,* and drew Avlóna from the level ground near the sea, returning to dinner before noon. At this meal, the overbearing and violent

---

27 'Everybody writes – write your name also.'

---

*   The Nubian servant of his German hosts.

political thunderings of Herr S—— against all monarchs, tyrants, kings, autocrats, etc. (they had received new gazettes from Austria), was so profoundly disagreeable, that I was rejoiced to know that two horses had arrived, with which, the Black being my guide, I was to visit the monastery of Aghia Marína di Svernéz, in a little island about two miles from Avlóna.

* * * *

The party there was increased by a Vúniote, who had been one of Lord Byron's guards at Missolonghi. He told me some anecdotes of the poet, but on such slight authority, I write them not down. As for my hosts, the news of the Emperor's flight from Vienna* had made them more full of political excitement than ever; between their pipes they thumped their table destructively, predicting with sinister glee all sorts of bloodshed and downfall of tyrants. In vain did I attempt to change the current of discourse; but when they proceeded to some long and violent tirades against 'England and the English', I broke through my role of passive listener, and having much the advantage of my hosts in fluency of Italian, took the liberty of telling them what I thought of their illbreeding in thus victimizing a guest who might by possibility not quite agree with all their opinions – requesting earnestly that we might henceforth talk about pelicans, or red mullet, or whatever they pleased, so that we eschewed politics.

October 31. Tepeléne
Nearer Tepeléne we met many peasants, all in white caps and kilts, and of a more squalid and wretched appearance than any I had yet seen; the whole of this part of Albania is indeed most desolate, and its inhabitants broken and dejected. Their rebellion under Zulíki seems to have been the last convulsive struggle of this scattered and disarmed people, and the once proud territory of Alí Pashá is now ground down into a melancholy insignificance, and wellnigh deprived of its identity.

It was nearly three p.m. ere the last tedious windings of the valley disclosed the great mountain Trebushín and its neighbour of Khórmovo, visible now from base to summit – each calmly

---

* The emperor Ferdinand I was eventually in December 1848 forced to abdicate in favour of his nephew Franz Josef I.

towering in bright purple below peaks of glittering snow. Beneath them the junction of the two rivers Viósa and Bantja forms the long promontory of Tepeléne,[28] whose ruined palace and walls and silver-toned mosque give a strange air of dreamy romance to this scene, one of the most sublime and simple in Albania and certainly one most fraught with associations ancient and modern.

* * * *

At the end of the space enclosed by the walls and overhanging the river is a single mosque – solitary witness of the grandeur of days past; – and beyond that, all the space, as far as the battlement terrace looking north and west is occupied by the mass of ruin which represents Alí's ruined palace. The sun was sinking as I sat down to draw in what had been a great chamber, below one of the many crumbling walls – perhaps in the very spot where the dreaded Alí gave audience to his Frank guests in 1809 – when Childe Harold was but 24 years old and the Vizír in the zenith of his power.[29] The poet is no more; – the host is beheaded, and his family nearly extinct; – the palace is burned, and levelled with the ground; – war and change and time have, perhaps, left but one or two living beings who, forty years back, were assembled in these gay and sumptuous halls. It was impossible not to linger in such a site and brood over such imaages, and of all the scenes I have visited the palace of Alí Pashá at Tepeléne will continue most vividly imprinted on my recollection.

November 1. Near Arghyró Kastro
All through the cultivated grounds which I have passed since I entered the vale of the Derópuli district, the costumes of the Greek female peasantry have been very pleasing and various: dark blue or red capotes, fringed and tasselled most fancifully and prettily. 'These,' quoth Giorgio, 'are Greeks! – Greeks, signore! We are not among Albanians now, Signore! let us be thankful we had gone out of the reach of those *poveri disperati! Quí siamo in Epiro, Signore! ringraziamo il cielo,** we are among Epirotes!' (For though the country opposite Corfú is distinctly known as Albanian, the

---

28 Tepeléne, anciently Antigoneia.
29 *Childe Harold*. Canto II. 56.

---

*   'Poor desperate people! Let's thank Heaven we're here in Epiro, Sir.'

innocent traveller who happens to speak of its natives to one of themselves as 'Albanians' finds himself in as wrong a position as if he should address Messrs A. and B. and C., residents at the Cape of Good Hope, as so many Hottentots.)

November 4. Between Arghyró Kastro and Zítza
We halted at the *khan* of Episkopí, close to a little stream full of capital watercresses which I began to gather and eat with some bread and cheese, an act which provoked the Epirote bystanders of the village to ecstatic laughter and curiosity. Every portion I put into my mouth, delighted them as a most charming exhibition of foreign whim, and the more juvenile spectators instantly commenced bringing me all sorts of funny objects, with an earnest request that the Frank would amuse them by feeding thereupon forthwith. One brought a thistle, a second a collection of sticks and wood, a third some grass; a fourth presented me with a fat grasshopper – the whole scene was acted amid shouts of laughter, in which I joined as loudly as any. We parted amazingly good friends, and the wits of Episkopí will long remember the Frank who fed on weeds out of the water.

November 6. Ioánnina
Among my letters is one from a friend* asking me to accompany him to Cairo, Mount Sinai, and Palestine, an offer not to be lightly refused; yet to avail myself of it, I must go hence directly to Malta and Alexandria. But I am the more inclined to do this, by the increasing cold of the weather, and from the small chance of making further progress in drawing among Albanian scenes at this late season. I determine, then, if possible, to come back a second time to Albania to 'finish' Epirus, before I return in the summer of the following year to England; and meanwhile resolve finally to start tomorrow for Arta and Prévezya, and so by the Ionian Isles to Malta with all speed. Meanwhile my friend, C.M.C——, between whom and myself the monks of Athos drew their cholera cordon, passed through Yannina but two days ago; and this chance of rejoining him at Prévezya or in quarantine – not to speak of the necessity of timing one's departure by certain steamers – all contribute to my decision; thus, therefore, I arrange the final page of my tour in Albania.

---

*   John Cross, with whom Lear toured Egypt in February 1849 before a recurrence of Lear's fever cut the trip short.

Part II

24 April to 9 June 1849

May 2. Kamarína

At three or four, in a pause between showers, I attempted to reach the rock of Zálongo, immediately above the village. This was the scene of one of those terrible tragedies so frequent during the Súliote war with Alí. At its summit twenty-two women of Súli took refuge after the capture of their rock by the Mohammedans, and with their children awaited the issue of a desperate combat between their husbands and brothers, and the soldiers of the Vizir of Yannina.* Their cause was lost; but as the enemy scaled the rock to take the women prisoners, they dashed all their children on the crags below, and joining their hands, while they sang the songs of their own dear land, they advanced nearer and nearer to the edge of the precipice, when from the brink a victim precipitated herself into the deep below at each recurring round of the dance, until all were destroyed. When the foe arrived at the summit the heroic Suliotes were beyond his reach.

But this is only one of many such acts which, during the Suliote war, furnished some of the most extraordinary instances on record of the love of liberty.[30]

May 3. Between Kamarína and Arya

During this morning's ride I have seen upwards of twenty large vultures; but now, the ornithological denizens of this wide tract of marshy ground are storks, which are walking about in great numbers, and their nests are built on the roofs of the houses, clustered here and there in the more cultivated part of the district. Snakes and tortoises also were frequent during the morning, concerning which last animals Andréa** volunteers some scientific intelligence, assuring me that in Greece it is a well-known fact that

---

30 The rock of Zálongo is famous also for other combats between the Suliotes and the soldiers of the Vizír.

---

* The women were Christian klephts who had resisted both Alí Pashá and the Turks.
** Andréa Vrindisi, of Patras: an excellent guide and dragoman in every respect and worthy of high recommendation. [E.L.'s note.]

they hatch their eggs by the heat of their eyes, by looking fixedly at them, until the small tortoises are matured, and break the shell.

May 5. Between Zermí and Súli
Descending the hill of Zermí we came in less than an hour to the vale of Tervitzianá, through which the river of Súli flows ere, 'previously making many turns and meanders as if unwilling to enter such a gloomy passage', it plunges into the gorge of Súli. We crossed the stream, and began the ascent on the right of the cliffs, by narrow and precipitous paths leading to a point of great height, from which the difficult pass of the Súliote glen commences. And while toiling up the hill, my thoughts were occupied less with the actual interest of the scenery, than with the extraordinary recollections connected with the struggles of the heroic people who so lately as forty years back were exterminated or banished by their tyrant enemy. Every turn in the pass I am about to enter has been distinguished by some stratagem or slaughter: every line in the annals of the last Suliote war is written in characters of blood.[31]

---

31 As some notice of the Súliote history may be desirable, I add as much matter as is necessary to illustrate the subject. The mountain of Súli may be conjectured to have been occupied by Albanians about the thirteenth or fourteenth century, and when the greater part of the surrounding country lapsed to the Mohammedan faith, this race of hardy mountaineers adhered firmly to Christianity.

   During the eighteenth century the Súliotes carried on a predatory warfare with the surrounding territories of Magaríti, Paramythía, etc., but when Alí Pashá, under pretext of reducing disaffected districts to the obedience due to the Sultan, had subdued all the surrounding tribes, the inhabitants of Súli found that he was an enemy, determined either by craft or force to dispossess them of their ancestral inheritance. From 1788 to 1792, innumerable were the artifices of Alí to obtain possession of this singular stronghold; in the latter year he made an attack on it, which nearly proved fatal to himself, while his army was defeated with great slaughter. In 1798, after six years of bribery and skirmishing, a portion of the territory of Súli was gained by the Mohammedans, through treachery of some of the inhabitants, and thenceforward the accounts of the protracted siege of this devoted people is a series of remarkable exploits and resolute defence, by Súliotes of both sexes, seldom paralleled in history.

   Every foot of the tremendous passes leading to Súli was contested in blood ere the besieger gained firm footing; and after he had done so, the rock held out an incredible period, until famine and treachery worked out the downfall of this unfortunate people.

   Then, in 1803, many escaped by passing through the enemy's camp, many by paths unknown to their pursuers; numbers fled to the adjacent rocks of Zálongo and Seltzo, others destroyed themselves, together with the enemy, by

But my reflections were interrupted by a disagreeable incident: in a rocky and crabbed part of the narrow path, the baggage horse missed footing and fell backward; fortunately, he escaped the edge of the precipice; but the labour and loss of time in rearranging the luggage was considerable; and when we had scaled the height, and I sat looking with amazement into the dark and hollow abyss of the Acheron, a second cry and crash startled me – again the unlucky horse had stumbled, and this time, though safe himself, the baggage suffered; – the basket containing the canteen was smitten by a sharp rock, and all my plates and dishes, knives, forks, and pewter pans – which F.L.* had bequeathed to me at Patrás – went spinning down from crag to crag till they lodged in the infernal[32] stream below. These delays were serious, as the day was wearing on, and the 'Pass of Súli' was yet to be threaded. This fearful gorge cannot be better described than in the words of Colonel Leake:** 'A deep ravine, formed by the meeting of the two great mountains of Súli and Tzikurátes – one of the darkest and deepest of the glens of Greece; on either side rise perpendicular rocks, in the midst of which are little intervals of scanty soil, bearing holly oaks, ilices, and other shrubs, and which admit occasionally a view of the higher summits of the two mountains covered with oaks, and at the summit of all with pines. Here the road is passable only on foot, by a perilous ledge along the side of the mountain of Súli; the river in the pass is deep and rapid and is seen at the bottom falling in many places over the rocks, though at too great a distance to be heard, and in most places inaccessible to any but the foot of a goat or a Súliote.'

I shall not soon forget the labour it cost to convey our horses through this frightful gorge. In many places the rains had carried away even what little footing there had originally been, and

---

gunpowder, or in a last struggle; or threw themselves into the Acheron, or from precipices. Those of these brave people who ultimately escaped to Párga crossed over to Corfú, and thence entered the service of Russia and France. Many, since the days of Greek independence, have returned to various parts of Epirus, or Greece; but they have no longer a country or a name, and the warlike tribe who, at the height of their power formed a confederacy of sixty-six villages, may now be said to be extinct.

32 The river of Súli is the Acheron of antiquity.

---

*   Franklin Lushington, with whom Lear had toured classical Greece in March and
     April 1849.
**   *Travels in Northern Greece* by Colonel William Martin Leake (1835).

nothing remained but a bed of powdered rock sloping off to the frightful gulf below; and all our efforts could hardly induce or enable each horse to cross singly. The muleteer cried, and called on all the saints in the Greek calendar; and all four of us united our strength to prevent the trembling beast from rolling downwards. There were three of these *passi cattivi*,* and the sun was setting. I prepared to make up my mind, if I escaped the Acheron, at least to repose all night in the ravine.

* * * *

At Alí Pashá's castle

I gazed on the strange, noiseless figures about me, bright in the moonlight, which tipped with silver the solemn lofty mountains around. For years those hills had rarely ceased to echo the cries of animosity, despair, and agony; now all is silent as the actors in that dreadful drama.

Few scenes can compete in my memory with the wildness of this at the castle of Kiáfa, or Súli-Kastro; and excepting in the deserts of the peninsula of Sinai, I have gazed on none more picturesque and strange.

May 7. Párga

About nine we arrived at beautiful and extensive groves of olive, for the cultivation of which Párga is renowned; they clothe all the hills around, and hang over rock and cliff to the very sea with delightful and feathery luxuriance. At length we descended to the shore at the foot of the little promontory on which the ill-fated palace and its citadel stood; alas, what now appears a town and castle consists of old ruined walls, for Párga is desolate. A new one built since the natives abandoned the ancient site, is, however, springing up on the shore, and with its two mosques is picturesque: this, with the rock and dismantled fortress – the islands in the bay, and the rich growth of olive slopes around, form a picture of completely beautiful character, though more resembling an Italian than a Greek scene; but it is impossible fully to contemplate with pleasure a place, the history of which is so full of melancholy and painful interest.**

---

*   Bad passes.
**   The British had abandoned this Christian stronghold to Alí Pasha in April 1819.

A dark cloud hangs over the mournful spot. Would that much which has been written concerning it were never read, or that having been written it could be disbelieved!

A lodging was found me in a very decent house and shelter against the heat of midday was grateful. In the afternoon and evening I made many drawings from either side of the promontory of Párga. From every point it is lovely, very unlike Albanian landscape in general, and partaking more of the character of Calabrian or Amalfitan coast scenery. But in spite of the delightful evening, and the sparkling white buildings that crowned the rock at whose feet the waves murmured, the whispering olives above me, the convent islets, and the broad bright sea beyond, in spite of all this, I felt anxious to leave Párga. The picture, false or true, of the 10th of April 1819 was ever before me, and I wished with all my heart that I had left Párga unvisited.

May 15. Between Métzovo and Metéora

We passed also more than one *khan* by the road, and usually at these places the Albanian guards asked us questions, and insisted on seeing passports which they had not the slightest idea of reading. As a proof of this, on my taking out by mistake the card of a hotel-keeper at Athens, the Palíkar* snatched at it hastily, and after gravely scrutinizing it, gave it back to me, saying, 'Good; you may pass on!' At the next guardhouse I confess to having amused myself by showing a bill of Mrs Dunsford's Hotel, at Malta, and at another the back of an English letter, each of which documents were received as a *teskeré.*** So much for the use of the Dervení guards, placed by the Turkish Government to take accurate cognisance of all passers-by.

* * * *

We arrived at Kastráki, a village nestled immediately below these gigantic crags, at sunset. I do not think I ever saw any scene so startling and incredible; such vast sheer perpendicular pyramids, standing out of the earth, with the tiny houses of the village clustering at the roots.

---

* An Albanian militia-man.
** Passport.

With difficulty – for it is the time when silk-worms are being bred in the houses, and the inhabitants will not allow them to be disturbed – Andréa procured a lodging for me in the upper part of a dwelling, formed as are most in the village, like a tower, the entrance to which, for the sake of defence, was by a hole three feet high. Here, after having gazed in utter astonishment at the wild scenery as long as the light lasted, I took up my abode for the night. The inhabitants of this place, as well as of Kalabáka (or Stagús),[33] are Christians, and every nook of the village was swarming with pigs and little children. 'Πολλα πιδλια,' said an old man to me, as the little creatures thronged about me, 'δια τον νερόν χαλόν.'* What a contrast is there between the precipices, from 500 to 600 feet high, and these atoms of life playing at their base! Strange, unearthly-looking rocks are these, full of gigantic chasms and round holes, resembling Gruyère cheese, as it were, highly magnified, their surface being otherwise perfectly smooth. Behind the village of Kastráki, the groups of rock are more crowded, and darkened with vegetation; and at this late hour a sombre mystery makes them seem like the work of some genii, or enchanter of Arabian romance. Before the dwellings, a slope covered with mulberry trees descends to the river, and grand scenes of Thessalian plain and hill fill up the southern and eastern horizon.

May 16. Kastráki
I went very early with a villager to visit and sketch the monasteries. Truly they are a most wonderful spectacle; and are infinitely more picturesque than I had expected them to be. The magnificent foreground of fine oak and detached fragments of rock struck me as one of the peculiar features of the scene. The detached and massive pillars of stone, crowned with the retreats of the monks, rise perpendicularly from the sea of foliage, which at this early hour, six a.m., is wrapped in the deepest shade, while the bright eastern light strikes the upper part of the magic heights with brilliant force and breadth. To make any real use of the most exquisite landscape abounding throughout this marvellous spot, an artist should stay here for a month: there are both the simplest and most classic poetries of scenery at their foot looking towards

---

33 Anciently Aeginium.

---

* 'Many children because of the good water.'

the plain and mountain; and when I mounted the cliffs on a level with the summit of the great rocks of Metéora and Baarlám, the solitary and quiet tone of these most wonderful haunts appeared to me inexpressibly delightful. Silvery white goats were peeping from the edge of the rocks into the deep, black abyss below; the simple forms of the rocks rise high in air, crowned with church and convent, while the eye reaches the plains of Thessaly to the far-away hills of Agrafa. No pen or pencil can do justice to the scenery of Metéora. I did not go up to any of the monasteries. Suffering from a severe fall in the autumn of last year, I had no desire to run the risk of increasing the weakness of my right arm, the use of which I was only now beginning to regain, so the interior of these monkish habitations I left unvisited; regretting that I did so the less, as every moment of the short time I lingered among these scenes, was too little to carry away even imperfect representations of their marvels.

* * * *

The plains [between Trikkala and Nomí] grew wider and wider. We pass a few villages, each more widely apart from its neighbour than the preceding, and by degrees I feel that I am really in Thessaly, for width and breadth now constitute the soul and essence of all the landscape. To the north only the distant form of Olympus rears itself above a low range of hills; and to the south the hills of Agrafa and Oeta are gradually becoming less distinct. Before me all is vast, outstretched plain, which never seems to end. Agriculture and liveliness are its predominant characteristics. It is full of incident; innumerable sheep, goats, horses, buffali, and cattle, corn or pasture-land, peasants' huts, hundreds of perambulating storks, give a life and variety everywhere. And then so green, so intensely green, is this immense level! and the peasant women, in their gay, fringed and tasselled capotes – how far handsomer than any Greeks I have seen!

May 19. Tempé
Leaving Monsieur Hippolyte,* I went onward into Tempe, and soon entered this most celebrated 'vale' – of all places in Greece that which I had most desired to see. But it is not a 'vale', it is a

---

*   A Frenchman living in Ambelaki.

narrow pass – and although extremely beautiful, on account of the precipitous rocks on each side, the Peneus flowing deep in the midst, between the richest overhanging plane woods, still its character is distinctly that of a ravine or gorge.

In some parts the pass (which is five or six miles from end to end), is so narrow as merely to admit the road and the river; in others the rocks recede from the stream, and there is a little space of green meadow. The cliffs themselves are very lofty, and beautifully hung with creepers and other foliage; but from having formed a false imagination as to the character of 'Tempe's native vale',* I confess to having been a little disappointed. Nevertheless, there is infinite beauty and magnificence in its scenery, and fine compositions might be made, had an artist time to wander among the great plane trees on the border of the stream: a luxuriant wooded character is that which principally distinguishes it in a pictorial scene from other passes where there may be equally fine precipices bounding a glen as narrow. Well might the ancients extol this grand defile, where the landscape is so completely different from that of any part of Thessaly, and awakes the most vivid feelings of awe and delight, from its associations with the legendary history and religious rites of Greece.

* * * *

In some meadows near a little stream flowing into the Peneus were several camels, which are frequently used about Saloníki and Katerína, etc. They were very ragged and hideous creatures, and offered a great contrast to the trim and well-kept animals of our Arabs, which we had so familiarly known in our journey through the desert of Suez and Sinai. But as I returned towards Tempe I perceived a young one among the herd, and I rode a little way towards it spite of the clamorous entreaties of the Yannina muleteer. I had better have attended to his remonstrances, for the little animal (who resembled nothing so much as a large white muff upon stilts), chose to rush towards us with the most cheerful and innocent intentions, and skipping and jumping after the fashion of delighted kids, thrust himself into the way of our three horses with

---

* The allusion is probably classical, but may possibly refer to line 86 of William Collins's 'The Passions: An Ode to Music' (1747): 'They saw, in Tempe's vale, her native maids'.

the most facetious perverseness. One and all took fright, and the muleteer's reared, threw him and escaped. There was much difficulty in recapturing the terrified animal, and when we had done so forth came the little muffy white beast once more, pursuing us with the most profuse antics over the plain and rendering our steeds perfectly unmanageable. To add to our discomfiture, the whole herd of camels, disapproving of the distance to which we were inveigling their young relation, began to follow us with an increasingly quick trot; and we were too glad to ford the stream as quickly as possible and leave our gaunt pursuers and their foolish offspring on the opposite side.

May 20. Lárissa
On my return to Larissa there is but just time to make one drawing of dark Olympus ere a frightful thunderstorm, with deluges of rain, breaks over the plain and pursues me to the city. It continues to pour all the afternoon, and I amuse myself, as best I can, in Hassán Bey's house. It is a large mansion, in the best Turkish style, and betokening the riches of its master. It occupies three sides of a walled courtyard, and one of its wings is allotted to the harem, who live concealed by a veil of close lattice work when at home, though I see them pass to and fro dressed in the usual disguise worn out of doors. I watch two storks employed in building on the roof of that part of the building. These birds are immensely numerous in Thessaly, and there is a nest on nearly every house in Lárissa. No one disturbs them; and they are considered so peculiarly in favour with the Prophet that the vulgar believe the conversion of a Christian as being certain to follow their choice of his roof for their dwelling; formerly a Christian so honoured was forced to turn Mussulman or quit his dwelling, – so at least they told me in Yannina, where two pair have selected the Vice-Consul's house for their abode. It is very amusing to watch them when at work, as they take infinite pains in the construction of what after all seems a very ill-built nest. I have seen them, after twisting and bending a long bit of grass or root for an hour in all directions, throw it away altogether. That will not do after all, they say; and then flying away they return with a second piece of material, in the choice of which they are very particular; and, according to my informants at Yannina, only make use of one sort of root. When they have arranged the twig or grass in a satisfactory manner, they put up their heads on their shoulders, and clatter in a mysterious manner

with a sound like dice shaken in a box. This clattering at early morning or evening, in this season of the year, is one certain characteristic that these towns are under Turkish government, inasmuch as the storks have all abandoned Greece (modern), for the Greeks shoot and molest them; only they still frequent Lárissa, and the plain of the Spercheius, as being so near the frontier of Turkey that they can easily escape thither if necessary. This is foolishness in the Greeks, for the stork is most useful in devouring insects, especially the larva of the locust, which I observed in myriads on the plains near the entrance of Tempe and I counted as many as seventy storks in one society, eating them as fast as possible, and with great dignity of carriage.

That part of the roof of the harem which is not occupied by storks, is covered with pigeons and jackdaws; a humane attention paid to the lower orders of creation being always one of the most striking traits of Turkish character.

The storm continues all night. The air of Lárissa is heavy and close, and so much threatens fever, that I resort to quinine in no little quantities.

May 23. Volo
Alas! the woes of Thessaly! It is again pouring with rain, and the wind is set in southerly, so that once and for altogether I give up all idea of sailing to Athos.

The horses are ordered, and as soon as Andréa can get about I start at length to return to Yannina.

As I ride away Volo, its gulf, and the scattered villages on the hills of Magnesia, seem truly beautiful; but to what purpose should I linger? Tomorrow, and tomorrow, may be equally wet. Mount Athos! Mount Athos! All my toil has been in vain, and I shall now most possibly never see you more!*

June 9. Sayádes, in Corfú
I was out of quarantine on the 5th and have passed some pleasant days in the town since, though not so much so as formerly. 'All things have suffered change.' Lord Seaton's family and many others I knew are gone.

Good old Andréa Vríndisi I have paid and sent off to Patrás; and today I am on board the Malta steamer *Antelope* and am sailing

---

* Lear was to visit and paint Mount Athos in 1856.

through the Ionian Channel for the ninth time. Off Párga: there are the mosques, silvery-white; there, high up beyond the plain, is the dark hill of Súli. There is the fatal hill of Zálongo – the point of Prévezya.

At sunset Sappho's leap – Leucadia's rock of woe. The mountains of Tchamouriá fade away and I look my last on Albania.

At midnight the moon rises over dark Ithaca, and lights up the Bay of Samos, where we stay half an hour.

Sunrise. – Patrás once more and the pearly-tinted Mount Voidhiá. Noon. – Gay Zante, bright and bustling as ever.

And so, with the last point of Zákynthus and the dim, distant mountain of Cephalonia, ends my journey in the lands of Greece.

from Journals of a Landscape Painter in Southern Calabria, Etc. *(1852)*

Ye poppular author & traveller in
Albania & Calabrià, keepinge his feete warme

1. Ye traveller.
2. Ye Railwaie rugge.
3. Ye author his vestmentes.
4. his hatteboxe.
5. Ye Cheste of draweres
6. Ye chaire
7. Ye large cheste.
8. Ye washingtable
9. Ye dressing table.
10. Ye traveller his bootes.
11. Ye sparkling looking glasse.
12. Ye table.
13. Ye tinne tubbe
14. Ye china tub.
15. Ye matting rolled uppe.
16. Ye quadrangular
    pincushione.
17. Ye jugge.
18. Ye flaskes of gunnepowder.
19. Ye picklejarres.
20. Ye beautiful chaire made of
    wickerworke
21. Ye peaceful cherubbes that
    appeared to ye author
    when 25. he fell asleepe.

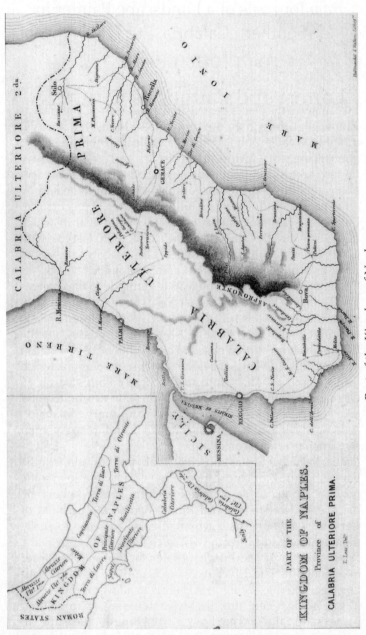

Part of the Kingdom of Naples

from Journals of a Landscape Painter in Southern Calabria, Etc. *(1852)*

Like many of the places Lear visited in the 1840s, Calabria was a remote territory in the autumn of 1847. Moreover, it was in a highly volatile political state, and Lear in the prevailing atmosphere of incipient uprising and revolutionary undercurrents was frequently suspected of being some sort of spy. The first part of this journal is brought to an end by what turned out to be a revolutionary flurry, a precursor to the larger scale movements of the following year in which insurgents briefly gained power, and then lost it, with Garibaldi eventually having to flee. Lear describes the city of Reggio, which had revolted and was under attack, as 'undergoing evil', which suggests his attitude to the changes at this time to have been more conservative than neutral. In some respects this is unsurprising, given his close personal and professional ties to the English governing classes, and the threat which revolution posed to his livelihood as an English artist in Rome. 'What *is* the use of all these revolutions which lead to nothing?' he wrote to Chichester Fortescue on 16 October 1847, though he turns the question to a quite good joke – 'as the displeased turnspit said to an angry cookmaid'. A decade later, however, he saw Italian resistance to Austrian domination as a beacon of hope.

Lear says that he has chosen to avoid politics, and that the book is a 'guide for landscape-painters'. He was also in some ways a guide to his companion, John Proby (whom he discovered later to be Lord Proby, heir to the earldom of Carysfort), a young man who had come to Rome to study painting and had earlier in 1847 travelled with Lear in Sicily. Proby died only eleven years later, at 35, and his sister maintained he had never recovered from the arduous pace Lear set. The rule of their travels was to allow for digression if something interesting beckoned them away from their plans, and the book has a roughing-it pleasure in experiencing 'much simplicity, much cordiality, and heaps more dirt'. Some of the people they encounter are evoked as comical and nonsensical, but Lear also gives us a sense of the local perspective from which England is a land of absurdity, and English travellers in Calabria self-evidently absurd. The book includes plenty of impressive description and funny incident, though it lacks the classical radiance and edge-of-Europe wildness of the *Journals in Albania*.

Preface

To the present Volume of Journals but little preface is requisite: they were written during tours made in the autumn of 1847, throughout the southern of the three Calabrian Provinces, and in that of Basilicata.

Few places visited by the author have not already been fully described in the accurate and interesting travels of the Hon. Keppel Craven.[1] Mr Swinburne has written a notice[2] of many places in Calabria, though his observations are principally confined to the coast; and the western road by the sea has been well and amusingly treated of in a little book called *A Tour in Calabria*, by Arthur Strutt.[3] The older notices[4] of the province are so confused or so cumbrous, as to be little read or known.

While some villages in this, the most southerly portion of the beautiful kingdom of Naples, have, however, hitherto remained unexplored by Englishmen, and others, till now unillustrated by views, are for the first time made known to the public, – the general

---

1   A *Tour through the Southern Provinces of the Kingdom of Naples, by* the Hon. R. Keppel Craven. 1821.

2   *Travels in the Two Sicilies,* by Henry Swinburne, Esq. 1785.

3   *A Pedestrian Tour in Calabria and Sicily,* by Arthur J. Strutt. 1842.

4   Alberti (Fra Leandro), *Descrit. di tutta l'Italia.* Venetia: 1596; P. Marafioti (Girolamo), *Antichità di Calabrià.* Padova: 1601; *Giustiniani, Dizionario del Regno di Napoli.* 1797.

aim of the writer to make his journal a Landscape-painter's Guide-Book will stand as an apology for his having sometimes described ground already better treated of in the above-mentioned works.

The mode of travel which I and my fellow-wanderer* adopted while these journals were written, was the simplest, as well as cheapest – we performed the whole tour on foot; except that in Basilicata some of the high roads were well got over in a carriage. In Calabria, a horse to carry our small amount of baggage, and a guide, cost us, altogether, six *carlini* daily[5] – no very heavy expenditure; but as there are no inns in that province except on the coach-road, which skirts the western coast, the traveller depends entirely on introductions to some family in each town he visits.

The tour in the more northern provinces was undertaken under somewhat different circumstances. The long journeys on the high road, or over the plains near the east coast of Italy, do not offer sufficient inducement to pedestrian exercise. In no country, perhaps, can greater contrasts be found, than between the far-stretched campagna of Apulia or the dreary ridges of part of Basilicata, and the fertile gardens, the wondrous coast scenes, or the purple gorges of the heart of Calabrian mountains.

Wishing to confine these journals strictly to the consideration of landscape, I have said as little as possible of events which occurred in 1848,** and their sequel. Yet it is but right to add, that some provincial families, whose suspicions and apparent want of hospitality marked them in our eyes as unlike their compatriots, were but too well justified in keeping themselves aloof from any strangers, whose motives for visiting this country were but little understood, and whose presence might possibly have compromised them in the event of disturbances which, they may have been aware, were on the eve of occurring.

LONDON,
September 15, 1852.

---

5   Little more than two shillings.

---

*   His fellow-traveller was John Joshua Proby (1823–58), a young Irishman who had probably been one of Lear's pupils in Rome. They had travelled together in Sicily in May and June 1847.

**   The nationalist and revolutionary uprisings in Italy in 1848.

Calabria

July 25. 1847
The very name of Calabria has in it no little romance. No other province of the kingdom of Naples holds out such promise of interest, or so inspires us before we have set foot within it, – for what do we care for Molise, or Principato? or what visions are conjured up by the names of Terra di Lavoro, or Capitanata? But – Calabria! – No sooner is the word uttered than a new world arises before the mind's eye, – torrents, fastnesses, all the prodigality of mountain scenery, – caves, brigands, and pointed hats, – Mrs Radcliffe and Salvator Rosa,* – costumes and character, – horrors and magnificence without end. Even Messina derives its chief charm from the blue range of mountains and the scattered villages on the opposite shore, – Reggio glittering on the water's edge, – Scylla on its rock, where the guide-books (by a metaphor) say you may hear (large?) dogs barking across the straits, – the lofty cloud-topped Aspromonte, and the pearl-pale cliffs of Bagnara. Yet this land of pictorial and poetical interest has had but few explorers; fewer still have published their experiences; and its scenery, excepting that on the high road, or near it, has rarely been portrayed, at least by our own countrymen.

July 29. Reggio
We could get no guide until noon, an arrangement not ill-fitting with our plan of sleeping the first night at Motta San Giovanni, on our way to Bova: so at two we prepared to start. We had engaged a muleteer for an indefinite time: the expense for both guide and quadruped being six *carlini* daily; and if we sent him back from any point of our journey it was agreed that his charges should be defrayed until he reached Reggio. Our man, a grave tall fellow of more than 50 years of age, and with a good expression of countenance, was called Ciccio,[6] and we explained to him that our plan was to do always just as we pleased – going straight ahead or

---

6 'Ciccio' is short for 'Francesco,' in the Neapolitan kingdom states. In the Roman states it is 'Cecco'.

---

* The famous 'Gothic' novelist Ann Radcliffe (1764–1823), and the Italian painter Salvatore Rosa (1615–73).

stopping to sketch, without reference to any law but our own pleasure; to all which he replied by a short sentence ending with – 'Dógo; díghi, dóghi, dághi, dà' – a collection of sounds of frequent recurrence in Calabrese lingo, and the only definite portion of that speech we could ever perfectly master. What the 'Dógo' was we never knew, though it was an object of our keenest search throughout the tour to ascertain if it were animal, mineral, or vegetable. Afterwards, by constant habit, we arranged a sort of conversational communication with friend Ciccio, but we never got on well unless we said 'Dógo si,' or 'Dógo no' several times as an *ad libitum* appoggiatura, winding up with 'Díghi, dóghi, dághi, dà,' which seemed to set all right. Ciccio carried a gun, but alas! wore no pointed hat; nothing but a Sicilian long blue cap. Our minds had received a fearful shock by the conviction forced on them during our three days' stay at Reggio, namely, that there are NO pointed hats in the first or southern province of Calabria. The costume, though varying a little in different villages, is mainly the same as that throughout Sicily, and it is only in the provinces of Catanzáro and Cosenza where the real (and awful) pyramidal brigand's hat is adopted. Ciccio tied four packets (one of vestments, etc., another of drawing materials for each man), plaids, umbrellas, etc., on a quiet-looking steed, touching whose qualities its owner was wholly silent, thereby giving me, who go by contraries in these lands, great hope that it might be worth a good deal, for had it been a total failure one might have looked for a long tirade of praises: and so, all being adjusted – off we set.

The road led over the torrent-bed and by the Villa Musitano, through suburban villages for two or three miles, and for a considerable distance we passed numerous odoriferous silk factories,[7] and many detached cheerful-looking houses, with lofty *pergolate*[8] or vine trellises spanning and shading the whole public road from side to side. Beyond, the broad dusty highway was uninteresting in its foregrounds, but the blue straits of Messina were ever on our right, with Etna beyond, while on the left a wall of hills, with Castel San Nocito and San Vito perched on their summits, sufficed for men who were all alive for impressions of

---

7 The cultivation of silkworms is carried on to a great extent in Calabria, especially in the territory of Reggio.

8 *Pergola*, or *Pergolata*, is the general name for any balcony or trellis covered with vine.

Calabrese novelty. Always in sight also was the town of Motta San Giovanni, our night's resting-place, but so high up as to promise a stout pull to reach it.

When in fullest sight of Mongibello, we turned from the coast and began to ascend the hills. For a while the path lay on the northern side, and at every turn we looked over a wider expanse of the beautiful garden-plain of Reggio, broken by the lines of its white torrents, and backed by the straits and hills of Messina; but afterwards we wound up a path closely shut in betwixt high sandy banks, or placed on the edge of clay ravines looking over slopes thickly planted with dwarf vines. High winds prevented our making any drawing, and indeed it was nearly Ave-Maria[9] when we had risen above the weary sandy gorges immediately below the town, which stands at a great elevation, and overlooks earth and sea extensively. With little difficulty we found the house of Don Francesco Marópoti, who received us with hospitality, and without show of ceremony, only apologizing that, owing to his being alone in this his country residence, our reception could not be in point of fare and lodging all he could wish. Indeed this worthy person's establishment was not of the most *recherché* kind, but I had warned my companion (hitherto untravelled in these regions) that he would probably meet with much simplicity, much cordiality, and heaps more of dirt throughout Calabria. There is always in these provincial towns a knot of neighbours who meet in the house of the great man of each little place, to discuss the occurrences of the day for an hour or two before supper; already a long perspective of such hours oppressed me, loaded with questions about Inghilterra and our own plans and circumstances. *'Cosa c'e da vedere in Bagaládi?'*[10] said our host's coterie with one voice, when they heard we wanted to go there, – and one elder was fiercely incredulous, proposing that, if, as we said, we were in search of the beautiful or remarkable, we should set out directly for Montebello or Mélito, or any place but Bagaládi. He also explained the position and attributes of England to the rest of the society, assuring them that we had no fruit of any sort, and that all our bread came from Egypt and India: and as for our race, with a broad contempt for minute distinctions, he said we were *'tutti Francesi'*, an assertion

---

9   Ave-Maria is half an hour after the sun sets at all times of the year, when it is then dark in Italy, and the computation of hours, 1, 2, 3, etc., recommences.
10 'What should there be to see in Bagaládi?'

we faintly objected to, but were over-ruled by – '*in somma – siete sempre una razza di Francesi: è lo stesso.*'[11]

At last the clique departed, and we sate down with Don Francesco to supper, an unostentatious meal, accompanied by tolerable wine, but with a rural style about the service, etc., more resembling that in the remoter villages of the Abruzzi than of the towns near any of the provincial capitals of the northern Neapolitan provinces. There was, however, no want of good will or good breeding, and we were neither bored by questions nor pressed to eat, nor requested to sit up late; so we soon retired, and, on perceiving very clean beds, were not slow in congratulating ourselves on the prosperous commencement of our Calabrian tour.

* * * *

August 2

A repetition of yesterday – was passed in drawing about the rock town of Bova. The Bovani take a great interest in our performances; and Don Antonio* makes a sonnet thereon, which I append,[12] notwithstanding it is in praise of my sketches, as a specimen of 'unpublished' Calabrese poetry.

11 In a word, you are a sort of Frenchman; it's all the same.
12 ALL' EGREGIO DISEGNATORE PAESISTA SIG. EDOARDO LEAR; NEL DIPINGERE DELLE VEDUTE NELLA CITTÀ DL BOVA.**

SONETTO

Salve genio d'Albione! oh come è bello,
Veder natura su le pinte carte
Figlie del tuo pensier, del tuo pennello
Dal vero tratte con mirabil arte!
Io là veggo le roccie, ed il castello
Le case, il campanile, e quasi in parte
Tutta la patria mia: e il poverello
Che dal monte per giù vi si diparte.
E se per balze e valli, e boschi ombrosi,
Molto questa contrada all' arte offria
Italia è bella pur nei luoghi ascosi.
Ed ivi l' amico lasci, cui il desio
Di memoria serbar pei virtuosi
Gli scalda il cor, perché desir di Dio.   [*Continued overleaf*]

*   Don Antonio Marzano, their host in Bova.
** 'To the esteemed landscape artist Mr Edward Lear, on his painting of the views in the city of Bova.'

Yet, in the elegancies of society, the Marzani are far behind most families of similar position in the Abruzzi provinces, however their equals in every kind of hospitality and good-nature. To-morrow we start for Staíti, San Angelo di Bianco, and San Luca, on the way to Santa Maria di Polsi, one of our greatest objects of curiosity in Calabria Ulteriore I.

August 3
Hardly could we persuade the domestics to accept of three *carlini*, even in remuneration for washing our linen. As we started from Bova ere the earliest sunbeams had changed Etna from a blue to pale rosy tint, the worthy Don A. Marzano bade us a hearty adieu, entreating us to write to him from whatever part of the world we might be in, generally, and from Gerace in particular.

Descending the narrow street of steep stairs, – for whosoever leaves Bova must needs so descend, unless he be a bird, – we passed the public prison, and lo! glaring through the bars was the evil countenance of the woman whom, in the tavern-hut of Condufóri, we had remarked as a species of Medusa: she had been sent hither last night for having murdered one of her fellow Turchi or Turche. The broad dark shades of morning filled the deep valley below the mountain, as the winding pathway led us on from wood to wood throughout a delicious vale, at the lowest end of which a mill and stream, with a few cottages, added a charm to the wild scene; and still through the thick foliage magnificent peeps of overtowering Bova were seen from time to time. And having passed the *fiumara* at the foot of the ridge crowned by the aerial city, we began to

---

A friend sends me the following translation of the foregoing verses:

> Genius of Albion, hail! what joy to see
>   The landscapes glowing on the tinted board,
> Fair children of thy thought, so wondrously
>   Drawn with thy magic brush from nature's hoard!
> I see the rocks, the frowning citadel,
>   As line by line the well-known shapes unfold, –
> The houses, and the tall tower with the bell,
>   And there a peasant wandering down the wold.
> Ah! if these glens, and vales, and shady groves,
>   Yield to the pencil matter without end,
> Among the scenes where artist seldom roves,
>   How fair is Italy! There, O my friend,
> Thou leav'st me, hoping, as a good man should,
> To live within the memory of the good.

Palizzi

ascend once more a brown cistus-covered hillside, with giant naked-armed oaks in the foreground, and the vast blue forest-clothed mountains of Aspromonte closing the landscape on all but the southern side. As the time for our mid-day halt came on, and the heat began to be rather troublesome, we came in sight of Palizzi, a most singular town, built round an isolated rock commanding one of the many narrow valleys opening to the sea. Coming, as we did, from the high inland ground, we arrived at the top of Palizzi, the castle of which is alone visible from the north side, so that to reach the level of the stream and lower town, it is necessary to descend a perfect ladder between houses and pergolas, clustered in true Calabrese style among the projecting cactus-covered ledges of the parent rock from which they seemed to grow. No wilder, nor more extraordinary place than Palizzi can well greet artist eye. Leaving P—— to finish a drawing I went forward to seek some shelter against the heat, and, reaching the castle, soon found myself in the midst of its ruined area, where, though full of incidental picturesqueness – namely, a cottage, a pergola, seven large pigs, a blind man, and a baby, I could get no information as to the whereabouts of the taverna; until alarmed by the lively remonstrances of the pigs, there appeared a beautifully fair girl who directed me down to the middle of the town: the light hair, and Grecian traits, like those of the women of Gaeta, seemed to recall the daughters of Magna Graecia.

The streets of Palizzi, through which no Englishman perhaps had as yet descended, were swarming with perfectly naked, berry-brown children, and before I reached the taverna I could hardly make my way through the gathering crowd of astonished mahogany Cupids. The taverna was but a single dark room, its walls hung with portraits of little saints, and its furniture a very filthy bed with a crimson velvet gold-fringed canopy, containing an unclothed ophthalmic baby, an old cat, and a pointer dog; all the rest of the chamber being loaded with rolls of linen, gems, gourds, pears, hats, glass tumblers, puppies, jugs, sieves, etc.; still it was a better resting-place than the hut at Condufóri, inasmuch as it was free from many intruders. Until P—— came, and joined with me in despatching a feeble dinner of eggs, figs and cucumber, wine and snow,* I sate exhibited and displayed for the benefit of the landlord, his wife, and family, who regarded me with

---

* A pudding, with main ingredients of egg-white and sugar.

unmingled amazement, saying perpetually, '*O donde siete?*' – '*O che fai?*' – '*O chi sei?*'[13] And, indeed, the passage of a stranger through these outlandish places is so unusual an occurrence, that on no principle but one can the aborigines account for your appearance. 'Have you no rocks, no towns, no trees in your own country? Are you not rich? Then what *can* you wish *here?* – *here*, in this place of poverty and incommodo? What *are* you doing? Where *are* you going?' You might talk for ever; but you could not convince them you are not a political agent sent to spy out the nakedness of the land, and masking the intentions of your government under the thin veil of pourtraying scenes, in which they see no novelty, and take no delight.

Going out to explore the lower part of the town, I could not resist making a sketch of its wonderful aspect from below; the square towering rock of Palizzi seems to fill the whole scene, while the houses are piled up from the stream in a manner defying all description. But to transfer all this to paper was neither easy not agreeable; the afternoon sun reflected from the crags of the close and narrow valley, making it like an oven, besides that every available bit of standing ground is so nearly covered with intractable cactus-bushes as to be utterly vexatious; and, add to their alarming prickles, and the frying heat, that the stream was full of soaking hemp, the poisonous stench of which was intolerable, and that all the juvenile unclothed population of the town came and sate over against me, and it may be perceived, that to sketch in Palizzi, though it be truly a wonder in its way, is indeed a pursuit of knowledge under great difficulties.

We left this town at three p.m., and made for Staíti, where we were to sleep, and, keeping always distant some miles from the sea, began to ascend the hill of Pietrapennata. From the north side, Palizzi appears totally different in form, and is one of those Poussinesque scenes so exquisite in character, and so peculiar to Italy. The village of Pietrapennata contains nothing remarkable, but from the height immediately above it, one of the most glorious landscapes bursts into view. What detached and strange crags! what overhanging ilex and oak! what middle-distance of densest wood! what remote and graceful lines, with the blue expanse of the eastern sea, and the long plains of the eastern side of Italy! The

13 'Oh where *do* you come from? – Oh what *are* you going to do? – Oh who *can* you be?'

setting sun prevented our sketching, but we resolved positively to return to this most exquisite scenery, from Staíti, which now towered above us on the opposite side of a deep dark gully, filled with wondrous groups of giant ilex. As we slowly toiled up to this most strange place, wholly Calabrese in aspect, with its houses jammed and crushed among extraordinary crevices, its churches growing out of solitary rocks, and (what forms the chief character of these towns) all its dwellings standing singly – the Zampognari[14] were playing, and all the peasant population thronging upwards to their evening rest. Here, too, were the first symptoms of local colour in costume, the women wearing bright blue dresses with broad orange borders, and all we saw gave promise of real unmixed Calabrian characteristics, unspoiled by high roads and the changes of all-fusing and assimilating civilisation.

Don Domenico Musitani, the chief man of the place, to whom the never-failing care of the Consigliere da Nava* had recommended us, was sitting in the Piazza – an obese and taciturn man, who read the introductory letter, and forthwith took us to his house; which, among many unpleasing recollections, will certainly ever rank as one of the most disagreeable. Life in these regions of natural magnificence is full of vivid contrasts. The golden abstract visions of the hanging woods and crags of Pietrapennata were suddenly opposed to the realities of Don D. Musitani's rooms, which were so full of silkworms as to be beyond measure disgusting. To the cultivation of this domestic creature all Staíti is devoted; yellow cocoons in immense heaps are piled up in every possible place, and the atmosphere may be conceived rather than described; for there is no more sickening odour than that of many thousand caterpillars confined in the closest of chambers. Almost did we repent of ever having come into these Calabrian lands! After the usual refreshment of snow and wine, we waited wearily for supper; at times replying to the interrogatories of our host on the subject of the productions of Inghilterra, and right glad when dismissed to what rest might be found in couches apparently clean, though odious from the silkworms all around them; but necessity as well as poverty makes the traveller acquainted with strange bed-fellows.

---

14 Peasants who play on the Zampogne, a sort of bagpipes used in Southern Italy.

---

* One of Lear's contacts in Reggio.

* * * *

August 7. Between San Luca and Polsi
We were obliged to walk as fast as possible, that we might arrive at Polsi by daylight, and as we ascended, the labour was not a little severe. It was twenty-two o'clock* when we reached a fountain very high up in the mountain, yet the brown-garbed guide said three hours were still requisite to bring us to our night's lodging. Clear streams, trickling down at every step to the great torrent, refreshed us, and soon we left the valley, and began to climb among oak woods, till the deep chasm, now dark in the fading daylight, was far below our feet.

A circuitous toil to the head of a second large torrent, skirting a ravine filled with magnificent ilex, brought us to the last tremendous ladder-path, that led to the '*serra*', or highest point of the route, wherefrom we were told we should perceive the monastery. Slowly old Ciccio and his horse followed us, and darker grew the hour. '*Arriveremo tardi*,' quoth he, '*se non moriamo prima – díghi, dóghi, dà!*'[15] But alas! when we did get at the promised height, where a cross is set up, and where, at the great *festas* of the convent, the pilgrims fire off guns on the first and last view of this celebrated Calabrian sanctuary – alas! it was quite dark, and only a twinkling light far and deep down, in the very bowels of the mountain, showed us our destination. Slow and hazardous was the descent, and it was nine o'clock** ere we arrived before the gate of this remote and singular retreat. It was a long while before we gained admittance; and the Superiore, a most affable old man, having read our letter, offered us all the accommodation in his power, which, as he said, we must needs see was small. Wonder and curiosity overwhelmed the ancient man and his brethren, who were few in number, and clad in black serge dresses. 'Why had we come to such a solitary place? No foreigner had ever done so before!' The hospitable father asked a world of questions, and made many comments upon us and upon England in general, for the benefit of his fellow-recluses. 'England,' said he, 'is a very small place,

---

15 'We shall arrive late, if we do not die before we get there.'

---

*   See Lear's note on p. 242 above. 'Twenty-two o'clock' would be two and a half
     hours before sunset.
**   Here reverting, presumably, to English time-keeping.

although thickly inhabited. It is altogether about the third part of the size of the city of Rome. The people are a sort of Christians, though not exactly so. Their priests, and even their bishops, marry, which is incomprehensible, and most ridiculous. The whole place is divided into two equal parts by an arm of the sea, under which there is a great tunnel, so that it is all like one piece of dry land. *Ah – che celebre tunnel!'* A supper of hard eggs, salad, and fruit followed in the refectory of the convent, and we were attended by two monstrous watch-dogs, named Assassino and Saraceno, throughout the rest of the evening, when the silence of the long hall, broken only by the whispers of the gliding monk, was very striking. Our bedrooms were two cells, very high up in the tower of the convent, with shutters to the unglazed windows, as a protection against the cold and wind, which were by no means pleasant at this great elevation. Very forlorn, indeed, were the sleeping apartments of Sta Maria di Polsi, and fearful was the howling of the wind and the roaring of a thunder-storm throughout the night! – but it was solemn and suggestive, and the very antithesis of life in our own civilized and distant home.

* * * *

August 13. Siderno
Descending to the River Novito, whose broad *fiumara* runs from the mountains north of Gerace to the sea, we ascended the hill of Siderno, and passed through that town, a large, but not picturesque place. The costumes of the peasantry are, however, becoming more marked in character; the women all wear deep-blue dresses, with four-inch broad orange or pink borders, and their heads are covered with black or white panni-cloths, adjusted as in the province of Terra di Lavoro. Throughout this, and all our walks hitherto, the civility and friendliness of every person we meet is most agreeable. Hence, leaving the Marina di Siderno on the right (it is said to be a thriving place among the little ports of this coast), we descended towards the sea in a northerly direction, and after many a long lane, by olive-grounds and fig-gardens, reached the beach. Rocella, on its rocky cape, always a beautiful object even from Gerace, becomes more and more beautiful as one advances towards it; but the hour grew late, and so low was the sun, that it was only by hard running that I reached a spot, among aloes and olives, by the sea-side, near enough to draw the fine outline before

me. When the sun had set, there were yet three miles to the town, over a flat ground, intersected with deceitful ravines, so that delays in approaching it were as unexpected as unavoidable. Troops of peasants passed us, playing the Zampogne merrily; dark grew the sky, and the stars were bright, as we arrived at the foot of the suburbs of Rocella – once a stronghold of the Caraffa family – now a collection of scattered houses below, and a knot of others on the double fortress rock. Don Giuseppe Nanni, to whom our letter directed us, we were told lived close to the castle; so up we went to the upper rock, through black arches and passages to a piazza surrounded by houses, all, as we could see, by their ragged walls against the sky, in utter ruin.

Ciccio shouted aloud, but no signs of life were given in the total darkness. We tried this turning – it was blocked up by a dead wall; that way you stumbled among sleeping horses; the next path led you to the precipice. We despaired, and remained calling forth 'ai! ai! Don Giuseppe Nanni! Oo! ooo! ai! ai!' till we were hoarse, but there was no other way of attracting attention. At last (as if there had been no steps taken at all to arouse the neighbourhood), a man came, as it were casually, forth from the dark ruins, holding a feeble light, and saying mildly, *'Cosa cercate?'*[16] 'We seek Don Giuseppe Nanni's house,' said we. 'This is it,' said he. So we walked, with no small pleasure, into the very place under whose windows we had been screaming for the last hour past. It was a very old palazzo, with tiny rooms, built against a rock, and standing on the extreme edge of the precipice towards the sea. As usual, the family received us cordially – Don Giuseppe, and Don Aristide, the Canonico,* and Don Ferdinando; and during the doleful two hours preceding supper, we sat alternately watching the stars, or listening to the owl-answering-owl melody in the rocks above our heads, or fought bravely through the *al solito*** questions about the tunnel, and the produce of Inghilterra, though I confess to having been more than once fast asleep, and, waking up abruptly, answered at random, in the vaguest manner, to the applied catechetical torture. I will not say what I did not aver to be the natural growth of England – camels, cochineal, sea-horses, or gold-dust; and as for the *célèbre*

---

16 'What do you want?'

---

*   The priest.
** Usual.

tunnel, I fear I invested it drowsily with all kinds of fabulous qualities. Supper was at last announced, and an addition to our party was made in the handsome wife of Don Ferdinando, and other females of the family, though I do not think they shared greatly in the conversation. Vegetables and fruit alone embellished the table. The world of Rocella particularly piques itself on the production and culture of fruit; and our assertion that we *had* fruit in England, was received with thinly hidden incredulity.

'You confess you have no wine – no oranges – no olives – no figs; – how, then, *can* you have apples, pears, or plums? It is a known fact that *no* fruit does or can grow in England, only potatoes, and nothing else whatever – this is well known. Why, then, do you tell us that which is not true?'

It was plain we were looked upon as vagabond impostors.

'*Ma davvero*,' said we, humbly; '*davvero abbiamo de' frutti – e di piu, ne abbiamo certi frutti che loro non hanno affatto.*' Suppressed laughter and supercilious sneers, when this assertion was uttered, nettled our patriotic feelings.

'*O che mai frutti possono avere loro che non abbiamo noi? O quanto ci burlano! Nominateli dunque – questi frutti vostri favolosi!*'

'*Giacché volete sapere,*' said we; '*abbiamo* Currants – *abbiamo* Gooseberries – *abbiamo* Greengages.*'

'*E che cosa sono Gooseberries e Gringhegi?*' said the whole party, in a rage; '*non ci sono queste cose – sono sogni.*'[17]

So we ate our supper in quiet, convinced almost that we had been telling lies; that gooseberries were unreal and fictitious; greengages a dream.

* * * *

August 16. Stilo
When a landscape painter halts for two or three days in one of the large towns of these regions, never perhaps to be revisited by him,

---

17 'But indeed we *have* fruit; and, what is more, we have some fruits which you have not got at all.'

'Oh what fruit can you possibly have that we have not? Oh how you are laughing at us! Name your fruits then – these fabulous fruits!'

'We have currants, gooseberries, and greengages.'

'And what are gooseberries and greengages? There are no such things – this is nonsense.'

the first morning at least is generally consumed in exploring it: four or five hours are very well spent, if they lead to the knowledge of the general forms of the surrounding scenes, and to the securing fixed choice of subject and quiet study to the artist during the rest of his stay. So many and so exquisite are the beauties of Stilo, that to settle to drawing any of them was difficult, and after having glanced at all the notabilia close to the town, I employed the rest of the morning in walking to Bazzano and Bigonzi, two villages on the farthest outskirts of Calabria Ulteriore I, in face of the mountains among whose depths lie the ruins of the famous Norman convent of Santo Stefano del Bosco. The gorge between Stilo and Bazzano is excessively grand, but the villages were not such as to tempt me to sketch them; the morning's walk, however, was delightful, if only for the opportunity it offered of observing the universally courteous and urbane manners of the peasantry. It is probable that no stranger had ever visited these wild and unfrequented nooks of a province, the great towns of which are themselves out of the route of travellers; but no one met or overtook me on the way to Bigonzi without a word or two of salutation; there were few who did not offer me pears, and parties of women laden with baskets of figs would stop and select the best for us. Nor did anybody ask a question beyond, 'What do you think of our mountains?' or 'How do you like our village?' In the town of Stilo we were sometimes followed by not less than fifty or a hundred people, but ever with the utmost good feeling and propriety. The well-bred population of Stilo we shall ever remember with pleasure.

* * * *

August 18. Castel Vetere
By the aid of the placid Ciccio and his horse, we crossed the swollen river, and, ascending wearily to the town, found it, though mean in appearance from below, full of houses of a large size and indicating wealth and prosperity.

To that of Don Ilario Asciutti we went, narrowly escaping the mid-day autumn thunder-storm, and found a large mansion, with a hall and staircase, ante-room, and drawing-room very surprising as to dimensions and furniture; the walls were papered, and hung with mirrors, prints, etc.; chiffoniers, tables, and a book-case adorned the sides of the rooms, and there were foot-stools, with other unwonted objects of trans-Calabrian luxury. The *famiglia* Asciutti were polite and most friendly; there were two smart sons, just come from college at Naples; a serene and silent father; and last, not least, an energetic and astute grandsire, before whose presence all the rest were as nothing. The Nonno[18] Asciutti was as voluble as Conte Garrolo;* but with more connected ideas and sentences, and with an overpowering voice; an expression of '*L'état, c'est moi,*' in all he said and did. The old gentleman surprised us not a little by his information on the subjects on which (*àpropos de bottes*) he held forth – the game laws of England, and Magna Charta, the Reformation, the Revolution of 1688, Ireland, and the Reform Bill. He was becoming diffuse on European politics, having already discussed America and the Canadas, and glanced slightly at slavery, the East and West Indies and the sugar trade, when, to our great satisfaction, all this learning, so wonderful in the heart of Magna-Grecia,** was put a stop to by the announcement of dinner. The silent son, and the two gay grandsons, listened to their elder relative's discourse, but took no part therein; and we, however superior the matter of the oration might be, greatly longed to exchange the orator for dear, little, fussy Conte Garrolo.

In the large dining-room were assembled many female and juvenile Asciutti, all very ugly; – hitherto we are not struck by Calabrian female beauty in the higher orders, though many of the peasant girls are pretty. The ladies spoke not during dinner, and the whole weight of the oral entertainment fell on the erudite grandfather, who harangued loftily from his place at the end of the table. It was Wednesday, and there was no meat, as is usual on that day in South Italian families. 'It would be better,' said the authoritative elder, 'if there were no such a thing as meat – nobody ought to eat any meat. The Creator never intended meat, that is the flesh of quadrupeds, to be eaten. No good Christians ought to eat flesh – and why? The quadruped works for man while alive, and it is a shame to devour him when dead. The sheep gives wool, the ox ploughs, the cow gives milk, the goat cheese.' – '*Cosa fanno per noi i lepri?*'[19] – whispered one of the grandsons. '*Statevi zitt'!*'[20]

---

18 Grandfather.
19 'What do the hares do for us?'
20 'Hold your tongue!'

---

*   Their host in Bovalino a week earlier.
**   The ancient Greek cities of Southern Italy, founded from about 750 BC onwards.

shouted the orator. 'But fish,' continued he – 'what do they do for us? Does a mullet plough? Can a prawn give milk? Has a tunny any wool? No. Fish and birds also were therefore created to be eaten.' A wearisome old man was the Asciutti Nonno! but the alarming point of his character was yet to be made known to us. No sooner, dinner being over, did we make known our intention of proceeding to sleep at Gioiosa on account of our limited time, than we repented having visited Castel Vetere at all. '*O Cielo! O rabbia! O che mai sento? O chi sono? O chi siete?*'[21] screamed the Nonno, in a paroxysm of rage. 'What have I done that you will not stay? How can I bear such an insult! Since Calabria was Calabria, no such affront has ever been offered to a Calabrian! Go – *why* should you go?' In vain we tried to assuage the grandsire's fury. We had staid three days in Gerace, three in Reggio, two in Bova and in Stilo, and not one in Castel Vetere! The silent father looked mournful, the grandsons implored; but the wrathful old gentleman having considerably endangered the furniture by kicks and thumps, finally rushed down stairs in a frenzy, greatly to our discomfiture.

The rest of the family were distressed seriously at this incident, and on my sending a message to beg that he would show us a new palazzo he was constructing (himself the architect), for the increased accommodation of the family Asciutti, he relented so far as to return, and after listening favourably to our encomiastic remarks, bade us a final farewell with a less perturbed countenance and spirit.

There are many fine views of Castel Vetere, which has somewhat in it of the grandiose and classic, from whatever point regarded, but we left it with less agreeable impressions than those we had carried from most of the larger Calabrian towns, partly from the feeling that we had vexed our host's family, and partly that it was yet so far to go to Gioiosa, that old Ciccio, with more than one admonitory growl, would not allow us to pause to sketch – no, not even for a quarter of an hour. Soon – after passing over high ground, from which the last views of ancient Caulon were very noble – we entered the downward course of the Meano, which, eternally winding over white stones, shut us in between high banks, till we came, at sunset, in sight of Rocella on its double rock; this, together with the river-bed, we bid farewell to by taking a

---

21 'Oh heavens! Oh rage! Oh what do I hear? Oh who am I? Oh who are you?'

route parallel to the coast, as far as the Fiume Romano, which we ascended for an hour, till we arrived at Gioiosa, apparently a large and well-built town, on the banks of a narrow part of the stream. The house of the Baron Rivettini, to whom we had letters, was large and imposing, but the Baron was not within, and the servants, with none of that stranger-helping alacrity of hospitality, so remarkable in more northern provinces of the Regno di Napoli, appeared too much amazed at the sudden arrival of '*due forestieri*',[22] to do anything but contemplate us; and, to speak truth, neither our appearance, considering we had toiled through some rain and much dirt all the afternoon, nor our suite, consisting of a man and a horse, were very indicative of being *comme il faut*. With difficulty we obtained leave to rest in a sort of ante-office, half stable, half kitchen, while a messenger carried our letter of introduction to the Baron Rivettini. When he returned, quoth he, 'The Baron is playing at cards, and cannot be interrupted; but, as there is no *locanda* in the town, you may sleep where you are.' Unwashed, hungry, and tired as we were, and seeing that there was nothing but an old rug by way of furniture in this part of the Baron's premises, we did not feel particularly gratified by this permission, the more that P—— was rather unwell, and I feared he might have an attack of fever; neither did the domestics offer us caffè, or any other mitigation of our wayfaring condition. 'Is there no caffè?' '*Non c'è*.'[23] 'No wine?' '*Non c'è*.' 'No light?' '*Non c'è*.' It was all '*Non c'è*.' So said I, 'Show me the way to the house where the Baron is playing at cards.' But the proposal was met with a blank silence, wholly unpropitious to our hopes of a night's lodging; and it was not until after I had repeated my request several times, that a man could be persuaded to accompany me to a large palazzo at no great distance, the well-lighted lower story of which exhibited offices, barrels, sacks, mules, etc., all indicative of the thriving merchant. In a spacious *salone* on the first floor sate a party playing at cards, and one of them a minute gentleman, with a form more resembling that of a sphere than any person I ever remember to have seen, was pointed out to me as the Baron by the shrinking domestic who had thus far piloted me. But excepting by a single glance at me, the assembled company did not appear aware of my entrance, nor, when I addressed the Baron by his name, did he break off the thread of his

---

22 'Two strangers.'
23 'There is none.'

employment, otherwise than by saying, '*Uno, due, tre, – signore, si – quattro, cinque, – servo quo, – fanno quindici.*'[24]

'Has your Excellency received an introductory letter from the Cavalier da Nava?' said I.

'*Cinque, sei, – si, signore, – fanno undici,*'[25] said the Baron, timidly. This, thought I, is highly mysterious.

'Can I and my travelling companion lodge in your house, Signor Baron, until to-morrow?'

'*Tre e sei fanno none,*'[26] pursued the Baron, with renewed attention to the game. '*Ma perchè,*[27] *signore?*'

'*Perchè,* there is no inn in this town; and, *perchè,* I have brought you a letter of introduction,' rejoined I.

'*Ah, si si si, signore,* pray favour me by remaining at my house. – Two and seven are nine – eight and eleven are nineteen.' And again the party went on with the Giuoco.

There was an anxiety, and an expression of doubt and mystery on the faces of all the party, which, however, did not escape my observation, and I felt sure, as I left the room, that something was wrong; though, like King Coal's prophet of traditional celebrity, 'I knew not what that something could be.'

When I returned to the Palazzo Rivettini, all the scene was changed. Coffee was brought to us, and a large room was assigned for our use, while all the natural impulse of Calabrese hospitality seemed, for a time at least, to overpower the mysterious spell which, from some unknown cause, appeared to oppress those inhabitants of Gioiosa with whom we were brought in contact. But the magic atmosphere of doubt and astonishment returned in full force as other persons of the town came in to the evening *conversazione.* Few words were said but those of half-suppressed curiosity as to where we came from; and the globose little Baron himself gradually confined his observations to the single interrogative, '*Perchè?*' which he used in a breathless manner, on the slightest possible provocation. Supper followed, every part of the entertainment arrayed with the greatest attention to plenty and comfort; but the whole circle seemed ill at ease, and regarded our looks and movements with unabated watchfulness, as if we might

---

24 'One, two, three, – yes, sir, – four, five, – your servant, Sir, – make fifteen.'
25 'Five, six, – yes, Sir, – make eleven.'
26 'Three and six are nine.'
27 'Why, what for?'

explode, or escape through the ceiling at any unexpected moment; so that both hosts and guests seemed but too well pleased when we returned to our room, and the incessant *'Perchè? perchè? perchè?'* was, for this evening at least, silenced.

By all this mystery – so very unusual to the straightforward and cordial manners of these mountaineers – there was left on my mind a distinct impression of some supposed or anticipated evil. 'Coming events cast their shadows before.'*

August 19. Gioiosa
As usual, we rose before sunrise, 'O *Dio!* perchè?' said the diminutive Baron Rivettini, who was waiting outside the door, lest perhaps we might have attempted to pass through the keyhole. A suite of large drawing-rooms was thrown open, and thither caffè was brought with the most punctilious ceremony. My suspicions of last night were confirmed by the great precision with which our passports were examined, and by the minute manner in which every particular relating to our eyes, noses, and chins, was written down; nor was it until after endless interrogatories and more *'perchès'* than are imaginable, that we were released. But our usual practice of taking a small piece of bread with our coffee renewed the universal surprise and distrust of our hosts.

'*Pane!*' said the Baron, 'perchè *pane? O Cielo!*'

'I never take sugar,' said P——, as some was offered to him.

'*Sant' Antonio, non prendete zucchero?* perchè? *O Dio!* perchè *mai non prendete zucchero?*'[28]

'We want to make a drawing of your pretty little town,' said I; and, in spite of a perfect hurricane of *'perchès'*, out we rushed, followed by the globular Baron, in the most lively state of alarm, down the streets, across the river on stepping-stones, and up the opposite bank, from the steep cliffs of which, overhung with oak foliage, there is a beautiful view of Gioiosa on its rock.

'*O per carità! O Cielo! O San Pietro! cosa mai volete fare?*' said the Baron, as I prepared to sit down.

'I am going to draw for half-an-hour,' said I.

'*Ma* – perchè?'

And down I sate, working hard for nearly an hour, during all

---

28 'Do you not take sugar?' etc.

---

* Proverbial.

which time the perplexed Baron walked round and round me, occasionally uttering a melancholy –

'*O signore, ma* perchè?'

'Signore Baron,' said I, when I had done my sketch, 'we have no towns in our country so beautifully situated as Gioiosa!'

'*Ma* perchè?' quoth he.

I walked a little way, and paused to observe the bee-eaters,[29] which were flitting through the air above me, and under the spreading oak branches.

'*Per l'amor del Cielo, cosa guardate? Cosa mai osservate?*'[30] said the Baron.

'I am looking at those beautiful blue birds.'

'Perchè? perchè? perchè?'

'Because they are so very pretty, and because we have none like them in England.'

'*Ma* perchè? perchè?'

It was evident that do or say what I would, some mystery was connected with each action and word; so that, in spite of the whimsical absurdity of these eternal what fors and whys, it was painful to see that, although our good little host strove to give scope to his hospitable nature, our stay caused more anxiety than pleasure. Besides, his whole demeanour so strongly reminded one of Croaker* – 'Do you foresee anything, child? You look as if you did. I think if anything was to be foreseen, I have as sharp a look out as another,' – that it was no easy task to preserve a proper degree of gravity.

His curiosity, however, was to be tried still further; for, having heard that Gioiosa was famous for the manufacture of sugarplums or confetti, we had resolved to take some hence to Gerace, to give to little Cicillo and Maria Scaglione; but when we asked where confetti could be purchased, the poor Baron became half breathless with astonishment and suspense, and could only utter, from time to time, '*Non è possibile! Non è possibile! O gran Cielo! Confetti? confetti?* perchè *confetti? Non è possibile.*'[31] We proved, however, that sugarplums we were determined to have, and forthwith got the

---

29 Merops Apiaster.

30 'For the love of Heaven, what are you looking at? What do you perceive?'

31 'It is not possible! it is not possible! O great Heaven! Sugarplums? *Why* sugarplums', etc.

---

*   A baleful pessimist in Goldsmith's *The Good-Natured Man* (1768).

direction to a confectioner's, whither we went and bought an immense quantity, the mystified Baron following us to the shop and back, saying continually 'perchè, perchè, *confetti! O Cielo!* perchè?' We then made all ready to start with the faithful Ciccio, and, not unwillingly, took leave of the Palazzo Rivettini, the anxious Baron thrusting his head from a window, and calling out, '*Ma fermatevi*, perchè? Perchè *andatevi? Statevi a pranzo*, perchè *no?* Perchè *ucelli?* Perchè *disegni?* Perchè *confetti?* Perchè perchè, perchè, perchè?'[32] till the last *'perchè'* was lost in distance as we passed once more round the rock, and crossed the river Romano.

Long did we indulge in merriment at the perturbation our visit had occasioned to our host, whom we shall long remember as 'Baron Wherefore'. Nevertheless, a certainty impresses me that so much timidity is occasioned by some hidden event or expectation.

Merrily we went through the long garden lanes which stretch away seaward from Gioiosa, over a rich tract of country most luxuriant in vegetables and fruit. Soon we left the coast once more, and winding round the uninteresting olive-clad hill of Siderno, ascended to Agnano, a village on the hill-side above the river Novito, the valley of which stream separates it from the rock of Gerace. From Agnano the eye looks into the very heart of the ravine of the Novito; and high above it on the west below stupendous cliffs, stands Cánalo, a village at the entrance of the Passo del Mercante, a wild route leading across the mountains to the western side of Calabria.

To Cánalo we were bound; it had been described to us by our friends in Gerace as '*Un luogo tutto orrido, ed al modo vostro pittoresco*';[33] and although Grotteria and Mammola were named in the same category, we could not devote time to all three.

We rested an hour at Agnano, with Don Nicòla Speziati, to whom we had a letter; but although there were mines of iron or copper in the neighbourhood which we ought to have gone to see under Don Nicòla's guidance he being the agent for the works – yet we neglected to do so, preferring the search after landscapes of Cánalo to exploring scenes of utility made illustrious by the recent visit of King Ferdinand and his Queen. All the Court had arrived in the preceding autumn on the coast in a steamer, and came hither

---

32 'But stop – *why* do you go? Stay to dinner; *why* not? *Why* birds? *Why* drawings? *Why* sugarplums', etc.
33 'A place altogether horrible; and, after your fashion, picturesque.'

from the Marina of Siderno on a vast crowd of donkeys, collected by the peasantry for the occasion. 'Maestà,' said the owner of the ass on which the royal traveller rode, 'no one else can ever ride on this donkey: it shall have a bit of ground and a stable to itself for the rest of its honourable life. I wish, nevertheless, Maestà, that I had another; for though the honour is great, yet I have no other mode of getting my livelihood.' The King, say the villagers hereabouts, gave the acute countryman all the dollars he had about him, and settled a small pension on him besides for life.

The view of Cánalo from the ravine of the Novito is extremely grand, and increased in majestic wonder as we descended to the stream through fine hanging woods. Having crossed the wide torrent-bed – an impracticable feat in winter – we gradually rose into a world of stern rocks – a wilderness of terror, such as it is not easy to describe or imagine. The village itself is crushed and squeezed into a nest of crags immediately below the vast precipices which close round the Passo del Mercante, and when on one side you gaze at this barrier of stone, and then, turning round, perceive the distant sea and undulating lines of hill, no contrast can be more striking. At the summit of Cánalo stands a large building, the Palazzo of Don Giovanni Rosa, the chief proprietor of the place, an extremely old man, whose manners were most simple and kind. 'My grandchildren,' said he, 'you are welcome to Cánalo, and all I can do for you will be too little to show you my goodwill'; and herewith he led us to the cleanest of rooms, which were to be ours during our stay, and apologized for any '*mancanza*'[34] we might find. 'You must excuse a bad fare today, but I will get you better to-morrow,' quoth Don Giovanni Rosa. The remainder of the afternoon we employed in wandering about the town and its most extraordinary environs, where masses of Titan rock threaten to crush the atoms of life that nestle beneath them. I have never seen such wondrous bits of rock scenery. Meanwhile, old careful Ciccio never lost sight of us; he was always silent, contenting himself by following our footsteps as attendant and guard, lest excess of enthusiasm might hurry us over one of the fearful precipices of Cánalo.

August 20
Every spot around this place possesses the very greatest interest,

---

34 Deficiency.

and is full of the most magnificent foreground studies. All the morning we drew on the hill-sides, between the town and Agnano; and very delightful were those morning hours, passed among the ever-changing incidents of mountain scenery – the goats and cattle among the tall oaks, the blue woody hills beyond. At dinner-time, good old Don Giovanni Rosa amused and delighted us by his lively simplicity and good breeding. He had only once in his long life (he was 82) been as far as Gerace, but never beyond. 'Why should I go?' said he; 'if, when I die, as I shall ere long, I find Paradise like Cánalo, I shall be well pleased. To me "*Cánalo mio*" has always seemed like Paradise – *sempre mi sembra Paradiso, niente mi manca.*'[35] Considering that the good old man's Paradise is cut off by heavy snow four months in the year from any external communication with the country round, and that it is altogether (however attractive to artists) about as little a convenient place as may well be imagined – the contented mind of Don Giovanni was equally novel and estimable. The only member of our host's family now living is a grandson, who was one of our party, a silent youth, who seemed never to do or say anything at any time. Our meals were remarkable, inasmuch as Paradiso cookery appeared to delight in singular experiments and materials. At one time a dish was exhibited full of roasted squirrels, adorned by funghi of wonderful shapes and colours; at another, there were relays of most surprising birds: among which my former ornithological studies caused me to recognize a few corvine mandibles, whose appearance was not altogether in strict accordance with the culinary arrangements of polite society.

Over all the doors which connected the suite of apartments we lived in, were rude paintings of various places, by a native artist, with their names placed below each. There were Naples and Rome, Vesuvius and Etna, London, Paris, Constantinople, and Saint Helena; but as most of these views contained three similar fuzzy trees, a lighthouse, and a sheet of water, or some such equally generic form of landscape, we were constrained to look on names below as more a matter of form than use.

The peasantry of Cánalo were perfectly quiet and well-behaved, and in nowise persecuted us in our drawing excursions. Only a poor harmless idiot followed us wherever we went, sitting below the rock or path we took for our station, and saying, without

35 'My Cánalo always seems Paradise to me, I am in want of nothing.'

intermission, '*O Inglesini! dateci un granicello – wh——ew!*'[36] the which sentence and whistle accompaniment he repeated all day long. Stern, awful scenes of Cánalo! Far, far above, along the pass to the western coast, you could discover diminutive figures threading the winding line among those fearful crags and fragments! or deep in the ravine, where torrents falling over perpendicular rocks echoed and foamed around, might be perceived parties of the women of Cánalo spreading out linen to dry, themselves like specks on the face of some enormous mass of stone; or groups of goats, clustered on some bright pinnacle, and sparkling in the yellow sunlight. Cánalo and its rocks are worth a long journey to behold.

August 21

After dinner at noon, we made our last drawings in this singular place, and bade adieu to the Casa Rosa, with its clean, airy, neat rooms, its painted doors, its gardens, vines, and bee-hives, and its agreeable, kind, and untiringly merry master, old Don Giovanni Rosa. The pleasant and simple hospitality of Cánalo had once more restored us to our former admiration of Calabrian life and its accompaniments, which the little casualties of Gioiosa and Castel Vetere had begun to diminish.

Instead of returning to Agnano, we kept a downward route in the channel of the Novito. Throughout this valley there are interesting scenes of cultivation; the patch of *gran turco* or Indian corn, the shelving terraces of olives, and the cottages here and there, covered with luxuriant vine. Once opposite Gerace, we crossed the river, and gradually ascended to the town, which, with its crumbling white rock, is very grand and simple in form from the northward approach.

On arriving at the Palazzo Scaglione all the family were delighted to welcome us back, including little Cicillo and his sister, to whom the sugarplums were a source of high edification; and it was great sport for us to tell them of all our adventures since we had left them, save that we did not dilate on the facetiae of the Baron Rivettini. All Gerace was in a fever of preparation for a great *festa*, to take place on the following day; and in the evening P—— and I, with Padre Abbenate and Don Gaetano Scaglione, inspected the site of the entertainment, which was

---

36 'O, little Englishman, give me a farthing!'

arranged at the west end of the rock, on the platform by the ruined castle. Here were Zampognari and booths, and dancing and illuminations, all like the days and doings of Tagliacozzo in the *fête* of 1843,[37] but on a smaller and more rustic scale. The Sottintendente, Don Antonio Buonafede, was presiding at the preliminary festivities. There was also, as in the Abruzzo, a temporary chapel erected in the open air, highly ornamented, and decked with figures of saints, etc.; but the usual accompaniments of dancing were expected to be rather a failure, as the Bishop of Gerace had published an edict prohibiting the practice of that festive amusement by any of the fairer sex whatever, so that poor Terpsichore* was to be represented only by the male gender.

August 22
We passed all the morning, being left to our own devices by the good people of our host's family, in a quiet shade on the great rocks east of Gerace.

Parties from all sides of the country were winding up the sides of the ravine to the *festa*; but there was little or no costume, the black skirt, worn mantilla-wise after the fashion of the Civita-Castellanese, being the only peculiarity of dress in Gerace.

In the late afternoon we all repaired to the walls of the town to gaze at the procession of the saint's image, followed by the inmates of every one of the monasteries, and by all the ecclesiastics of the place. On the rocky platform, far below Gerace, yet elevated high above the maritime plain, are several convents, and far, far over the terraces of crags, among which they are built, the long line of the procession crept slowly, with attendant bands of music and firing of cannon – a curious scene, and not easy to pourtray. Hence, as evening was closing and the last golden streams of sunset had ceased to gild the merry scene, we came to the castle, where hundreds of peasants were dancing to the music of the Zampognari; black-hooded women ranged in tiers on the rock-terraces, sate like dark statues against the amber western sky; the gloomy and massive Norman ruins frowned over the misty gulf beneath with gloomier grandeur; the full moon rose high and formed a picturesque contrast with the *festa* lights, which sparkled

---

37 See *Illustrated Excursion in Italy*, McLean. [For Lear's account of the *fête* see above, pp. 144–8.]

---

* The Greek muse of dancing.

on the dark background of the pure heaven; and all combined to create one of those scenes which must ever live in the memory, and can only be formed in imagination, because neither painting nor description can do them justice.

After supper all the Scaglione family wished us a hearty farewell – and may all good betide them! as kind a set of folk as stranger or wayfarer has met anywhere at any time. The days we passed with them will always be recollected with feelings of kindliness for their hearty welcome and friendly hospitality. Separated as Gerace is, though the chief town of a district, from the more civilized parts of Italy, its inhabitants marry chiefly among families in the immediate neighbourhood, and very rarely out of the province. Among the richer classes a few years of youth are passed away at Naples, where the sons attend schools and colleges, and the daughters are educated in nunneries; but after their return to their rocky fortress city, they seldom quit its precincts; and the changes of seasons, as they busy themselves with the agricultural produce of their sea-shore plains, and inland river vales, or the little politics of so narrow a space, alone vary the monotony or calm of Calabrian existence in these days, when mediaeval party wars and the romance of brigandage are alike extinct.

* * * *

August 23. Castelnuovo
Far below us was Castelnuovo, one of the towns which have arisen from the scattered remnant of those ruined by that fatal period of devastation and depopulation so well described above,* when the whole of the western side of Calabria was so fearfully afflicted. Standing on an elevated site above the plain, this modern and unpicturesque successor to the former city exhibits long streets flanked by low one-storied houses, with bright red-tiled roofs, and in no part of its composition does it offer any loophole for admiration, or capability of artistic picturesqueness. We at length arrived at it after a long descent from the hills, and soon found the house of Don Vincenzo Tito, to whom our letter was addressed. Don Vincenzo, who seemed a wealthy proprietor, with a dwelling full of conveniences, seemed to hesitate as to his reception of us;

---

*   In an excerpt taken from the Hon. R. Keppel Craven's *A Tour through the Southern Provinces of the Kingdom of Naples* (1821), describing the earthquake of 1783.

but after a long scrutiny, and many interrogations, he apparently decided in our favour, and, showing us some good rooms, ordered a dinner for us anew, his own being finished. But the manner of our host was abrupt, restless, and uneasy; and his frequent questions, as to whether we had heard anything from Reggio, etc. etc., gave me a stronger suspicion than ever that some political movement was about to take place. Although long accustomed to hear that some change of affairs was anticipated in the kingdom of Naples, and equally in the habit of studiously remaining as far as I could in ignorance of all political acts or expressions, I half concluded that now, as often before, the suspicious reserve of Don Vincenzo, and possibly that of Baron Rivettini also, proceeded from some false rumour afloat. Nevertheless, I confess that more than one trifling occurrence in the last two days had increased my feeling that 'something is about to happen'.

Be this as it might or not, the afternoon passed in wandering around Castelnuovo to obtain some characteristic views of its position, and of the great plain it stands on. This is not easy; studies of tall graceful olives, and Claude-like richness of distance, are innumerable, but the choice among such scenes is difficult. I sate me down by the side of a broad torrent-bed, and drew one of many landscapes; all perfectly pastoral, calm, and elegant, and essentially different in their outline and expression to the scenes of Eastern Calabria.

Before supper we were penning out our drawings in Don Vincenzo's room, and we seemed to puzzle him much by our professional labours and obstinate ignorance, real or assumed, of political events. We have adopted this quiet mode of passing the evening hours of late, as a passive refuge from the persecution of continual interrogations; for the interest our sketches awaken in the families where we may chance to be, fully occupies their attention.

We shall devote tomorrow morning to a visit to San Giorgio, which, by a description of its castle, seems worthy of a walk; and we think of making a chance dash at Polístena, one of the numerous villages dotted over the great plain of cultivation, and to me interesting, as being the native place of one of the best Neapolitan painters – Morani* – whom, years ago, I had been acquainted with in Rome.

---

* Vincenzo Morani (1809–70).

August 24

By long lanes, through the immensely extensive olive-grounds, and by descents into earthquake-marked ravines, – by crossing torrent-beds, and walking in irrigated gardens, we came in three hours to the foot of the hill of San Giorgio, which is an isolated ridge, running out from the central range of hills, and crowned most magnificently with a town and castle. Among the numerous grand positions of towns in this varied land, San Giorgio may bear an eminent place. Thick foliage clothes the steep sides of its pyramidal hill, and its houses are crowded together on plateaux of rock, or are piled up into spires with a beauty and abundant variety striking even in Calabria. As you rise up to its many entrance-paths, the broad blue plains of Gioia and the glittering sea are peculiarly lovely. The costume of the women is here perhaps the best we have yet seen in Calabria, and the wearers certainly the handsomest; but, excepting the interesting groups of figures, the interior of the town of San Giorgio had but little to repay a visit. We lingered awhile in the Piazza, wandered through two or three of its streets, and soon decided on bending our steps to an onward route. Descending once more by olive and chestnut shades to the plain, we arrived, by ten, at Polístena, a large town, where riven rocks, a broken bridge, shattered walls, and desolate streets, bore witness to the fatal catastrophe of 1783.[38]

We easily found the house of Morani's family – '*Quel pittore famoso*',[39] as the town's-people called him, and entering it, were welcomed by his mother and sisters, who seemed pleased that any stranger should inquire after his dwelling. 'These,' said two very nice girls, throwing open the door of a small room, 'are all the works we possess done by our brother'; little supposing that to an Englishman one of the portraits possessed the highest possible interest. It was a small drawing made from Sir Walter Scott during his visit to Naples; and though neither remarkable for beauty of execution, nor pleasing as a likeness, it was highly interesting as the last record of that great man taken from life. '*Si dice questo qui essere uno scrittore famoso*,'[40] said our two hostesses. There, too, was Pio Nono,* a sketch just made from nature.

---

38 Polístena is represented in Pacichelli's work as a fine city.
39 'That famous painter.'
40 'They say that this was a famous author.'

---

* Pope Pius IX (1792–1878), Pope since 1846, and especially popular in 1847 for his sympathy with Italian nationalist aspirations.

August 30. Reggio

We set out for our day's expedition to the hills of Basilicò at early dawn, and retraced our steps along the high road to Naples, nearly as far as Gallicò, a village which stands at the foot of the mountains, and is exquisitely picturesque, owing to its wide streets being entirely webbed and arched over with a network of *pergolate*. Here, as it was Ciccio's native village, we paid a visit to his cottage, where his wife and family gave us heaps of fine figs and grapes, and did all they could to welcome us in their way.

Toiling up a *fiumara* we ascended hence to Calanna, a castellated village, placed in a grand rocky pass; after making a drawing of which, we continued to ascend the hills – looking back on ever-widening views of the Straits and Etna, and forwards towards the heights of Basilicò, on the hills of Aspromonte. But the forests which all the world of Reggio talked of were little worth looking at; those who had described them to us had never seen either Polsi, or Pietrapennata; and we were sadly disappointed with the result of our exertions. At length we reached some few men who were at work at the *Sega*, or sawpits, placed on the highest part of the mountain; these laughed at our questions about 'large oak trees', and grinned incredulously with odd signs which we could not make out. 'Oak trees are all bosh,' said they, 'and you know that as well as we; but as for the men you seek we assure you they are *not* here: but we do not say they are not at Santo Stefano, that village you see below.' In vain we said we sought no persons. 'You are wise to keep your own counsel,' was the reply. So again we saw there was some mystery we could not unravel. Therefore, voting the mountain of Basilicò an imposture, we left it, and came straight down to Reggio. Possibly, after all, we had not gone high enough up in the hills to discover the gigantic oaks. We returned by a different route, and before we reached Reggio it was dark.

August 31

We crossed to Messina, paying twelve *carlini* for a boat, which we took for ourselves. In the fine old cathedral, and in the exquisite views from the higher parts of the city, there is sufficient amusement for travellers, and we, besides, had colours, paper, and wandering artist conveniences of all kinds to look after.

September 1

For three *carlini* I recrossed the Straits in one of the public boats, leaving P—— at Messina to join me at Reggio on the 4th. A fair wind soon placed me on the Calabrian shore, where I found the faithful Ciccio awaiting me with welcome, and a considerable piece of eloquence ending with Díghi-dóghi-dà as usual.

By one o'clock all was in readiness for starting, my passport, as well as a letter from Consigliere da Nava to a proprietor in Mélito, where I am to sleep to-night for the purpose of visiting Pentedatilo, that strange rock-town which we had seen from Bova, and which at all risks I had resolved to examine. So I set off in a *caratella*, for three ducats, all by the dusty pergola-covered high-road of July 29; the views of Etna increasing in magnificence as I approached Capo dell' Armi, to the extreme point of which a *strada carrozzabile** is carried, and where I found Ciccio and his horse already arrived. Leaving the carriage we then struck inland, as the sun was getting low, by mule-routes crossing the frequent *fiumaras* here joining the sea. On advancing, the views of the wondrous crags of Pentedatilo become astonishingly fine and wild, and as the sun set in crimson glory, displayed a truly magnificent and magical scene of romance – the vast mass of pinnacled rock rearing itself alone above its neighbour hills, and forming a landscape which is the *beau-idéal* of the terrible in Calabrian scenery. On the sea-shore, a few miles below Pentedatilo, stands Mélito, a large town, the most southerly in all Italy, and ere we reached it, we arrived at the house of D. Pietro Tropaea, in the outskirts, whose residence is a kind of ill-kept villa; for albeit Don Pietro gave me a most friendly welcome, it is not to be disguised that his *casino*** was of the dirtiest; and when I contemplated the ten dogs and a very unpleasant huge tame sheep, which animated his rooms, I congratulated myself that I was not to abide long with them.

Moreover, it appeared to me that some evil, general or particular, was brooding over the household, which consisted of a wife, haggard and dirty in appearance, and agitated in a very painful degree; an only son, wild and terrified in every look; and a brother and nephew from Montebello, strange, gloomy, and mysterious in aspect and manner. The host also apologized for being ill at ease and unwell. The singular uneasiness of the whole

---

*   *caratella*: a small carriage; *strada carrozzabile*: a road suitable for carriages.
**   A small house.

party increased presently at the sound of two or three guns being fired, and Donna Lucia Tropaea, bursting into tears, left the room with all the family but Don Pietro, who became more and more incoherent and flurried, imparting the most astounding revelations relative to his lady and her situation, which he declared made all his family and himself most afflicted and nervous.

These excuses for so remarkable a derangement as I observed in the manner of all the individuals of the family did not deceive me, and I once more suspected, more strongly than ever, that 'something was to be foreseen'. This feeling was confirmed at supper-time when the assembled circle seemed to have agreed among themselves that it was impossible to conceal their alarm, and a rapid succession of questions was put to me as to what I knew of political changes about to take place immediately. 'Had I heard nothing? Nothing? Not even at Reggio?' 'Indeed I had not.' '*Ma che!* it was folly to pretend ignorance; I must be aware that the country was on the very eve of a general revolution!' It was useless to protest, and I perceived that a sullen ill-will was the only feeling prevalent towards me from persons who seemed positive that I would give no information on a subject they persisted in declaring I fully understood. So I remained silent, when another brother from Montebello was suddenly announced, and after a few whispers a scene of alarm and horror ensued.

'*È già principiata la revoluzione!*'[41] shrieked aloud Don Pietro; sobs and groans and clamour followed, and the moaning hostess, after weeping frantically, fell into a violent fit, and was carried out, the party breaking up in the most admired disorder, after a display, at least so it appeared to me, of feelings in which fear and dismay greatly predominated over hope or boldness.

As for me, revolution or no revolution, here I am in the toe of Italy all alone, and I must find my way out of it as best I may; so, wrapping myself in my plaid, and extinguishing the light, I lay down in the front room on the bed allotted me, whose exterior was not indicative of cleanliness or rest.

Hardly was I forgetting the supper scene in sleep, when a singular noise awoke me. After all, thought I, I am to encounter some real Calabrian romance, and as I sate up and listened the mysterious noise was again repeated. It proceeded from under my bed, and resembled a hideous gurgling sob four or five times

---

41 'The Revolution has already begun.'

reiterated. Feeling certain that I was not alone, I softly put out my hand for that never-to-be-omitted night companion in travelling – a phosphorus box, when before I could reach it my bed was suddenly lifted up by some incomprehensible agency below, and puffing and sobs, mingled with a tiny tinkling sound, accompanied this Calabrian mystery. There was no time to be lost, and having persevered in obtaining a light in spite of this disagreeable interruption, I jumped off the bed, and with a stick thrust hastily and hardly below the bed, to put the intruder, ghostly or bodily, on to fair fighting ground, – Baa — aa — a! —

Shade of Mrs Radcliffe!* it was the large dirty tame sheep! So I forthwith opened a door into the next room, and bolted out the domestic tormentor.

* * * *

September 2
At the hour of one in the night we reached Reggio, and here the secret divulged itself at once.

How strange was that scene! All the quiet town was brilliantly lighted up, and every house illuminated; no women or children were visible, but troops of men, by twenties and thirties, all armed, and preceded by bands of music and banners inscribed, '*Viva Pio IX*', or '*Viva la Constituzione*', were parading the high street from end to end.

'*Cosa x'è stata,*[42] *Ciccio?*' said I.

'*O non vedete,*' said the unhappy muleteer, with a suppressed groan. '*O non vedete? É una rivoluzione! Díghi, dóghi, dà!*'

No one took the least notice of us as we passed along, and we soon arrived at Giordano's Hotel. The doors were barred, nor could I readily gain admittance; at length the waiter appeared, but he was uproariously drunk.

'Is Signor P—— arrived by the boat from Messina?' said I.

'*O che barca! O che Messina! O che belle rivoluzione! Ai! ao! Orra birra burra – ba!*' was the reply.

'Fetch me the keys of my room,' said I; 'I want to get at my *roba*' –

---

42 'What has happened?'

---

*   See note to p. 240.

'*O che chiavi! O che camera! O che roba! ai, ai!*'*

'But where are the keys?' I repeated.

'*Non ci sono più chiavi,*' screamed the excited cameriere; '*non ci sono più passaporti, non ci sono più Ré – più legge – più giudici – più niente – non x'è altro che l'amore la libertà – l'amicizia, e la costituzione – eccovi le chiavi – ai! o-o-o-o-oorra birra bà!!*'[43]

Without disputing the existence of love, liberty, friendship, or the constitution, it was easy to see that matters were all out of order, so, taking Ciccio with me, I went hastily through the strangely-altered streets to Cavaliere da Nava's house. From him, whom with his family I found in serious distress, I heard that a concerted plot had broken out on the preceding day; that all the Government officials had been seized, and the Government suspended, he (da Nava), the Intendente, and others being all confined to their houses. That the telegraph and the castle still held out, but would be attacked in a day or two; that the insurgents, consisting mostly of young men from the neighbouring towns and villages, had already marched into Reggio, and were hourly increasing in number; that on the opposite shore, Messina was also in full revolt; and that the future arrangements of the Government could only be known after time had been allowed for telegraphic communication between Reggio and Naples. The Government *impiegati*** are all naturally dejected, as nothing of their future fate is known, except so much as may be divined from the fact that no one has hitherto been maltreated. Thus, the agitation of the people at Montebello and Mélito; the suspicions of Don Tito, and of the woodmen at Basilicò, and even those of the fat Baron Rivettini, were all fully explained and justified; for whether those persons were for or against Government, the appearance of strangers on the very eve of a preconcerted revolt was enough to make them ask questions, and put them all in a fuss.

I returned to the inn. As for what I should do, there seemed no will of my own in the matter; I might be arrested, or executed as

---

43 'There are no more keys there are no more passports, no more kings, no more laws, no more judges, no more nothing! Nothing but love and liberty, friendship and the constitution!'

---

*   Lear doesn't translate all that Ciccio and the waiter say: 'O don't you see? It's a revolution!' 'O what boat? O what Messina? O what a fine revolution!' etc. 'O what keys! O what room! O what clothing! ai, ai!'

** Officials.

either a rebel or a royalist – as things might turn out; so there was nothing for it but to wait patiently.

All that long night the movement increased: large bodies from Santo Stefano, and other places – most of them apparently young mountaineers – thronged into Reggio, and paraded the streets, singing or shouting '*Viva Pio Nono*', with banners, guns, swords, and musical instruments.

September 3
No boat stirs from Messina. I watch on the beach in vain. I sit with Da Nava and his perplexed family. The telegraph works away incessantly; but there is no attempt to stop it, and no attack on the castle. If there is no movement in the northern provinces, troops will certainly march hither, and, in any case, steamers will come, and this wretched town will assuredly be bombarded into annihilation or repentance. On the other hand, Messina will as surely undergo the same fate, and the more probably, inasmuch as it is of more importance. Nevertheless, as P—— is detained there, and I cannot ascertain what extent of fighting therein prevails (owing to no boats having put off from the Messinese shore), it appears to me better to go over to him if possible.

So, by hard work, I persuaded some very reluctant boatmen to take me: and I quit the Da Nava family with regret, for a cloud of uncertainty seems to hang over all Southern Italy, and the foreshading gloom of it has earliest reached this remotest place.

After intolerable waiting for five hours with a boat-load of depressed and anxious natives, we were towed by oxen as far as Villa San Giovanni, and thence (the sea was rough and the wind contrary) came over to a point about a mile from Messina, where we landed out of reach of the guns of the fort. Here I was glad at Nobile's Hotel to rejoin P—— , whose suspense had been equal to mine. The revolt at Messina has occasioned the death of fourteen or fifteen men; but the Government has firm hold of the citadel. Distress and anxiety, stagnation and terror, have taken the place of activity, prosperity, security, and peace. A steamer comes from Malta tomorrow, and I resolve to return to Naples thereby; for to resume travelling under the present circumstances of Calabria would be absurd – probably impossible.

September 4
Two war-steamers are at Reggio, and firing is heard, though the

details of action are of course unknown to us. The poor town is undergoing evil I fear, nor will it be wonderful that it does so; for that 400 or 500 men should seize and hope to hold permanently a distant part of a large kingdom, unless assisted by a general rising, appears to be the extreme of folly, and can only, whatever the cause of complaint, meet with ultimate ill-success and probably with severe chastisement.

No steamer comes, and we remain at Messina.

September 5
The steamer arrives from Malta, P—— and I go on board, and at six in the evening we sail. Soon the sparkling line of Reggio ceases to glitter on the purple waters; soon we pass the Faro; and the Rock of Scylla, the headland of Nicótera, and the long point of Palmi recede into faint distance.

I leave the shores of Calabria with a grating feeling I cannot describe. The uncertainty of the fate of many kind and agreeable families – Da Nava, Scaglione, Marzano, etc. – it is not pleasant to reflect on. Gloom, gloom, overshadows the memory of a tour so agreeably begun, and which should have extended yet through two provinces. The bright morning route of the traveller overcast with cloud and storm before mid-day.

September 15. Avellino
After numberless irritations from the lies and subterfuges of drivers – for the race of *vetturini** around Naples are odious to deal with – we finally set off at ten a.m.

The road lies through cheerful places: gardens, cottages, and numerous villages and towns are always in sight; but after leaving Prata and Pratola on the left, and Montefuscolo on a high hill beyond, the country grew more and more uninteresting as we approached the mid vertebral line of Italian mountains, here more broken and less striking in appearance than in any other part of the Regno. A tedious descent to the valley of the River Calore, with some monotonous undulations, followed, till we reached Grotta Minarda, during our journey to which the outline of the town of Ariano on the east, and on the west that of Monte Vergine, formed

---

* *vetturini*: drivers. In the much shorter second part of the book, Lear describes his travels from September 11–October 4 in more northerly parts of Calabria, the Principata Citeriore, Basilicata, and Terri di Bari (see map, p. 236).

the principal, or rather the only, features of a wide expanse of country. Picturesquely speaking we were by no means pleased with this part of his Neapolitan Majesty's dominions; but we trusted to find compensation for such barrenness of interest, in Apulian plains, Norman castles, and Horatian localities, by and by to be visited. At a tavern below Grotta Minarda we dismissed our *vetturino*, and dined on the universal and useful Italian omelette and maccaroni.

But now came the difficulty. Where should we go next? and how should we get there? Melfi might be reached in two whole days; but as we wished to devote an hour or so to the 'Mofette',[44] if we could find it, Frigento appeared to us as the most fitting place to sleep at; for although it did not seem clearly understood whether the infernal basin was nearest to Frigento or to Sant' Angelo de' Lombardi, yet the latter place was too far off to be reached before night. Had we been at Gioiosa in Calabria, the Baron Rivettini might well have said, *'Perchè!* do you go to such a disagreeable place as the Mofette? – *Perchè!'*

Much search and earnest persuasion produced a half-witted old man with a donkey which might carry our small quantity of luggage, and after long hesitation he agreed to go with us to the Mofette, the way to which he knew, though, he said, he should not tempt Providence by going very near the spot. He also held out indistinct views of accompanying us all the way to Melfi if he were well paid. The more enlightened inhabitants of Grotta Minarda also said that we should have no difficulty in finding a delightful home at Frigento in the house of Don Gennaro Fiammarossa, who they declared was the wealthiest and most hospitable of living men – '*È tutto denaro, è tutto cuore: possiede Frigento, possiede tutto.*'[45] So we set off resolving to confide our destinies to the care of Don January Redflame, who is all money and all heart, possessing Frigento in particular, and everything else in general.

Frigento was immediately before our eyes, standing on a very ugly clay hill, and although the grandeur of shifting clouds, storm, and a rainbow did their best to illumine and set off the aspect of the land, yet we were obliged to confess that our journey lay over

---

44 'Le Mofette' is the name by which the lake or pool of Amsanctus is known; identified by Antiquarians (see Craven, Swinburne, etc.) with the description.. in Virgil, 'Est locus, Italiae medio, sub montibus altis', etc. ['It is the place in the middle of Italy, beneath the high mountains', *Aeneid*, Book 7, line 563.]

45 'He is all money and all heart: he possesses Frigento – he possesses all things.'

a most wearily monotonous country. Nor, on arriving at the foot of the bare hill of Frigento, had we any wish to make acquaintance with Don January Redflame for the sake of his native place; and it was not until we had peeped into a very unsatisfactory *osteria* at the high-road-side, that we reluctantly resolved to ascend the dismal and ugly cone before us. At the miserable little town of Frigento itself we made one more trial, but the only taverna was so palpably disgusting, that it was not to be thought of as a place of sojourn, even by us, tried Calabrian travellers; and thus we were at length driven to appeal to the hospitality of the benevolent Don Gennaro, whose house is the only large one in the town. Everything in his mansion betokened wealth, and we contemplated with pleasure the comfortable hall with crockery and barrels, and all kinds of neatness and luxury; and until Don Gennaro came, we were pressed to take a glass of wine by the steward and his very nice-looking wife.

But lo! the great January arrived, and all our hopes were turned to chill despair! *'How* grieved he was not to be able to have the pleasure of receiving us, none but he could tell'; – this he said with smiles and compliments, yet so it was. He was expecting an aunt, four cousins (*anzi, cinque*[46]), three old friends, and four priests, who were to pass through Frigento on their way to a neighbouring town; they might come and they might not, but he dared not fill his house. But what of that? There was a capital inn at Frigento, one of the very best in Italy; he would take us there himself; it was time we should be sheltered for the night. And forthwith he led the way out into the street, overwhelming us with profuse expressions of compliment – *'Signori miei gentilissimi e carissimi illustrissimi padroni garbati e cortesi, – amici affezionatissimi,'* etc., till, to our dismay and surprise, he stopped at the door of the very filthy *osteria* which we had ten minutes ago rejected with abhorrence as impracticable and disgusting.

'Viaggiatori culti, eccellentissimi Giovani, ecco qui l'albergo qui troverete tutto, tutto, tutto, tutto, tutto,'[47] said our friend; and, bowing and smiling to the very last, he retreated hastily towards his own house, leaving us very distinctly 'sold', and not a little enraged at Don January Redflame's proficiency in the art of humbug, though

---

46 'Nay, five.'
47 'Polished travellers – excellent young men, here is the inn; here you will find everything – everything.'

we excused him for not desiring to house unknown wanderers in these days of unsettled events.

We turned away from the man 'all money and all heart', and came indignantly down the hill wishing ourselves in Calabria, and composing our minds to the necessity of passing the night at the one-roomed *osteria* at the hill-foot. Here, at least, we found civility, though there was little but the bare walls of the taverna to study: a stove filled up one side of a little chamber, half of which was used as a stable; yet when our new muleteer had cooked us some poached eggs, we made ourselves tolerably comfortable by the fireside, and finally slept well in a granary on large heaps of grain, which had the advantage of cleanliness as well as novelty when considered as beds. The furniture of our dormitory was simple to the last degree: the before-named wheat-heaps, long strings of onions depending from above, and numerous round boxes of eggs below.

* * * *

September 23. Castel del Monte
While riding over the Murgie,* slowly pacing over those stony hills, my guide indulged me with a legend of the old castle, which is worth recording, be it authentic or imaginary. The Emperor Frederick II** having resolved to build the magnificent residence on the site it now occupies, employed one of the first architects of the day to erect it; and during its progress dispatched one of his courtiers to inspect the work, and to bring him a report of its character and appearance. The courtier set out; but on passing through Melfi, halted to rest at the house of a friend, where he became enamoured of a beautiful damsel, whose eyes caused him to forget Castel del Monte and his sovereign, and induced him to linger in the Norman city until a messenger arrived there charged by the emperor to bring him immediately to the Court, then at Naples. At that period it was by no means probable that Barbarossa, engaged in different warlike schemes, would ever have leisure to visit his new castle, and the courtier, fearful of delay, resolved to hurry into the presence and risk a description of the building which he had not seen, rather than confess his neglect of

---

*   The name of this part of the province of Bari.
**   Lear means the Emperor Frederick I (c.1123–90), known as 'Barbarossa'.

duty. Accordingly he denounced the commencement of Castel del Monte as a total failure both as to beauty and utility, and the architect as an impostor; on hearing which the emperor sent immediately to the unfortunate builder, the messenger carrying an order for his disgrace, and a requisition for his instant appearance in the capital. 'Suffer me to take leave of my wife and children,' said the despairing architect, and shutting himself in one of the upper rooms, he forthwith destroyed his whole family and himself, rather than fall into the hands of a monarch notorious for his severity.

The tidings of this event was, however, brought to the emperor's ears, and with characteristic impetuosity he set off for Apulia directly, taking with him the first courtier-messenger, doubtless sufficiently ill at ease from anticipations of the results about to follow his duplicity. What was Barbarossa's indignation at beholding one of the most beautiful buildings doomed, through the falsehood of his messenger, to remain incomplete, and polluted by the blood of his most skilful subject, and that of his innocent family!

Foaming with rage, he dragged the offender by the hair of his head to the top of the highest tower, and with his own hands threw him down as a sacrifice to the memory of the architect and his family, so cruelly and wantonly destroyed.

* * * *

September 25. Venosa
The castle of Venosa[48] is a fine old building of the fifteenth century; it is inhabited at present by Don Peppino Rapolla and his lady. Hither, attended by Don Nicóla,* whom I in vain endeavoured to detach from us, we repaired at early morn, and sate down before it to draw, our polite host lingering by our sides, until, on my telling him that we might be fixed for two or three hours, he at length withdrew. Afterwards we crossed the ravine, and drew the town of Venosa, with its old churches and picturesque houses, and the purple Monte Voltore behind, – one of the most pleasing

---

48 Erected in the fifteenth century by Perro di Balzo, Prince of Altamura and Venosa.

---

* Don Nicóla Rapolla, their host in Venosa. Don Peppino is one of his brothers.

landscapes I had seen in this part of the Regno.

At noon we paid a visit to the castle and its inmates. Don Peppino has modernized one of the great halls into a very delightful drawing-room, where a grand piano and sofas harmonize well with old carved chairs and ornamented ceilings; its pretty and ladylike mistress being the chief charm of the *salon*.

We explored the whole of this old feudal fortress: a long winding stair leads to fearsome dungeons, their sad and gloomy walls covered with inscriptions, written by the hands of despairing captives. Most of these mournful records are dated in the early years of the sixteenth century, and a volume of ugly romances might be gathered from the melancholy list. Then there were four stables to see, each made to hold fifty horses; and a deep moat round the whole castle, with other etcetera – 'quae nunc describere',* etc.

Returning at noon to the Casa Rapolla, we found the dinner-hour fixed at three – woe to us for the fashionable hours of our hospitable hosts! – through which arrangement we fear our afternoon sketching must be relinquished. Don Peppino and his wife were of the party, and the entertainment was excellent in all respects. The conversation is often on English literature – Shakespeare, Milton, etc., on whom there are various opinions; but all agree about *'quel Autore adorabile, Valter Scott!'*** The Canonico reads one of the *romanzi* once a month, and the whole family delight in them; and are also equally conversant with other known English writers. The cuisine is of a much more *recherché* kind than is usually met with in the provinces, and we are particularly directed to taste this dish of *seppia* or cuttlefish, or to do justice to those mushrooms. The wines, moreover, are superexcellent, and the little black olives the best possible; and all things are well served and in good taste.

---

* 'which now to describe'.
** 'that adorable author, Valter Scott!'

'A Leaf from the Journals of
a Landscape Painter
(The Journey to Petra)'
(1858, 1897)

'A Leaf from the Journals of a Landscape Painter (The Journey to Petra)'. Written from journal entries of 1858, published posthumously in Macmillan's Magazine (1897)

Lear described Petra in a letter to Lady Waldegrave on 27 May 1858: 'Petra was the capital of the Nabathoean (or Idumoean) Kings, who reigned in Jerusalem as Herods, and it was one of them who built Masada. The magnificence of Petra is not to be told, I mean the magnificence of combined ruin, splendour of sepulchral architecture and excavated temples, united to the most romantic mountain or rock scenery and the most beautiful vegetation.' It is situated in the Edom mountains of south-western Jordan; nowadays it is part of the tourist trail, but in the 1850s it was a hazardous place to visit, as Lear's narrative dramatically bears out.

He started from Hebron with an escort of fifteen men, planning to remain a week at Petra. The journey through the desert inspires some lively comedy about camels and squabbling incomprehensible foreigners, closer to hostile racial stereotyping than is usual for Lear. But the desert landscape and Petra itself evoke also some of his most magnificent landscape description, rapturous and precise, and at times reminiscent of passages from Coleridge's notebooks and letters. Lear's Suliot servant Giorgio Kokali helps him to transpose the romantic feeling into his own territory of the comic sublime: '"Oh master," said Giorgio (who is prone to culinary similes), "we have come into a world where everything is made of chocolate, ham, curry powder, and salmon."'

This was the only part of Lear's Journals that his executor, Franklin Lushington, saw through to publication, in *Macmillan's Magazine* for April 1897. Lear must have prepared the piece for publication. He may have withheld it because he felt that his *sang-froid* in a crisis might seem boastful (Learence of Arabia?), and perhaps he would have toned down its anti-Arab sentiment. The robbery is really a high Victorian imperial adventure, with the landscape painter behaving, as Peter Levi says, 'as coolly as a Waterloo veteran'.

Hebron Quarantine Building, April 7, 1858
In came my dragoman, Abdel, with various Arabs, and lastly no less a person than the Sheikh of the Jehaleen himself, no other than Abou Daôuk or Defr Alla, the guide to Petra of Robinson* in 1838, and later of De Saulcy.** A child might have read the old Arab's face, which was expressive of an amount of cunning and avarice hardly to be exceeded in one man's countenance. Abdel says, beamingly, that he has made a compact with the Sheikh that I shall go with an escort of fifteen to Petra, to remain there a week, and to return by the Dead Sea, where I am to remain four days between Es Zuweirah and Ain Gedi, for the sum of £30, which is to include the expense of camels and all etcetera.

April 9
We are all moving long before daybreak. Myriads of gay little grasshoppers jump up like spray from the grass at each footfall as I walk. The camels appear good, a matter of great import for such a journey. Mine is a very handsome and young one, and behaves himself tranquilly. Giorgio's looks as if he had been boiled or shaved, but is spare and active. Then there is a huge white Hubblebubble who is evidently a *pièce de résistance* for all the goods the others decline to carry, one for Abdel, one for the Sheikh Salah, the chief guide (who is called the brother of Abou Daôuk), and one

---

*   Edward Robinson, author of *Travels in Palestine and Syria* (1837) and *Biblical Researches in Palestine, Mount Sinai, and Arabia Petraea: A Journal of Travels in the Year 1838* (1841).

**   Félicien de Saulcy (1807–80), a historian from the entourage of Napoleon III, completed several scientific missions around the Dead Sea area during the period from 1845 to 1869.

more for luggage, complete the tale of six. But this last individual turns out to be a violent party, and refuses to be loaded, particularly opposing all attempts to make him carry the cage of poultry, as an uncamel-like and undignified burden. Altogether the din of snarling, growling, screaming, and guggling was considerable; and the lean Jehaleen attendants, of whom there are fifteen, seem a very filthy and incapable lot by way of escort. But it is useless to complain; the Petra journey is to be made now, so be it made as best it may.

April 10

Looking back towards Hebron we are now so high as to be able to see the long plain and mountains drawn out westward in rosy and opal lines, beautifully remote.

A steep descent, down which I walk, leads to a narrow wady, immediately below the last and highest portion of the Sufâa ridge; and this crossed, we begin the ascent, winding slowly and in silence along the narrow paths which for long ages have been the tracks by which this part of the desert is passed. A portion of the view towards the east now suddenly bursts upon the eye – a pale, strange world of sand and rock, plain and hilly undulations; the broad, faint-hued Arabeh beyond, with the clear ultra-marine Moab mountains and what seems a portion of the south end of the Dead Sea to the left. To this glimpse succeeded an hour and a half of threading very hot, close-walled gorges in the mountain at the top of the Sufâa pass, which at 2 p.m. brought us to the full view of the whole eastern prospect – a view most marvellous and not to be easily forgotten. Just before we reached this particular spot, the camels had been unluckily sent round to descend the pass by an easier route than the steep footpath, so that, as I had left my book on my own beast, I was without materials; otherwise the eastern summit of Nukb-es-Sufâa would have tempted me to try a large sketch of it. And yet, though I resolved to remember this lesson of the inconvenience of parting with my tools, I half rejoiced that I was unable to commence the task of pourtraying a scene the chief attributes of which were its astonishing beauty of colour and its infinite detail of forms and masses of rock and sand. I lingered long on this point (old Salah making use of the halt to eat a large luncheon of snails), and it seemed impossible that one could ever weary of contemplating so strange a glory and beauty as that outspread desert and mountain horizon presented. Even the usually silent Suliot said: 'They do well to come to such places who can; no one could believe in such a beautiful world as this unless he saw it!' The whole tract of plain below the Edom mountains is apparently a broad level, of the loveliest lemon-coloured rosy pink, and pearly white delicate hues. Mount Hor, and the hollow lotus-land of Petra, seen from hence, seem almost to blend and melt into the southern sky; while the nearer portion of the Arabeh and all around to the Wady Fikkreh immediately below the height we stood on, is fretted and wrinkled and slashed into miraculously twisted and barred cuts and hollows of brown, orange, chocolate, or snuff-coloured tints. Quite beneath my feet are inconceivable grim chasms, along the downward stretching edges of which my diminished camels creep like flies. I made the descent of the pass or steep eastern side of the mountain on foot, the only pleasant method of reaching the bottom; for although the descent does not appear very formidable, it really is so, since the path leads over vast, slippery, inclined slabs of limestone, often entirely smooth and bare, and affording an insecure foothold for laden beasts. But what a scene of stoniness and cragginess – points and chasms – black grimness, exquisite colours, and strange, wild forms! What strata of giant boulders and rock-forms below! What tawny vastness of lion-coated ridges above! all lit up with the golden light of the afternoon sun – a splendour of wonder – a bewildering, dreamlike, unfinished world – bare, terrible, stupendous, strange, and beautiful!

April 11
As we were progressing towards Mount Hor over a gravelly tract dotted at intervals with shrubs, a little gazelle started up and ran off, three of the Arabs and black Feragh* following it with speed unencumbered by much dress. After twenty minutes the Ishmaelites gave in, but Ebony still held on, and in twenty-five minutes from the first start had tired down the beautiful little creature, which he brought back triumphantly to me, when Giorgio took charge of it. That evening, however, was the last of its life, for without food it soon drooped; and knowing it must have died if left at large, we gave up Giorgio's idea of taking it back to Corfú. I unwillingly gave orders for its flesh to be turned into meat, and its four slender legs into handles for paper-cutters.

---

* 'A black slave of the Haweitât … guide in chief to the wonderful valley of Petra', Lear explains in the entry for 9 April.

April 13

Clear pale sky before sunrise, with long rosy clouds floating pennon-like round the harsh jagged outline of Hor. A particularly early start was ordered, that the mountain might be ascended before the hotter part of the day; but this precautionary measure was, to say the least, modified by the wicked camel's twisting himself viciously against the first rocks he encountered, and shooting all the luggage into a deep hole below. 'I am quite sick of camels,' says the traveller in the East. So I walked onwards and upwards for four hours, glad to be away from the wearisome janglings and yells of my unpleasant suite, and longing with increasing impatience for the first glimpse of Petra's wonders. Every step opened out fresh interest and beauty in the wild scenery; immense chasms and vast views over strange boundless desert unfolded themselves at each turn of the winding path up the steep mountain; and at one spot the intensity of giant-crag solitude, deepest rifts and high pinnacles of naked rock, was more wondrous than anything I have ever seen except the sublimity of Gebel Musa and Sinai. About nine we reached the highest part of the mountain ascent, and passing the ridge immediately below the rocks of Gebel Haroun (Aaron's mountain), now upon our left, entered the first or upper part of Wady Mousa on its western side. But it was nearly another hour before, still descending by winding tracks, we reached the first cavern tombs and the first coloured rocks. The slow advance chills with a feeling of strange solitude the intruder into the loneliness of this bygone world, where on every side are tokens of older greatness, and where between *then* and *now* is no link. As the path wandered among huge crags and over broad slabs of rock, ever becoming more striped and glowing in colour, I was more and more excited with curiosity and expectation. And after passing the solitary column which stands sentinel-like over the heaps of ruin around, and reaching the open space whence the whole area of the old city and the vast eastern cliff are fully seen, I own to having been more delighted and astonished than I had ever been by any spectacle. Not that at the first glance the extent and magnificence of this enchanted valley can be appreciated: this its surprising brilliancy and variety of colour, and its incredible amount of detail, forbid. But after a while, when the eyes have taken in the undulating slopes terraced and cut and covered with immense foundations and innumerable stones, ruined temples, broken pillars and capitals, and the lengthened masses of masonry on each side of the river that runs from east to west through the whole wady, down to the very edge of the water – and when the sight has rested on the towering western cliffs below Mount Hor, crowded with perforated tombs, and on the astonishing array of wonders carved in the opposite face of the great eastern cliff – then the impression that both pen and pencil in travellers' hands have fallen infinitely short of a true portrait of Petra deepens into certainty. Nor is this the fault of either artist or author. The attraction arising from the singular mixture of architectural labour with the wildest extravagances of nature – the excessive and almost terrible feeling of loneliness in the very midst of scenes so plainly telling of a past glory and a race of days long gone – the vivid contrast of the countless fragments of ruin, basement, foundation, wall, and scattered stone, with the bright green of the vegetation, and the rainbow hues of rock and cliff – the dark openings of the hollow tombs on every side – the white river-bed and its clear stream, edged with superb scarlet-tufted blossom of oleander alternating with groups of white-flowered broom – all these combine to form a magical condensation of beauty and wonder which the ablest pen or pencil has no chance of conveying to the eye or mind. Even if all the myriad details of loveliness in colour, and all the visible witchery of wild nature and human toil could be rendered exactly, who could reproduce the dead silence and strange feeling of solitude which are among the chief characteristics of this enchanted region? What art could give the star-bright flitting of the wild dove and rock-partridge through the oleander-gloom, or the sound of the clear river rushing among the ruins of the fallen city? Petra must remain a wonder which can only be understood by visiting the place itself, and memory is the only mirror in which its whole resemblance can faithfully live. I felt, 'I have found a new world – but my art is helpless to recall it to others, or to represent it to those who have never seen it.' Yet, as the enthusiastic foreigner said to the angry huntsman who asked if he meant to catch the fox – 'I will try.'

April 14
By 4 a.m. I had packed up everything inside my tent, in case of accidents, and step out on the grassy terrace. What a scene! Groups of nine or ten Arabs, in all upwards of one hundred in number, are around the tents; many are quarrelling away among themselves at intervals; others watch every movement of Abdel, and are already

asking for sugar, coffee, bread, etc. Abdel and Salah tell them that the *gufr*, or tribute-money, is to be divided fairly, that it is first to be given to the Haweitât, and that they will settle with the fellaheen. The fellaheen say no Haweitât are come or will come, and declare loudly that they will have the tax for visiting their territory now. Our party reply – No; the money is to be given into the hands of the Haweitât by order of Abou Daôuk, Sheikh of the Jehaleen, and we can do nothing till they arrive: a declaration we persist in, though an immense uproar ensues. Suddenly great shouts are heard, and a body of twenty Haweitât really appear, who announce that their Sheikh is on the way, and that no money is to be allotted till that personage reaches the tents, on which the more demonstrative fellaheen protest and appear inclined to attack the twenty Haweitât, but evidently are not sufficiently united to follow any concerted plan, for presently two sets of them fall upon each other, while the Haweitât dispose themselves to remain quiet spectators. I begin to feel convinced that studied drawing in Petra will prove most difficult or impossible, for unless the Haweitât Sheikh brings a very large body of men with him, the different sets of these rabble fellaheen cannot be controlled, and they assuredly have not come so far for nothing. It seems to me that the affair is a trial of strength or right between them and the Bedaween, and that the latter, if only present in small numbers, are likely to be the losers. I therefore order Giorgio to close and watch my tent while I try a visit to Ed Deir, the highest temple far up the ascent to Mount Hor, reserving to the last my chances for a drawing of the theatre and the entrance to the Sik, on the ground that by the time I return from Ed Deir the fortune of the day may perhaps be changed for the better by the arrival of a sufficient number of friendly Arabs.

So under the paternal care of black Feragh and two of the Haweitât, I set out before sunrise to the western cliffs. We crossed the river-bed, and were soon involved in intricate passages among oleander, tamarisk, and large blocks of pale lilac, red and raspberry-ice-coloured stone, up which the pathway led, often by great flights of stairs cut in the stone, often over vast smooth surfaces, through narrow crevices, below gigantic genii-walls and demon-palatial darknesses. Both Arabs threaded the magic staircase with a rapidity I could hardly keep up, brushing the wild fig, thrusting aside the tamarisk, and startling the hoopoe, rockdove and partridge, until the report of a gun below, the echoes of which circled and reverberated like thunder among the

precipices, caused a sudden halt. The Black and Arabs listened
attentively, supposing, I imagined, that some disturbance had
commenced among the gentle villagers in the valley; a second shot
succeeded, but no further sound, so we began to ascend again
through the narrow ravine by a difficult labyrinth of rock-ladder
and tangled shrub and creeper hanging from the sides of the
striped gorge, till we came out on to a wider space, a wonderful
wilderness of coloured crags and chasms, and all kinds of
geological enormities. Here, ever looking about me, I suddenly saw
something move over a cliff far above, and as suddenly disappear.
I called to Feragh, and before I could fix his eyes in that direction,
I saw the same movement twice more, a form bobbing up and
down quickly. The three dark gentlemen held a rapid council
together, which ended in the two Arabs disappearing in a chasm,
and presently we saw them at intervals reappearing on the heights
far above. Shortly afterwards two reports were heard with shouts
and howls in proportion, and as I and the Black climbed upwards,
lo! a slain roe-deer fell toppling over from one of the tallest
precipices at our feet. Down came the two Haweitât; to cut off the
animal's head and double up the body over their shoulders was a
work of short time, and away and up we all rushed again in a
savage triumphal scramble, over still vaster blocks of stone, now
cut into a regular ascent of steps. The views from the heights above
the Meteora monasteries in Thessaly, or in parts of Zagori in
Albania, most nearly of all the landscapes I know resemble this
astonishing scene, but they have not the surprising colours by
which this is made all glorious and strange. At the finish of this
bewildering climb is a platform of moderate extent, and on one of
its sides is the temple or tomb called Ed Deir – solitary and striking,
cut in the solid rock like the Khasmé, but neither so beautiful in
colour nor so attractive in situation, yet a fit crown to the marvels
of the ascent. To me it seemed probably to be a temple, not only
from its position on the platform at nearly the summit of the
mountain, with the cut steps in the gorge leading up to it, but also
from the echoes of sound so distinctly produced from the opposite
rocks, a peculiarity not likely to have been overlooked by any
priesthood aware of the influence of natural sounds and scenes
over the mind. The whole spot had the air of an absolutely
enchanted region, and can never be forgotten by whoever has
penetrated so far.

As soon as we arrived here, the two Haweitât lit a fire, skinned the deer, cooked and ate the liver; but I interrupted their wild feast by the order to descend, as I did not know how much longer the ascent to the top of Mount Hor might occupy, and thought that if the Arabs in the valley below should molest me to the point of preventing much more study, I would rather get one view of the theatre and the Sik-chasm than any other, if only one. Moreover I had agreed with Abdel to be ready about ten o'clock to leave the valley altogether, if staying in it should become increasingly inconvenient. On regaining the ruined terraces above the stream in the valley, I was sorry to find nearly double the number of Arabs I had left there gathered round the tents, not fewer I suppose than 200 in all.

Many of these fellaheen were quarrelling violently with each other, and all were more or less insolent except only the Haweitât, whose Sheikh or headman had now arrived with ten others of his tribe, he riding on a white horse and clad in scarlet robes, but evidently unable with his small party to control the numerous and disorderly rabble around. I felt that I must now decide on my plans, and I was of opinion that no firmness on my part (as in the case of Robinson) of refusing to pay anything except on condition of being left in quiet and with stipulations as to a certain time for drawing, could have availed me anything, since there was here no one person to be relied on as exercising authority over the crowd. Nor, if the comparatively small body of Haweitât were to leave the place or get worsted by any united attack of the fellaheen, was there any guarantee that our tents and baggage would have been sacred in the eyes of the latter worthies. I therefore gave orders that our tents should be struck and the camels loaded, greatly vexed at the necessity of shortening my stay, but glad to have secured yesterday's drawings, and hoping that before these tasks were completed I should still have time to make a last drawing at the theatre.

My Jehaleen escort were not of the slightest use, and did nothing beyond begging me to leave the valley, old Salah alone persisting, in spite of increasing threats from the fellaheen, that he would only pay the *gufr* to the Haweitât, and Feragh busying himself with staving off on all sides the crowd of Arabs, who became more importunate and turbulent every minute, snatching at any object within their reach, and menacing the Jehaleen with their fire-arms.

Meanwhile the patient Suliot brought me some coffee, bread, and eggs, saying with his usual calmness that we had better eat a little, for it might be our last breakfast; and leaving him and Abdel to get all ready, I set off with Feragh and the two Haweitât to the theatre. When I turned to look back from the high ground leading to the Sik, no more picturesque scene could be imagined than that of the two tents surrounded by the agitated rabble in the midst of such singular and beautiful landscape, though the appearance of long lines of fresh straggling Arabs pressing towards the encampment by no means added to the pleasure I derived from the prospect.

I had not long to devote to my drawing from the upper part of the theatre; yet how vivid and enduring are the memories of that half-hour! The pile of vast rocks before me was dark purple and awful in the shadows of the morning, and the perpendicular walls of the wild rent of the Sik were indescribably grand, closed almost at their roots, but reflecting bright sky and white clouds in the stream which burst through them amid thickets of oleander and broom and rushed onward below the semicircle of the ancient theatre cut in the living rock below me. After I had made my sketch, I still felt a longing to see the Khasmé once more; and though through the gorge of the Sik the ill-omened Arabs still continued to come in small parties, I again stood before the wonderful temple. Both Feragh and the two Haweitât, however, positively withheld me from entering the Sik, saying that many of the Dibdiba Arabs were still on their way downwards. So I contented myself with entering the chamber of the Khasmé and wrote my name on its wall (the only place in which I can remember ever to have done so), feeling that if I should come by the worst in the impending affray, I might be thus far traced out of the land of the living. For a fray there was to be – great shouts had been heard for the last few minutes, and the Black became very anxious to get back to the eastern cliff, where he said the money was to be divided, and we should find the camels ready. As I returned down the stream, not unforeboding of mischief, loud and louder cries as from a great crowd echoed among the vast enchanted rock-world. I ascended the steep path leading to the tents, and saw thence our Jehaleen Sheikh's camel near the largest cave at the north end of the east cliff; the cave seemed full of Arabs, and at least a hundred were round its mouth. Others were running to the same point, and as I came in sight of the encampment terrace, I saw that Abdel and Giorgio were coming towards me with the camels, surrounded by a throng of the savages vociferating and mobbing them in their slow progress. A camel, be the exigency what it may, never alters its pace; if anything, the wicked camel on this occasion walked rather less quickly than usual, now and then looking round with an ineffable camel-grin, which said as plain as words, 'Don't you wish you may get me to move on?' There are some narrow steps in the rocks which I wished to pass, but could not before the unlovely community were upon me; so I was compelled to stand still while they rushed by me singly to the number of one hundred and fifty or thereabouts, on their way to their brethren at the cave's mouth. They were in a state of great excitement, and many yelled and threatened as they ran; a few pushed me or pulled my clothes, and one struck me in the face with one of my own hens, adding insult to injury. The last had gone on, when Abdel and Giorgio came up, and with them and the camels I proceeded to the entrance of the cave, where, said Abdel, 'Salah is in the pay of the money from the Arab of the Jehaleen to the Haweitât, and they all fight for about it with another to the other.'

Not only in the cave or tomb and around its mouth was the assembly clustered, but on the paths leading out of the valley northward, intimating very meaningly that we were not as yet to depart. From time to time violent outcries burst from the cave, and the mob without appeared to get more and more excited. Every minute gave plainer proof that the horde of savages was quite disunited and uncontrolled by any authority. More cries from within, and forth rushed twenty or thirty to the camels, which they dragged away from the helpless Jehaleen, when in another moment a larger number fell on the first party, and were for the time masters. The confusion of the scene and the fury of the Arabs increased with every moment, and I expected instantly to see a wholesale dismantling of the imperturbable and lofty Hubblebubble and the wicked camel, whose groans and shrieks of indignation at being pulled this way and that resounded through the valley. All the while, too, parties of the most villainous-looking fellaheen pressed closer on us, and began to insult and annoy us by twitching and jostling. So dense was the crowd, and so impossible any movement of escape, that there was literally but one course left us, that of appearing as far as possible indifferent to the violence one could not resist. For, as Abdel afterwards said, 'When it was one or two fire-temper younger in the striking or the shooting, so he all sudden dead.'

Presently a more supreme uproar arose at the cave's mouth, and

Abdel said that the money which we had brought for the pre-arranged ordinary *gufr* was awarded respectively by the Red Sheikh, but that the many-tribed crowds rejected the division, and immediately a large body of these odious Ishmaelites rushed out in a frenzy of fury with deafening cries, and hustled and dragged us from where we were waiting by the camels to the entrance of the cave. Even among these ruffians there seemed a divided mind, for while some pushed us on others endeavoured to hold us back, and with increasing menaces and ill-usage seemed anxious to proceed at once to a division of the spoil; a consummation only prevented by their want of union, each lot of thieves being fearful of the interference of all the others. The expression of intense rage in their disgusting faces as they put them close to mine, shrieking and howling out, '*Hât! hât!* – give us dollars!' would have been a study for a painter had the circumstances permitted: and it was not easy to keep up the passive air so needful at a time when each moment was adding to our cause of irritation. The tranquil and dignified dodge was however beneficial to our interests; for when one of the younger brutes seized my beard, he was severely rebuked by an elder for this peculiar development of impropriety, though there was no abatement of ear-nipping and arm-pinching, and the Suliot had a hard task to follow my orders and be quiet. Another and a greater clamour now rose again from the great cave, and a fresh supply of savages joined in the tumult outside. A party still more violent than the last succeeded in appropriating us; and these, holding my arms and unbuttoning all my clothing, extracted in a twinkling everything from all my many pockets, from dollars and penknives to handkerchiefs and hard-boiled eggs; excepting only my pistols and watch. Whether they left me these as calculated to carry dissension among themselves from their being unable to divide them, whether from knowing that no one among them could conceal an object of such value, or because they were aware that the fire-arms would be useless to them without percussion-caps, or from thinking the watch an infernal machine, I cannot tell.

During this scramble, in which the Suliot underwent a similar ordeal, the hubbub and yells were incessant, but the great weight of their anger fell upon the unlucky Abdel. 'We will kill your two Howadji, and not be cheated out of our money,' cried one. 'I,' bellowed a second, 'am the man who killed the dragoman two years ago – so you had better give us all you have'; and in less time than I can write it, they had pinioned him (for, though a powerful man, more than twenty were attacking him), had torn off his turban and thrown him on the ground, when, amidst the horrid uproar, I determined to make a last effort to prevent bloodshed if possible. The first pistol-shot would have been the signal for our instant sacrifice, which I believed was probable enough, because the quarrelling among the wretches themselves was becoming so frantic, and the whole scene one of such uncontrollable lawless- ness. I forced my way into the cave, by the very door of which all this was happening, threw myself on the Red Sheikh, who was re- dividing some of the money in the vain hope of appeasing the mob, and uniting to my small amount of Arabic a much larger persuasion of my hands, I pulled him up from his seat and to the door of the tomb, where Abdel was still struggling with his assailants. To these the Sheikh instantly proceeded to deal blows and immense abuse, saying at the same time to us: 'You must pay twenty dollars at once to these men of Dibdiba or I can do nothing for you; after that I will help you on if I can.' Further discussion would have been useless, so I ordered Abdel to pay the money, and immediately that particular body of aggressors wheeled off and left the field, howling and jumping like demoniacs.

The Red Haweitât Sheikh – who, to do him justice, had not seemed aware of the lengths to which the fellaheen were proceeding outside the cave – now mounted his horse, and with several of his followers urged on the camels beyond the last of the caves, and towards the path leading upwards and northwards out of the valley of Petra. He was not, however, allowed to assist us in escaping without fresh bodies of fellaheen making efforts to prevent him, some of them rushing on him and trying to drag him off his horse; nor until he had struck one down with his spear and others had been more or less seriously knocked about, was he able to follow us. In a quarter of an hour we turned out of Wady Mousa; the Red Sheikh, who was evidently still anxious at the anger and numbers of the rabble, left us to return to the cave, saying he must needs go back to prevent further mischief. The Jehaleen escort silently crept after their camels, shorn, alas! of all smaller ornaments, pipes, sacks, and, worst of all, of the whole remains of the poultry except two; and the Desert-Ships themselves began to step forth with their usual measured gait, the wicked camel persevering now and then in stopping to look round with a ridiculously plaintive expression of vexation at leaving the green valley and the pure water.

But hardly were we out of sight of the cliffs, steadily going up the track north-west towards Wady Nemula, when lo! new shouts were heard, and more than thirty guns bristled and sparkled up the hill-side. Headed by five of the most outrageous, and calling on us to stop or they would fire, on they came and surrounded us with their former violence, declaring that they had had no share of the money from the Haweitât, and would by hook or crook have it from us. Resistance was absolutely useless now as before, and the only policy was to save the luggage by giving up more money; after a long parley, seven dollars sent off the savages and left us free once more. Again we moved on, but as we proceeded upwards we saw that the Arabs who left us encountered a smaller party below, and that a row ensued between them; the end of the struggle being that the path again bristled with arms, and a fresh knot of twenty brought us to a halt once more in another ten minutes. Four dollars sent back these horseleeches, and again we proceeded, again to be brought up by ten of the vermin, more enraged than any on account of their longer run, who did not quit us till the last two dollars we had were disbursed to ensure our liberty. Had the Jehaleen had any desire of slaying their Ishmaelite brethren, we might have been a match for this last set, but the sound of gunshots would have attracted the main mob below, and we were still in the heart of the Fellah villages. Three more of the thieves came up with us in another quarter of an hour, and it was Abdel's policy to get them to accompany us as far as possible, until a few reluctantly extorted coppers convinced them that nothing else was to be got. And thus we passed the last hill, looking back into Wady Mousa; a memorable spot to me for more than its wonders and beauties, as I believe that at one time it was extremely probable that our lives would have been taken, not from any premeditated design or love of blood, but in the blind rage of so many furious savages. All along it appeared to me that each odious pack of robbers declined to take on itself the responsibility of unloading and seizing all the goods, because that action would have been the signal for an instant general scramble in which they might have been beaten off by stronger ill-doers. It was the intent of each one to get what he could with the least show of offence to the rest.

from Views in the Seven Ionian Islands *(1863)*

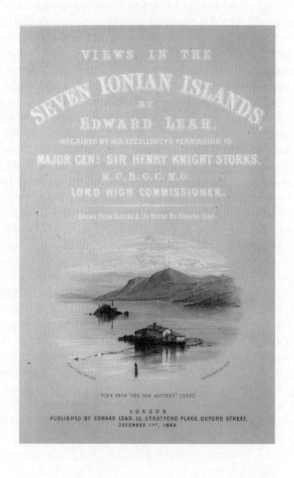

VIEWS IN THE

SEVEN IONIAN ISLANDS,

BY

EDWARD LEAR,

INSCRIBED BY HIS EXCELLENCY'S PERMISSION TO

MAJOR GEN: SIR HENRY KNIGHT STORKS.
K.C.B. G.C.M.G.
LORD HIGH COMMISSIONER.

DRAWN FROM NATURE & ON STONE BY EDWARD LEAR.

VIEW FROM "ONE GUN BATTERY" CORFÚ

LONDON
PUBLISHED BY EDWARD LEAR, 15, STRATFORD PLACE, OXFORD STREET,
DECEMBER 1ST, 1863.

from Views in the Seven Ionian Islands *(1863)*

This book interrupts the sequence of 'Journals of a Landscape Painter', and reverts to the more formal mode of lithograph with descriptive text which Lear had used for the second volume of *Illustrated Excursions in Italy*. Like the *Views in Rome* and *Illustrated Excursions*, it was published by subscription, and Lear had the onerous and demoralizing task of writing to 600 potential subscribers and then chasing up their three guinea payments. He produced it partly as a moneyspinner. His oil paintings had not been selling, and it was a good moment to cash in on the interest in the Ionian Islands just before their cession to Greece in 1864.

Corfú and the other islands had passed from Venetian to French rule in 1797, then to the British under the terms of the Congress of Vienna in 1815, and had stayed British in the face of growing Greek protests even after the founding of the modern Greek state in 1830. It was a strangely and uneasily multicultural place, with Italian the first language, Greek the official language of law and government, and most business in practice conducted in English under the British administration. But when Prince William of Denmark became King of the Hellenes in 1863, the cession of the Ionian islands to Greece was a condition in return for the anglophile monarch: Corfú and Paxos were neutralized militarily, and their fortresses demolished – hence Lear's note below to the vignette of what had formerly been 'One-Gun Battery' (see p. 302)

Lear had first visited Corfú in 1848, and spent his winters there from 1856 to 1863. He had mixed feelings about life in what was essentially a colonial outpost. 'A more rotten, dead or stupid place than this existeth not,' he wrote in a letter in 1857, and again, in 1861 'the aspect spiritual of this little piggywiggy island is much as a very little village in Ireland would be – peopled by Orangemen and papists – and having all the extra fuss and ill-will produced by a Court and small officials'. But he missed it when he had to leave: 'the farther I go from Corfú – the more I look back to the delight its beautiful quiet has given me,' he wrote in June 1863, when the beauty of the islands was fresh in his mind from the eight week tour he had made in March and April 1863 to gather views for the book.

The book was published without a map, but the map for the *Journals of a Landscape Painter in Albania* shows the position of the islands (see p. 167).

Introductory

The purpose of this Work is to offer to the Public a Collection of Views characteristic of the Scenery of the Seven Ionian Islands. To this intent I shall confine myself, so far as regards the literary part of the volume, to a short description of the Drawings, and to a few general remarks on the Scenery of each of the Islands. [...] At a time when so great a change in the destiny of these Islands is about to occur, the present book, illustrative of places, hereafter perhaps, to be as little visited by our countrymen as they have been familiarly known to them for nearly half a century, may have a more than ordinary claim to be thought interesting.

An Englishman could hardly travel in any part of Europe possessing in so remarkable a manner three different character-istics rarely found combined, viz. the beauty and variety of form and colour so generally prevailing on the shores of the Mediter-ranean; the associations of poetical and historical antiquity which pervade the classical land of Greece; and the hearty welcome and joyous hospitality which, at every stage of his journeying through the Islands, the tourist receives from his fellow-countrymen. Of these three distinguishing characteristics, the third is alike noticeable in all the Seven Islands: for while Corfú is greatly superior to the other six in exquisite delicacy of numberless landscapes, and while none can be compared with Ithaca in the classic interest for which every part of it is renowned, each of the Seven Islands is equally fixed in the memory of the traveller from its association with the friendly assiduity shown by all who are able to promote his plans.

I should be glad to acknowledge here the many and valuable kindnesses I have received during a residence of the greater part of six years in these Islands, not only from three Lords High Commissioners – the late Lord Seaton, Sir John Young, and Sir Henry K. Storks – but also from their Secretaries, Sir George F. Bowen, and Sir Henry Drummond Wolff. [...] Nor can I omit noting the never-failing courtesy and friendliness which have been shown me by the native inhabitants of the Islands, – whether as to the upper classes, in placing their houses at my disposal if I travelled in the more unfrequented districts, and by their welcome if I sojourned with their families; or, as to the peasantry, by their humbler, yet not less amiable, efforts to please and assist the traveller.

15 Stratford Place,
November 1863.

CORFÚ

First of the Seven Islands in importance, and the chief seat of the Government of the Septinsular Republic, Corfú is also superior to the other six, both in the beauty of its scenery, and of its position as regards the main-land. With the variety and delicacy of the former, that of none of the others can compare; and, with regard to the latter, it lies so close to the lofty mountain-ranges of Epirus, as to include the grand features of the opposite coast in most of the views which can be taken from its own central hills. Whilst the noble line of the snowy Albanian heights thus forms the magnificent background of every picture if you look to the East, on the West the broad sea spreads from the foot of romantic precipices; to the North rises the ever-beautiful Mount San Salvador; and, towards the South, are the long lines of Lefchimo and the Channel widening into the open Mediterranean. Everywhere the olive-tree grows in abundance and gracefulness; one of the greatest charms of Corfú being the perpetual framing of beautiful scenes by its twisted branches, and the veil-like glitter it throws around by its semi-transparent foliage.

The City stands on the sea, and contains no particularly

noticeable characteristic, except that from it the view towards the Channel and Eastern mountains is one of the loveliest the world can offer to those who delight in nature.

The population of the Island of Corfú, including that of the City, is about 68,000. The peasants are a picturesquely costumed race, though not so much so as those of Santa Maura or Cerigo.

VIGNETTE TITLE. VIEW FROM 'ONE-GUN BATTERY', CORFÚ
This little drawing represents a scene known to most of those who have been to Corfú , the 'One-Gun Battery' now being merely a level space at the end of the usual carriage-drive, at a distance of two or three miles from the City. Of the two small Island Monasteries shown in the Vignette, the farthest is, according to tradition, the ship of Ulysses turned into rock. Beyond, are the hills (south of Santi Dekka) above the village of Benitza.

CAPI DUCATO, OR SAPPHO'S LEAP,* SANTA MAURA
This grand cliff scene is at the South-western point of the island of Santa Maura, and is well worthy of a visit, though not reached without considerable trouble. The great rocks rise boldly from the dark, deep waters, often raging against their base; and the solemn effect of that part which is in shadow is enhanced, in the early morning, by the bright light sparkling on the white crags, which, fringed by the wild cypress, overhang the gloomy depth below.

On each of the two farthest cliffs are the remains of an ancient Temple – blocks of stone and scattered pottery; a spot once trodden by the feet of crowding votaries, now the haunt of the vulture and eagle.

VIEW FROM THE VILLAGE OF GALÁRO, ZANTE
This View, taken from a village on the slope of the western hills of Zante, shows the Plain of Currant-Vines before mentioned, which is only varied by scattered olive-trees and sparkling white villas.

The old nursery-rhyme –

If all the world were apple-pie,
And all the trees were bread and cheese –

---

*   The Greek poet Sappho (c.625–570 BC) was said to have thrown herself to her death from this spot, in some accounts out of unrequited love for Phaon.

supposes a sort of Food-landscape hardly more remarkable than that presented by this vast green plain, which may be, in truth, called one unbroken continuance of future currant-dumplings and plum-puddings.

To the left, the Drawing is bounded by the Castle Hill, behind which stands the City of Zante; and in the center is Mount Skopó. The foreground is full of Olives and of luxuriant Aloes, throwing out their flower-stems (not unlike Asparagus-stalks on a gigantic scale), shortly to burst into bloom.

from Journal of
a Landscape Painter in Corsica
(1870)

from Journal of a Landscape Painter in Corsica
(1870)

Lear's position in this book is that of a tourist in recognizably modern mode, as against the more ambitious adventurer of his earlier journals. He had grown older, too, and fatter, and travelled now by carriage instead of on foot and horseback. He made three tours of the island between April 9 and June 6 1868. The journals start rather gloomily in Ajaccio, bemoaning the lack of animation and colour in the locals and their garb, and – though he later discovers more to admire in the landscape and in the Corsicans – they mostly lack the sparkle and high spirits of the earlier books (in ways which a selection of the best excerpts will inevitably mask).

He was furnished with introductions by the French novelist Prosper Mérimée, whose *Colomba* had fictionalized a famous Corsican vendetta (Lear gets to meet the nephew of the title figure). Corsica had become a stabler place by 1868, though its divided history as first a Genoese and then from 1768 a French colonial possession produce some moments of tension for Lear, whose French is thought to be suspiciously less good than his Italian.

Preparation of the book was fraught with difficulties. Smith and Elder expressed interest in publishing the book provided the costs were kept low. With this in mind, Lear prepared one volume instead of the two he had wished, and went to trouble and expense in making wood engravings instead of the more expensive lithographs he would have preferred. On receipt of sample engravings, whose quality was disappointing, Smith and Elder pulled out of the venture. Another publisher, Bush, agreed to go ahead with the book 'if cheaply got up', with cheaper blocks for the engravings. Lear was very dissatisfied with the eventual quality of the illustrations, which he thought 'coarse and queer': readers can compare the illustration on p. 319 with those on pp. 154, 218 and 245 to get some sense of the differences. He worked hard on the book throughout 1869, and it appeared in time for Christmas that year (though it is dated 1870), costing one pound to subscribers and one pound ten shillings to other buyers.

Preface

In the years 1846, 1849, and 1852, I published illustrated journals of tours in Central and Southern Italy, and in Albania, three books which met with a successful reception from the Public, and were very kindly noticed by the Press.

The present volume consists of journals written with the same intent and plan as those which preceded them. They describe, nearly word for word as they were written, my impressions of the nature of the landscape in those portions of Corsica through which I travelled. It is possible that the literary part of this book may not prove of equal interest with that of the publications above named; not, indeed, from any want of merit in the subject, but because I have now no longer the help of friends who then kindly assisted me by their criticisms, especially the late Robert A. Hornby, Esq., and Richard Ford, Esq. But the aim of all these journals should be looked on as the same, simply to be aids to the knowledge of scenery which I have visited and delineated.

I passed last winter at Cannes, intending to return early in the spring to Palestine, for the purpose of completing drawings and journals for a work already partly advanced;* but circumstances having prevented me from carrying out this plan, I decided on going to Corsica, rather perhaps on account of its being a place near at hand and easily reached, than from any distinct impression as to the nature of the country, or from any particular interest in its history, inhabitants, or scenery. It is true that the Corsican

---

* Lear had planned to prepare his journals of tours to Crete and the Nile for publication.

mountains are sometimes visible from Cannes at sunrise, and latterly I had read M. Prosper Mérimée's beautiful little tale of *Colomba*,* the scene of which lies in Corsica; but I confess to having been chiefly led to think of going there by that necessity which the wandering painter – whose life's occupation is travelling for pictorial or topographical purposes – is sure to find continually arising, that of seeing some new place, and of adding fresh ideas of landscape to both mind and portfolio –

For all experience is an arch, wherethrough
Gleams the untravell'd world, whose margin fades,
For ever and for ever when I move.**

* * * *

A few words on the arrangements preliminary to such travelling may be allowed. Some there are who declaim against carrying much luggage, and who reduce their share of it to a minimum. From these I differ, having far more often suffered from having too little *roba* than too much. Clothing for travelling comfortably in hot or cold climates, such as must be experienced in the plains and mountains of an island so varied in formation as Corsica, and for different phases of social life during an extended tour; great amount of drawing material, folios, paper, etc.; an indian-rubber bath; above all, a small folding camp or tent bed, of good use in many a long journey in Albania, Syria, etc., and in which I am sure of sleep anywhere; these, mostly contained in a brace of strong saddle-bags, form a goodly assortment of luggage, and eventually I found it to be not one iota too much.

Then, as to travelling alone, the prospect of which is dreadful to some, I almost always do so by preference, because I cannot otherwise devote every moment to my work, or so arrange plans as to ensure their success. Sometimes, indeed, I have made exceptions to this rule, yet only in cases where my fellow-travellers were not only as eager draughtsmen as myself, and where I, being their senior, as well as instructor in sketching, could define and follow all my own plans exactly and without hindrance. Strictly

---

* In Mérimée's *Colomba* (1840), set in Corsica, Colomba tries to bring her brother Orso to avenge the murder of their father.
** Slightly misquoting Tennyson, 'Ulysses', lines 18-20 ('For' instead of 'yet'; 'the' instead of 'that').

speaking, however, it is long since I made any tours really alone, as various sharp illnesses have taught me the great inconvenience of doing so; and I have frequently been thankful for the care of a good servant who has travelled with me for many years. George Kokali, a Suliot, speaking several languages, sober, honest, and active, saves me all trouble and gives none; now carrying a weight of cloaks and folios and 'daily bread' for a twenty-mile walk or more, anon keeping off dogs and bystanders when I am drawing, or cooking and acting as house-servant when stationary; a man of few words and constant work.

April 9. Ajaccio
The night voyage,* though far from pleasant, has not been as bad as might have been anticipated. He is fortunate, who, after ten hours of sea passage can reckon up no worse memories than those of a passive condition of suffering – of that dislocation of mind and body, or inability to think straightforward, so to speak, when the outer man is twisted, and rolled, and jerked, and the movements of thought seem more or less to correspond with those of the body. Wearily go by

The slow sad hours that bring us all things ill**

and vain is the effort to enliven them as every fresh lurch of the vessel tangles practical or pictorial suggestions with untimely scraps of poetry, indistinct regrets and predictions, couplets for a new *Book of Nonsense* and all kinds of inconsequent imbecilities – after this sort –

Would it not have been better to have remained at Cannes, where I had not yet visited Theoule, the Saut de Loup, and other places?

Had I not said, scores of times, such and such a voyage was the last I would make?

Tomorrow, when 'morn broadens on the borders of the dark', shall I see Corsica's 'snowy mountain tops fringing the (Eastern) sky'?***

Did the sentinels of lordly Volaterra see, as Lord Macaulay says

---

*   From Nice to Ajaccio.
** Tennyson, 'Love and Duty', line 57.
*** Tennyson, 'A Dream of Fair Women', line 265 ('broaden'd').

they did, 'Sardinia's snowy mountain-tops', and not rather these same Corsican tops, 'fringing the southern sky'?*

Did they see any tops at all, or if any, which tops?

Will the daybreak ever happen?

Will two o'clock ever arrive?

Will the two poodles above stairs ever cease to run about the deck?

Is it not disagreeable to look forward to two or three months of travelling quite alone?

Would it not be delightful to travel, as J.A.S.** is about to do, in company with a wife and child?

Does it not, as years advance, become clearer that it is very odious to be alone?

Have not many very distinguished persons, Œnone among others, arrived at this conclusion?

Did she not say, with evident displeasure –

And from that time to this I am alone,
And I shall be alone until I die? –***

Will those poodles ever cease from trotting up and down the deck?

Is it not unpleasant, at 56 years of age, to feel that it is increasingly probable that a man can never hope to be otherwise than alone, never, no, never more?

Did not Edgar Poe's raven distinctly say 'Nevermore'?

Will those poodles be quiet? 'Quoth the raven, nevermore'.****

Will there be anything worth seeing in Corsica?

Is there any romance left in that island? Is there any sublimity or beauty in its scenery?

Have I taken too much baggage?

Have I not rather taken too little?

Am I not an idiot for coming at all? –

Thus, and in such a groove, did the machinery of thought go on, gradually refusing to move otherwise than by jerky spasms, after

---

* Macaulay, 'Horatius. A Lay made about the Year of the City CCCLX', lines 31–2.
** John Addington Symonds. It was for Symonds's daughter Janet that Lear wrote 'The Owl and the Pussycat'. He and Lear are the main speakers in 'Growling Eclogue', pp. 43–6, above.
*** Tennyson, 'Oenone', lines 179–80.
**** Poe, 'The Raven', lines 25, 48, 84, 96, 102.

the fashion of mechanical Ollendorff* exercises, or verb-catechisms of familiar phrases –

Are there not Banditti?

Had there not been Vendetta?

Were there not Corsican brothers?

Should I not carry clothes for all sorts of weather?

Must *THOU* not have taken a dress coat?

Had *HE* not many letters of introduction?

Might *WE* not have taken extra pairs of spectacles?

Could *YOU* not have provided numerous walking boots?

Should *THEY* not have forgotten boxes of quinine pills?

Shall *WE* possess flea-powder?

Could *YOU* not procure copper money?

May *THEY* not find cream cheeses?

Should there not be innumerable moufflons?

Ought not the cabin lamps and glasses to cease jingling?

Might not those poodles stop worrying? –

thus and thus, till by reason of long hours of monotonous rolling and shaking, a sort of comatose insensibility, miscalled sleep, takes the place of all thought, and so the night passes.

* * * *

On a nearer approach Ajaccio does not seem to me to present any special beauty or interest; no charm either of colour or architecture in public or other buildings salutes the eye of the painter. There are lines of respectable-looking, lofty, and bulky houses – they may be likened to great warehouses, or even to highly magnified dominoes – with regular rows of windows singularly wanting in embellishment and variety; but there is no wealth of tall campanile or graceful spire, no endless arches or perforations or indescribable unevennesses, no balconies, no galleries, as in most parts of Italy, in the dull lines of buildings here; no fragmentary hangings, no stripes, no prismatic gatherings of inconceivable objects, far less any gorgeous hues, as in Eastern worlds. Perhaps the place I thought of at first as being likest to Ajaccio was Rapallo, on the Riviera di Levante, a town, if I remember rightly, one of the least gay or ornamented on that beautiful coast.

Still more striking is the absence of colour, and of any peculiarity

---

*   H.G. Ollendorff (1802–65), author of foreign language textbooks.

of costume in the dress of both sexes. Almost all are in black, or very dark brown, and to a new comer who has travelled in the East and South everything has a dull and commonplace, not to say a mournful, air. The boatmen who convey me, my man, and luggage, to the shore, are quiet and solemn; and, on reaching the landing-place – ah, viva! once more the solid ground! – the sober propriety of demeanour in the groups standing round is remarkable; the clamour and liveliness of an Italian port, the wildness and splendour of an Eastern quay are alike wanting; the countenances of both men and women are grave, and the former have an inactive and lazy manner; so that, whether or not I am prejudiced by the damp and overcast gloom of the day, my first impressions of the Gulf of Ajaccio and of the capital of Corsica are not of a lively character. Among the notes I have had forwarded to me by the last post from friends in England who knew of my coming to this island, are some written by a naturalist, who mentions, among other creatures peculiar to Corsica, the *Helix tristis;* and, in my present mood, I feel that the melancholy snail was right when he chose a sympathetic dwelling.

* * * *

But how rural – now that I have explored most parts of Ajaccio – does this city seem! How little activity and movement in its streets! How abounding with children and how destitute of men! How scantily furnished is the sea with craft! How lazy seem a great portion of its inhabitants! The brisk little French soldiers alone redeem the dullness of the town scenes, their bright red trousers almost the only gleam of colour in a world of black and brown; their lively walk and discourse nearly the only signs of gaiety. City, quotha! might it not, O sympathetic *Helix tristis,* rather be called a village?

April 11. Ajaccio
There remains this plan, on which, after looking at the matter in all its bearings, I finally decide – namely, to hire a two-horse carriage for the whole time of my stay, paying for it so much daily, and using it for long or for short journeys, either as there may be much or little to draw, or according to the distance of halting places. In this way I should be free to make drawings in the neighbourhood of the principal towns, or to make excursions from them to various

points; and if any scene on the high road could not easily be returned to, owing to too great distance, I might halt my vehicle while I worked, or perhaps oftener send it on and walk; on the other hand, I could drive as quickly as possible through districts in which there is little of the picturesque. This plan of travelling, though apparently the most expensive, will economize time, and in the end, I believe, will prove the cheapest; for my object in coming to Corsica being that of carrying away the greatest possible number of records of its scenery, the saving some outlay will not compensate for a meagre portfolio, and I might ultimately discover the least costly process to be also the least satisfactory. In support of which hypothesis a fable taught me long years ago by one dead and gone recurs to my memory.

Once upon a time three poor students, all very near-sighted, and each possessing a single pair of horn-rimmed spectacles, set out to walk to a remote university, for the purpose of competing for a professorship.

On the way, while sleeping by the road-side, a thief stole their three pairs of horn-rimmed spectacles.

Waking, their distress was great: they stumbled, they fell, they lost their way; and night was at hand, when they met a pedlar.

'Have you any spectacles?' said the three miserable students.

'Yes,' said the pedlar, 'exactly three pairs; but they are set in gold, and with magnificent workmanship; in fact, they were made for the king, and they cost so much ——'

'Such a sum,' said the students, 'is absurd; it is nearly as much as we possess.'

'I cannot,' the pedlar replied, 'take less; but here is an ivory-handled frying-pan which I can let you have for a trifling sum, and I strongly recommend you to buy it, because it is such an astonishing bargain, and you may never again chance to meet with a similarly joyful opportunity.'

Said the eldest of the three students, 'I will grope my way on as I can. It is ridiculous to buy a pair of this man's spectacles at such a price.'

'And I,' said the second, 'am determined to purchase the ivory-handled frying-pan; it costs little, and will be very useful, and I may never again have such an extraordinary bargain.'

But the youngest of the three, undisturbed by the laughter of the two others, bought the gold-rimmed sumptuous spectacles, and was soon out of sight.

Thereon, No. I set off slowly, but, falling into a ditch by reason of his blindness, broke his leg, and was carried back, by a charitable passer-by in a cart, to his native town.

No. 2 wandered on, but lost his way inextricably, and, after much suffering, was obliged to sell his ivory-handled frying-pan at a great loss, to enable him to return home.

No. 3 reached the University, gained the prize, and was made Professor of Grumphiology, with a house and fixed salary, and lived happily ever after.

Moral – to pay much for what is most useful is wiser than to pay little for what is not so.

* * * *

Next as to baggage. Not knowing in the least what sort of accommodation is to be met with, I shall carry a good supply. Dividing my *roba*, and leaving part of it with my host, M. Ottavi, I shall take lots of drawing material, and clothing for hot and cold weather, besides my small folding bed; so that, with my servant's help, I may at least be as comfortable as in Albanian *khans*, Cretan cottages, or Syrian sheds. For it is certain that at 56 'roughing it' is not so easy as at 30 or 40, and if good rest at night is not to be procured, the journey may as well be given up, for there would be an end of work. Last of all, a fitting carriage and driver are to be found, and price, etc., agreed on.

Here is a visit from M. Martinenghi; he kindly offers to show me some pictures in his possession, some by Salvator Rosa, etc., and appears confounded at the little enthusiasm I express on the subject, and at my declining the proposal. In this hotel there resides an English lady – a Miss C.* – who has not only been here for some months, but has visited many parts of the island; and before I set off I shall venture on a visit to her, to get some hints about my journey.

Noon. — What is going to happen? A remarkable clattering noise fills the air. I look out of window, and behold a torrent of children – a hundred, at least – all carrying bits of wood, which they knock,

---

* Thomasina M.A.E. Campbell, author of *Notes on the Island of Corsica in 1868*, 'an unpretending excellent little book, written in a pleasant spirit', according to Lear's 'List of some of the principal Publications relating to Corsica'. Miss Campbell, we hear in Lear's journal, was 'a vast and man-like maiden' who 'goes roaring about Corsica'.

and bump, and rattle against all the railings, doorsteps, and walls, as their procession passes on. Now, in most southern places where Christians are desirous of celebrating Easter by triumphant noises, pistols and crackers are fired off at the proper time; every one who has been in Rome at that season is aware of the uproar made on the Saturday preceding Easter Day; and in the Maltese villages, at Alexandria, and other eastern cities, the hullabaloo is fearful. But here, in Corsica, no firearms of any sort are at present allowed to be in the hands of the people, and so the popular piety finds vent in this singular outburst of rattling pieces of wood, which, I am told, has a dim reference to Judas Iscariot, the thumps on the rails and stones being typical of what the faithful consider that person's bones, were he living, should receive.

April 12. Ajaccio
After dinner I visit Miss C., whose acquaintance indeed is well worth cultivating. Her interest in Corsica and all it contains is extreme. The collection of plants and natural history she has made in the island, and her drawings of the numerous fish found here, must have fully occupied her leisure through the winter; she has already accomplished some long mountain excursions, and really knows the island well. A person uniting great activity of mind, physical energy, good judgement and taste, as this lady appears to do, and bent on introducing Corsica to the English south-seeking public, may really become instrumental in bringing about great changes in Ajaccio.

April 15. Ajaccio
The kindly Miss C. has sent me a flask in place of the one lost, and calls from the window, cheerfully, 'You should have taken my man Jean! all your luggage will fall off! your horses will tumble! everything will go wrong!' Absit omen!* and finally we start at 3.30.

* * * *

Cauro
Hardly had I sat down to supper than I found I had committed an error, into which a little previous thought might have prevented my falling; yet, with the very best intentions, a man may sometimes

---

*   May this not be an omen!

'rush in where angels fear to tread'. One of the party spoke French with a Parisian accent, the others were Corsicans. '*Vous êtes donc Français, Monsieur?*' said I; a remark which directly produced a sudden chill and pause, and after that came this reply – '*Monsieur, nous sommes tous Français.*'* I had yet to learn that the words 'French' and 'Corsican' are not used by the discreet in this island; you should indicate the first by 'Continental', and the second by 'Insulaire' or *du pays*.** It is as well, indeed, to recollect that there are old men still living who can remember the hopes of Corsican independence even up to the end of the last century, and, consequently, all allusions by a stranger to differences of race are as well avoided, now that both people are under one government.***

The fact, too, that I spoke Italian with greater facility than French evidently puzzled my supper companions, and when I asked questions about the country, there was a kind of occult distrust observable; travellers in Corsica – in out-of-the-way places at least – are rare; might I not be a revolutionary agent? I asked about the wines made in the island, but when ill luck urged me to speak about Sardinian produce, dumbness or short replies ensued, and at once I found that Sardinia was a tabooed subject. The better I spoke Italian and the more I hesitated in French, the less respectable I became, and since at the commencement of travelling in a new country one has all to ask and learn, my numerous inquiries were received and answered with caution, and my evil genius having suddenly prompted me to ask something about the Straits of Bonifacio, there was again a full stop, and a sensation as if all Caprera-cum-Garibaldi**** were about to burst into the room.

April 19. Sartêné
At 5.30 a.m. I walk down the hill, and drawing more or less by the way, gradually reach my farthest point, the bridge over the Tavaria, a distance of some eleven kilometres, or seven miles. Such a walk here, at early morning, is unboundedly full of pleasant items; the whistle and warble of countless blackbirds, and the

---

*   'You are a Frenchman, then, Sir?' 'Sir, we are all Frenchmen.'
**   *du pays*: of the country.
*** Corsica was under Genoese rule until in 1768 it was handed over to the French, who subdued the nationalist revolt of Paoli in 1769.
**** Presumably suggesting an invasion of Italian nationalists following Garibaldi. Caprera is a small island off the north coast of Sardinia; the Straits of Bonifacio separate Sardinia and Corsica, only about ten miles apart at the nearest point.

frequent cuckoo's note; flowers everywhere, especially the red cyclamen, blue vetch, yellow broom, tall white heath, pink cranesbill, and tiny blue veronica; the great rocks – at this hour in deep shadow – overgrown with ivy, moss, and a beautiful red lichen; the slopes of fern and cystus; all these are on each side, and below there is ever the grand valley scene. I must linger yet another day at Sartené; indeed, a week would be a short stay in these parts for an artist who really wished to study this fine order of Corsican landscape.

About the seventh kilometre the road is lively by groups of peasants going up to the town on the *fête* day – lively, that is by movement, not by colour, for all are gloomily black, caps, beards, and dresses – trotting on little ponies, many of which carry two riders. While I sit drawing above the Tavaria bridge, a shepherd leaves his large flock of black sheep and stands by me. At length he says, 'Why are you drawing our mountains?' '*Per fantasia e piacere,*' I reply, 'for fun, and because it gives me pleasure to draw such beautiful places.' '*Puole,*' quoth he, '*ma cosa siggriffica?*' – That may be, but what is the meaning of it? – *da qualche parse d'Italia venite certo* – You come, it is plain, from some part of Italy; do you go about mapping all our country? – *facendo tutta la Corsica nostra dentr' una carta geografica?*' But I, who cannot work and talk at the same time, tell him so, on which he says, with an air of wisdom, '*Si capisce* – I understand' – and goes away apparently in the belief that I am constructing a political survey of the island.

At eleven it is time for breakfast, which G. has set, with cloaks and a folio for chair and table, below a large olive tree some way off the road; and Fatima* the plentiful has outdone herself by a selection of good things, cold lamb, eggs, tunny, and Sta. Lucia di Tallano wine. I have seen few spots more full of poetical beauty than this, which, though close to the high road, would be completely a solitude but for hosts of birds, of which the woods are full, especially blackbirds, titmice, and bee-eaters, with many jays and ravens, whose home is in the crags high up on Monte Lungo. But after midday, all these woodland and mountain dwellers cease to sing or cry, and the bright dead silence of southern noon succeeds to the lively freshness of morning. Once only a living stream of some eighty jet black goats suddenly passes along the green sward by the little brook, sneezing and snuffling after their

---

*   The hotelkeeper of Lear's hotel in Sartené.

Sarténé

fashion, and disappearing behind the great crags of granite, leaving silence as they had found it; little greenish lizards playing about the flat stones being now the only sign of life all around –

> For now the noonday quiet holds the hill;
> The lizard, with his shadow on the stone,
> Rests like a shadow.*

The whole scene recalls to me many a morning in Greece, and repeats the 'days that are no more'** as I had not supposed they could be brought back.

April 24. Porto Vecchio

Reaching the foot of the hills, at present covered with mist, we now begin to ascend towards the forests, and the road, one of the second class, called in Corsica, *Routes Forestières*, is henceforth carried, curving and winding with a steep ascent, up the face of the mountain; and though it is a good one, yet it has no parapet, and the fact of seeing mules pulling up a cart, the wheels of which are not more than an inch from the precipice's edge, by no means makes me more at ease in the carriage, from which I dismount, and thenceforth walk. My companion, the Maire,*** is full of cheery fun, and stories innumerable. Presently we pass a wild and singular-looking individual tending two or three goats, who waves his hand to M. Quenza with an air of lordly patronage, quite unlike the respectful obeisance I observe paid to him by other peasants. 'But this poor fellow,' says M. Quenza, 'is a harmless lunatic, and his present delusion is that he is King of Sardinia, which explains his magnificent manner.' A short time since the poor fellow was persuaded of a far less agreeable fact, for he believed that he had swallowed two gendarmes, and that the only remedy for this mishap was to eat nothing, in order to starve the intruders, which resolution he rigidly adhered to, till his own life was nearly sacrificed. When all but gone, however, he exclaimed, *'Ecco, tutti due son morti di fame!* – Both of them have died of hunger!' – and thereupon he resumed eating and work with joy.

---

* Tennyson, 'Oenone', lines 24–7 (omitting line 25, 'The grasshopper is silent in the grass').
** Tennyson, 'Tears, idle tears', line 10.
*** M. Quenza, the mayor of Porto Vecchio.

M. Quenza also tells many stories of the too-famous Colomba,[1] who was his aunt by marriage; she died only four years ago, and one of her sisters is still living. Among his anecdotes of that surprising female, he recounts that at one time the family who were in Vendetta with her own in their town Fozzano wished to build a tower, which would have commanded that of their antagonists. Colomba, therefore, improvised a party of her own people, who sat down to play at cards on the ground opposite the tower, and when they were settled she went out and joined them, as if observing the game, always dancing and dandling her baby at the same time. But in the dress of the child she had concealed a loaded pistol, and, watching her opportunity, suddenly shot one of the masons on the tower, replacing the pistol in the child's girdle under a shawl. The wildest confusion ensued; but the card players had their hands full of cards, and their guns all lying by their sides, while Madame Colomba, with both hands, was pacifying the screaming child, so that the party seemed guiltless, and a false direction was given to suspicion. This feat Colomba is said to have performed on two more of the builders, till the raising of the tower was deferred *sine die*.*

April 26. Ghisonaccio
Peter the coachman about this time, I being on foot, and he somewhat ahead, gets himself into disgrace, by reason of beating one of his horses unmercifully when it stumbled, I and my man being unable to prevent him, far less to moderate the astonishing current of oaths with which, in these paroxysms of fury, he accompanies his blows. But on overtaking him I tell him that patience may have an end, and that if he persists in disorderly behaviour, I will telegraph to Ajaccio for a new coachman, and leave him here. Whereon he says, '*Una cosa certa é che l'uomo deve sempre aver pazienza; quest' é una delle prime regole della vita* – One thing is certain, that a man should always be patient; and this, indeed, is one of the first rules of life!'

---

1 This lady was a celebrated leader in the Vendetta-wars at Fozzano, and is supposed to be the heroine of M. Mérimée's beautiful tale of the same name. – E.L.

---

* Without a specific date .

April 28. The Forest of Bavella
At the end of the descent stand two small foresters' houses on the short space of level ground between the four sides of this vale of Bavella; but here, at the twentieth kilometre from Solenzaro, the clouds burst, and violent torrents of rain make shelter welcome. Yet when the storm ceases for a time, and the sun gleams out through cloud, the whole scene is lighted up in a thousand splendid ways, and becomes more than ever astonishing, a changeful golden haze illumes the tops of the mighty peaks, a vast gloom below, resulting from the masses of black solemn pines standing out in deepest shadow from pale granite cliffs dazzling in the sunlight, torrents of water streaming down between walls and gates of granite, giant forms of trees in dusky recesses below perpendicular crags; no frenzy of the wildest dreams of a landscape painter could shape out ideal scenes of more magnificence and wonder.

* * * *

Once, when the horses had stopped, and I prohibited their being touched, Peter's volubility ceased from sheer want of power to continue; 'for', said he, 'I have no more breath, and besides I have sworn at everything, and there's nothing left to *bestemmiare* – to curse.' But at that moment the upraised voice of several cuckoos, who seemed rather than not to rejoice in the rain, was heard, and gave him a fresh impetus, for, with a poetical ingenuity worthy a better cause, he exclaimed, 'May all the parliament of heaven be so full of these nasty cuckoo birds that the saints and apostles will not be able to hear themselves or each other speak; and may every drop of rain turn into a million of snakes on its way from the sky downwards!' Assuredly Peter is a most unpleasant coachman.

May 1. Sarténé
My return to her hotel instead of going to the other inn greatly pleases poor Fatima, and she volunteers conversation and confidence to a degree at once surprising and mournful.

'Did you not,' said she, enumerating one by one the hotels I had been to, 'at Grosseto, at Olmeto, at Bonifacio, Porto Vecchio, and Solenzaro, find that all the hotels were kept by widows?'

'Yes,' said I.

'Have you written down this fact?'

'I have.'

'Then,' said the unhappy Fatima, 'write me down, too, a widow, and not only a widow, but *mille volte più infelice che tutte vedove* – a thousand times more unhappy than all widows!'

Whereon there followed a tremendous burst of tragic eloquence in the highest tones, and with gestures to match, telling how, after seventeen years of marriage, in which she had never given her husband the smallest cause for discontent – *la minima cagione di scontento* – he had forsaken her, faithlessly carrying off her servant girl, and settling in Sardinia under a changed name in a new hotel, had left the unfortunate Fatima, like the Ossianic heroine before alluded to, 'alone, upon the hill of storms'.

Fatima's opinion about the state of the culinary science in the other hotel at Sarténé was sufficiently sweeping, the cook there being, according to her, *'un disgraziato vecchio, chi forse settanta anni fà, sapeva far una frittura, – mai più di ciò; ed ora nemmeno tanto* – a miserable old man, who perhaps seventy years ago knew how to make an omelette, never anything more; and now not even that.'

May 2. Casalabriva

Just beyond the village of Casalabriva a wonderful spectacle strikes the eye, namely, a carriage with two horses, a lady and her maid therein, going, like the landscape painter, to 'see all Corsica'. It is Miss C., who is on her way to Sarténé and Bonifacio. We stop and discourse, the cheery nature of this pleasant lady being a happy set-off to the sad scene I had left at the sick man's house in Olmeto.* I recommended the lonely Fatima to Miss C.'s notice, but, unluckily, she has already written to secure rooms at the other inn; and so, as in the words of the song –

Too soon we part with pain,
To drive o'er dusty roads again, –**

Miss C. continuing to profess herself incredulous as to the safety of my luggage, and still predicting that some indefinite woe will befall me on account of my employing Peter, of whom, now that I am experienced as to his character, certainly very little good may be expected.

---

* Lear had visited a terminally ill Englishman, 'Mr B.', in Olmeto on April 17 and May 2; he died at the end of the month.
** Thomas Moore, 'The Meeting of the Ships', adapting lines 11-12 ('To sail o'er silent seas again').

* * * *

Once only during the afternoon, at a place where two or three houses (called by Peter, Bagni di Surbalaconi) combine with the fine bridge and the high road to indicate the vicinity of man, do I see any human life; here there is a little boy tending some goats. Peter, who is somewhat ahead, having dropped the apron of the carriage, the small boy picks it up, runs after the trap to give it to him, and returns to his goats; whereon I offer him the superfluity of Fatima's breakfast – to wit, two loaves of bread. But these are rejected with a solemn and decided shake of the head by the child; who, however, on my telling him that though white, they are really good bread, takes them after a time gravely, and thenceforth appears to think that he ought to do something in return. 'Perhaps,' says he, 'you might be pleased to know the names of my goats: one is Black-nose, another Silver-spot, that is Grey-foot, and this is Cippo. Cippo is quite the best goat in these parts, and likes to be talked to – *come un Cristiano* – just like a Christian – perhaps even, if you stand still, she may let you scratch the end of her nose and I will call her at once if you choose to try.' After which gratifying information the small boy prattles about the state of the corn, and the good it has gained from the last rains, with a quiet intelligence, and at the same time with a want of vivacity peculiar to Corsican life; until at a by-lane he says, 'The goats must go down here; so addio!' – and exit.

May 3. Cauro
A carriage road, I am told, leads to Aïtone and Valdoniello from Evisa, either by way of Porto or Vico.

Madame Paoloni's breakfast of trout and beefsteak, brains and caper sauce, Irish stew, *broccio*,* etc., good in quality and profuse in quantity, is, as usual, a curious contrast to the stairs and entry of her hotel, and is accompanied by the usual careful and obliging manners of Corsican innkeepers. When I leave the house, the hostess says, 'Do not pay me now, but stop as you return, and pay then.'

'But, not so,' I reply, 'for who can tell what may happen? Suppose I should die at Bastelica; you would then lose your money.'

---

* A Corsican cheese.

'In that case,' says Mdme Paoloni, 'although we are poor, and should miss your money, we should not feel the loss so much, because our sorrow for your death would be greater.'

Shortly after noon I went on towards Bastelica, which is twenty kilometres distant. Peter the oathful, who this morning has had some very bad fits of swearing and beating, but who is at present in a comparatively placid mood, says, 'At these villages I am very often asked who you are, and I always say you are the *Ministro delle Finanze* – the Finance Minister of England.'

'But why,' said I, 'do you say such a thing?'

'Oh, partly because you wear spectacles and have an air of extreme wisdom, and partly because one must say something or other.'

A Minister of Finance seems to be grim Peter's *beau idéal* of earthly grandeur, and he has frequently spoken of having accompanied the illustrious M. Abbattucci, late Minister of Finance, to the country residence of that personage at Zicavo. Now, as I was particularly in want of information concerning the road thither, I asked him one day, 'Did M. Abbattucci make the journey by Sta. Maria Zicché, or by the village of Bicchisano?'

'He went by Grosseto to Sta. Maria,' was the reply.

'But,' said I, 'as the way from Ajaccio to Zicavo is long, where did the minister stop, at Grosseto, or is there any other midway inn?'

'By no means,' said Peter, *'non si fermò punto, andava a giorno e notte* – he stopped nowhere, but travelled day and night. *Era mortissimo* – he was quite dead – that Minister of Finance – *e non era che sue cenere che si portava* – it was only his ashes that I took to Zicavo.'

* * * *

At kilometre eleven and a half is a neat little forest-house and a mill. The *guardiano* and his family, sitting outside their dwelling, make a picture, combined with groups of trees and the beautiful river, here close below the highway, and dashing foamily over its worn stones. Beyond this point the road makes a sharp turn, and for the moment Peter is lost sight of. Latterly his swearing has been so horrible, and his cruelty so odious, that I have thought at times that he is not quite sane; consequently, I have walked nearer the carriage, and it was only by the accident of my having stopped a little while at the forest house, to make some inquiries about the distance, that he had got considerably ahead, for here the ascent is not steep.

But on turning the corner of the road just mentioned there was a shocking sight, and one that became more so at each moment. Taking this opportunity of being alone Peter had given way to a burst of rage and violent blows with his whip handle on the poor beasts' heads. In vain did both I and Giorgio shout, running forward. Even then the carriage stood at right-angles to the side of the road, and not far from the edge of it, above the river, while at every blow the poor horses backed nearer to the ravine.

One more blow – carriage and horses are quite at the side of the precipice! –

Yet one more blow, struck with an infernal scream from bad Peter, and the horses back for the last time! And then –

Down, down, go all into the ravine!

Nothing was left on the road but the abominable old fellow, kneeling, and wailing to the Madonna and all the saints, whom a minute before he had been blaspheming.

I ran back to the corner of the road, whence I could see the forest house, to alarm the inhabitants; and, directly, they set off on the way up to help. Meanwhile, the Suliot was already down the steep. Happily, the hillside at this spot, the twelfth kilometre, is not nearly so precipitous as it is at a few yards distance either way, and a cluster of large chestnut trees had stopped the carriage and horses from rolling downward to the stream. One of the poor beasts was, notwithstanding, killed on the spot; the other, which G. had managed to extricate, was dreadfully lacerated by a sharp rock. The carriage, as may be supposed, was broken in pieces, and the luggage – literally fulfilling Miss C.'s prediction – had rolled farther down, among the rocks and fern.

The zeal with which the forester, his son, and friends, worked to get up the *roba* and the remaining horse, was most praiseworthy; and seeing so much energy where I had expected apathy, I internally resolved to be less hasty in future in characterizing Corsicans as lazy, on account of their being undemonstrative.

May 9. Sagona
The highway, now a winding road, follows the shore from point to point, till it climbs the last hills before you reach the promontory of the Greek colony.

* * * *

Carghésé, which you come upon all at once by a sudden turn of the road, is a larger place than I had expected to see, and is built with regular streets at right-angles to each other. Several scattered houses, among them the hotel and the old Greek church, are by the side of the high road, which here crosses the cape of Carghésé; but the chief part of the village stands lower down, facing the south; the Latin church, and a second Greek building, large and unfinished, are in the farther part of the settlement, nearer the end of the promontory, and the whole forms a singular and picturesque scene, greatly interesting to me from what I had heard of the migration of these Greek settlers from the Morea, and of the persecution which had at one time made their adopted land little less undesirable than their own.

I had told my Suliot servant not to speak Greek at first, by way of having some merriment when our knowledge of their language came to be suddenly known; but this plan fell through by my own inattention; for from a window of one of the first houses I pass, there looks out a Greek priest with a venerable beard and the well-known cap, who makes me a bow and waves his hand, to which salute I unthinkingly reply, 'Καλὴ σας ἡμέρα! – Good morning!' and naturally elicit 'Πῶς ὁμιλειτε Ρωμαϊκὰ? – What! do you speak Romaic?' for in the days when these Greeks came to Corsica, 'ἡ Ἑλληϲικὴ γλῶσσα* was unknown as such.

* * * *

On returning to the hotel [at Carghésé] an excellent dinner was provided – soup, a dish of pilaf (the first seen in Corsica), roast lamb, etc., and very tolerable wine, but the priest, who came to pay his promised visit, brought a bottle of far better quality. The colony, according to him, came to Corsica under Genoese protection, about 1626, and consisted of 600 or 700 Greeks from Vittolo in Maina, and he says that now the population of the village is 1,200, but much crossed by marriage with the islanders, and that even some Corsicans by descent are counted in that number. He describes the site of Paomia – the first settlement of these Spartan Moreotes, and burned some thirty years after their coming – as being distant about

---

*   The Hellenic language.

an hour's walk from here. After its destruction the colonies took refuge in Ajaccio for fifty years. They preserve their old ritual, but are all 'united Greeks', or, in other words, Papists. The priests, he says, may marry, and at first did so, but do not now. Long since they have disused all national costume, and very generally the use of the Greek language, which intermarriage and the settling of the islanders amongst them are fast obliterating, and it is evident that they seek to separate themselves as little as possible from Corsicans. Thus, in two or three more generations their family names will be the only remaining proof of their nationality. My acquaintance, Papa Michele, seems to have been superseded, unjustly, according to his own account, by the Bishop of Ajaccio, who has given his place to a curate from the Piana de' Greci, in Sicily. 'Perhaps,' says he, 'the *Préfet* may one day do me justice – νομίζω αὐτὸν, ἔπειτα τὸν θεὸν ἦναι ὁ Ηατήρ μου καὶ πρῶτος ἀνθρώπων – He, after the Lord, is (in my opinion) my father, and the first of men.'

May 12. The Forest of Aïtone

The trees near the entrance of the forest are not of great height, and for some distance inward are mostly more or less covered with a multitude of the bright white sacs or nests of the larvae of that remarkable insect, the *Bombyx processionalis*(?),* my first acquaintance with which I had made in the woods round Cannes. Here, in Aïtone, the smooth satin-like surface of these nests, shining like silver among the tall dark green pines, has a most curious effect; and not less strange, from time to time, are the long strings or processions – some of them ten or fifteen feet in length – of this extraordinary caterpillar crawling along the road, now parallel with its edge, now crossing it in unbroken file. In other parts, below trees more than commonly full of their nests, are great heaps, some of them as large as a half-bushel basket, of these creatures, apparently in a state of torpor, or only in motion towards the point from which their 'follow my leader' institution is about to take place. Now and then, in passing under trees loaded with these bombyx bags, the thought that one may plump into one's face is not agreeable, for the hairs which come from these animals on the slightest touch occasion excessive and even dangerous irritation.

---

*   The 'pine procession caterpillar (Bombyx processionis)', according to the notes at the end of the volume.

But the questions arise, on seeing such myriads of these wonderful little brutes – do the nests fall down by their own weight, owing to the increasing size of the caterpillars? Or do the inmates at a certain time open their nests and fall down 'spontaneous' to commence their linear expeditions? Do they, as some maintain, migrate in order to procure fresh food? It seems to me not so from what I have noticed of their habits; for though I have continually discovered them coming *down* the trunk of a pine tree, I have never seen any going up. Rather is not all this movement preliminary to burrowing in the earth (as, indeed, the peasants about Cannes say they do) previously to their transformation into chrysalides? Anyhow, they are a singularly curious, though not a pleasant lot of creatures, and their most strange habits are well worth observing.*

May 17. Ajaccio
Mellili** is one of the places that has left with me a stronger impression than most I have visited. The house, always inhabited in the early days of Napoleon by his father and Madame Letitia Buonaparte, is now neglected. Bequeathed by Cardinal Fesch to the municipality of Ajaccio, it is let to peasants, who keep sheep and pigs in the once probably well-cared-for grounds. The building, apparently an ordinary farmhouse or villa, tall, small-windowed, and with a forlorn look, presents nothing remarkable to the observer; many large grey rounded granite rocks are scattered near it; great growth of cactus, and long-armed thin-foliaged olive-trees with moss-grown stems. You pass beyond the house through a wilderness of vegetation, and find a level space covered with a tangle of cystus mixed with long grass and lupines, among which a few sheep are feeding; and at the edge of this sort of platform stands the great ilex tree – truly, as Valery says, *'un arbre historique'*, for its shade was the favourite retreat of Napoleon the First.***

This celebrated ilex tree – a large portion of which has been broken off by time or storms – is of great size, and stretches its venerable branches droopingly above the verdure and the stone seat it overshadows. Its tufted and thick foliage, almost yellow in colour, contrasts strongly with the green below and with the grey

---

* Lear refers the reader to the notes relating to this species of Bombyx at the end of the volume.
** The country house of the Bonaparte family.
*** The original edition included a vignette of the ilex tree.

olives on every side; beyond its dark black-brown stem and deep grey branches the blue gulf and hills gleam; and there is no sound to break the sad quiet of this once gay spot but the voice of the wild pigeon and the sweet harmony of many nightingales. Yet the undying spirit of the past seems to pierce the dim veil of years and neglect, to colour with life all this impressive and solitary place, and to people Mellili with visions of beauty and history connected with the family who, as children, played here unnoticed, but who grew up to be the most prominent objects in the sight of a wondering world. Madame Letitia, her five sons, four of them to sit in after years on thrones; and her three daughters, two of them to be queens. The boy Napoleon reading below the great oak, or pacing about what was then the garden, looking to those majestic mountains beyond the sea; in after days (1790) meditating on the fierce Buttafuoco letter (it is dated from Mellili), or on the whirlwind of change so soon to astonish Europe; ten years later, visiting once more, and for the last time, his favourite haunts, when the fortunes of Corsica were beginning to seem insignificant among those of so many states, and mainly of France.

Like the talking oak of the poet, could the aged tree but answer our questions, and be

– garrulously given,
A babbler in the land,*

what might he not tell us of the days when Elise, Caroline, and Pauline Buonaparte sported in its shade, undreaming of the crowns of Tuscany and Naples and the princely Borghese halls; when Joseph, Lucien, Louis, and Jerome played, and Napoleon paced and meditated below its branches. Melancholy Mellili, well does the repose of the neglected garden and the beautiful scenery around suit such memories!

May 18. Bocognano
Berlandi** tells me that he was away when I arrived, searching, with nearly all the people of the Bocognano villages, for a poor half-witted youth who has now been missing for four days. He says that every year deaths occur in these mountains from children or old persons losing their way in the thick *maquis,* or from being caught,

---

*   Tennyson, 'The Talking Oak', lines 23–4.
** The chief of police at Bocognano.

high up in the hills, by snow storms. Last autumn two little girls strayed from their home, only to be found (or rather their skeletons) when the snow melted, a month or two ago.

May 19. Bocognano
As I sit close to the village, I have at least the advantage of seeing all who come out of it on this side; but, alas, for the joyous singing of Italy! and for the gay dresses and beautiful laughing faces of Italian mountain girls as they leave the town for their work in the country! Here all things are triste and mute; mopy men in black, their hands in their pockets, lead out a single black goat to some pasture, the rope fastened to their arm; women in black dresses, and black kerchiefed, and with grave though not unpleasing faces, and grave manners, also lead forth one goat apiece. Slowly and lazily walk the men, slowly the women – mournful Corsican mountain homes and inhabitants. But on the other hand I am allowed to draw quite unmolested; two or three boys on their way to school stop to look at my work, and make intelligent remarks on it, but avoid giving me the least annoyance, some of them rebuking others if they stand ever so little in my way; and when, on more of them gathering round me, I suggest that it would be better they should go to school, one of the children says, quietly, '*E vero, sarebbe meglio, andiam* – It is true, it *would* be better, let us go' – and away they all walk. I never was in any country where so little trouble was given me by bystanders.

A walk through and beyond the village next occupied me; on the whole an air of neatness and tranquillity pervades it. Children are numerous but not idle, for one and all carry books, and are on their way to school. There are many pigs, too, for it is a land of chestnuts, and the hams and sausages of the chestnut-fed are famous. As I returned, M. Berlandi joined me, and took me to see the house from which Napoleon I so narrowly escaped with life in 1780, when pursued by his enemies of the Pozzo di Borgo faction. The building is now the *caserne* of the gendarmerie, and near one of the windows there formerly grew a tree, by the aid of whose branches the young Napoleon was enabled to leave the house at night and to fly to Ucciani, a village not far off, where the family Poggiani protected him. My informants state that at the death of the first emperor several persons of Ucciani received legacies of 5,000 and 6,000 francs, and that their descendants are still much favoured by Napoleon III.

* * * *

Corte

It was nearly dusk when I entered the city. Long ranges of many-windowed and very lofty houses form one side of the main road, which rises steeply to the centre and more level part of the town, and no lack is there here of bustle and life compared with the quiet of Ajaccio; even the swarms of children seem still more abundant. Suddenly, at the opening of the high street, running at right-angles to this first approach, transparencies and illuminations, bands of music, crowds of people, and universal movement greet my astonished senses. I had thought the bitterness and noise of *fêtes* was over with Sunday, but, on the contrary, this, the last of the three days, is the most violent and fuss-ful of the whole time allotted to rejoicing on this occasion, that of unveiling a statue of Marshal the Duc de Padoue, one of the first Napoleon's generals, and a native of Corte.

Every place was thronged, and it was with difficulty I could get through the crowd to the Piazza, and thence to the Hôtel de l'Europe. Here all was bustle and confusion. There were no vacant rooms; and as to where Domenico and my luggage might be found, no answer could be got; the general festivity seemed to have turned the heads of the good people of Corte. Group after group of people to whom I applied shrugged their ignorance on the subject. Nor were the efforts of Giorgio to find our driver and *roba* more fortunate, and we were meditating – as at Montenegro in 1866 – on the possible chance of passing the night in the street, when I remembered that M. Mérimée had procured me an introduction to Signor Corteggiani, President of the Tribunals, and residing in Corte. In such a difficulty, application to one of the gendarmerie is usually the best proceeding, and had I asked M. Lambert for a letter, I could have been saved all trouble, though Corte is not in his district; as it was, a gendarme took me to the Judge's house, though this was a step but little in advance, for M. Corteggiani was giving a dinner to the Duke, the General, and others, and the servants would not deliver my letter until next day. Meanwhile, as I remained on the staircase with the gendarme and others, that functionary, who had evidently entered fully into the festal hilarities of the day, made an absurd scene by shouting 'Proclaim your rank! call aloud your title! We gendarmes are the heart and beginning of all justice! We will see everything done for you!' till a domestic, thinking it would be wiser to end the matter at once, rushed upstairs with the letter, and shortly brought down the Judge's secretary, with directions to show me a lodging, and to apologize for his not being able to receive me at the moment.

Accordingly, I was taken to a tiny house, with a very dirty entrance, but containing one available decent bedroom, and a sort of public chamber, where they promised some supper. G. shortly joined me, with two wild-looking individuals bringing up the *roba*; but these men, being in a festive and elated state, asked fabulous sums for each article and on G. refusing to pay so much, a row ensued. The most outrageous of the 'savage men' kicked a saddle-bag downstairs, and was proceeding to further violence, when a compromise was come to by aid of the gendarme, and peace was finally restored. I had previously been told that the people of Corte had the reputation of being dirtier and more turbulent than any in the island, and, however unwilling to harbour unfavourable impressions, my first hour in this place tends to make me think the character is not undeserved.

May 23. Vescoveto
After coffee, I took leave of my landlord, M. Gravie, who said, *'Je ne crois pas, monsieur, que nous nous reverrons.'* On my asking him last night if he had ever revisited France, the poor old fellow said, *'Non, monsieur, je n'ai jamais vu la France depuis que je l'ai quittée, et maintenant je ne la reverrai plus.'** I do not think my worthy host was convinced that I was not a political agent of some sort, partly because it has always been a characteristic of Vescovato to mix itself up in or initiate surprising political events; and partly that, after all, it is very difficult for these people to reconcile the popular notion of a painter laboriously working his way from place to place with that of an elderly traveller speaking four languages, and going about with a carriage, luggage, and a servant. It is of no use to attempt explanations – *qui s'excuse s'accuse*** – and, therefore, silence is golden is the best rule of the traveller's life in these lands.

May 24. Bastìa
From 8 a.m. till 4 p.m. I pass the time in a hay-field below the

---

* 'I don't believe, sir, that we shall see each other again.' 'No, sir, I have not seen France since I left, and now I shall not see her again.'

** 'He who excuses himself accuses himself.'

friendly shade of olive trees, writing letters; a blazing fringe of
scarlet poppies and the blueness of sea beyond and sky above are
all day long a charm of glorious colour. A hoopoe or two comes
near now and then, and except these, no other bird but one, who
sits in a companionable way on the topmost bare bough of an
almond tree a few yards off, hour after hour, chattering with a soft
multitudinous kind of note, as if he were four or five birds instead
of one, chibbly-wibbly-twitter-witter unceasingly, unless when he
darts down to the ground to seize a beetle. This shrike – such at
least he seems to me – is a restless little fellow, flitting at times from
tree to tree, but always returning to his favourite broad branch
opposite where I lie. He gives me no little amusement; sometimes,
besides his continuous small chatter, he warbles with a good deal
of pleasing delicate variety.

May 26. Cap Corse
From the top of the ascent I now send back Domenico* and the trap,
and following the footpath which leads up from immediately
above the tablet rock, through aromatic *maquis*, to the old Capuchin
convent, I continue to mount the path, here broken and narrow, to
the tower, so-called, of Seneca.** But after toiling a good way up I
abandon the pilgrimage, because a thick mist covers the sea, and
not a symptom of the shores of Italy can be discovered; the coast
of Cap Corse is on this side thoroughly wild and rugged, but does
not seem to me to possess any particular interest; moreover, I am
disinclined to encounter any extra fatigue. The latter part of the
climb to this old tower – so G.*** informs me, who went to the top
– is very steep and difficult. The building itself, though of early
date, does not appear to have anything of Roman times in its
composition; rather it has been erected by the Pisans, or by the
Signori di Mare, who ruled this part of the island about the tenth
century. This theory, however, is treason in the estimation of the
good people of Luri, who firmly adhere to their opinion that Seneca,
the philosopher, was shut up in it. 'My father,' said one of the
inhabitants of the valley to me, 'told me that this was told to him

---

*　Young Domenico Casanova, a forester's son, who had replaced Peter as Lear's
　　driver, sometimes accompanied by the dog Flora, a rare exception to Lear's
　　dislike of dogs.
**　Seneca was exiled to Corsica for seven years. The original 1870 edition includes
　　a vignette of 'Seneca's tower'.
***　Giorgio.

by *his* father, and back from father to son for eighteen centuries; you see, therefore, that the story cannot be otherwise than true' – a position I did not attempt to combat. What is more to the purpose, so far as a painter is concerned, is that this rock and tower of Seneca are most picturesque; thick groups of ilex grow at the base of the pinnacle, and all the upper part of it is a bright bare rock.

* * * *

As we arrived at his village [Luri], the Maire presses me to have some refreshment at his house, but when I tell him I dare not lose a minute of working time, now that the sun is so rapidly mounting, and that the great heat and absence of shadow in the valley would soon stop my morning's labours, he leaves me with great good breeding to my own devices.

* * * *

At two p.m. I leave Piazza di Luri, and passing through the groves of aged white and grey-armed olives, and the rich abundance of fig, lemon, and walnut, soon arrive at the Marina of Sta Severa by the sea. Far beyond my expectations have been the interest and beauty of the valley of Luri, and long shall I remember its pleasant and industrious people, its quiet and shady gardens and woody hill slopes, and its lofty traditional beacon tower, with its tales of the Roman philosopher.

May 27. St Florent
Meanwhile this small place has been, since my arrival, a prey to amazement and curiosity, by reason of a war steamer which has suddenly appeared, and having steamed as far as nearly opposite St Florent, has gone back and disappeared behind the point on the west side of the gulf, making no sign. But at noon she returns, in company with the squadron of French ironclads, which in all the fullness of power and ugliness, are ranged opposite the town, and boats soon coming off, these events communicate to St Florent as much agitation and life as it is perhaps capable of receiving.

May 28. Ile Rousse
At 6.30 dinner was ready, served by a brisk damsel of no pretensions to beauty, but with a look of *espièglerie* and intelligence;

always she held a flower in her mouth; at the beginning of dinner it was a rose, latterly a pink. She waited also at a table where seven or eight 'continentals' – *employés* – were dining. The dinner was good and some Balagna cherries and cheese excellent.

Later, when the damsel – who greatly resembled a lady on a Japanese teacup – brought some coffee, I said, 'May I venture to ask, without offence, why you continually carry a flower in your mouth?' 'And,' retorted the Japanese, 'may I venture to ask, without offence, why you, a stranger, inquire about matters which are not your affairs, but mine?' '*Perdoni'*, said I, 'do not be angry; I only had an idea that there might be a meaning in your doing so.' Quoth she, '*Che cosa potrebbe mai significare?* – What could it possibly mean?' 'I thought,' said I, humbly, 'it might mean you were not to be spoken to; for how, with a flower in your mouth, could you answer?' Whereat the Corsican gravity gave way, and the hotel resounded with long peals of laughter from the Japanese.

May 29. Algayola
Fortunately for me, after some heavy showers, the weather became brilliant once more, in good time to array in its fullest beauty what is doubtless one of the finest portions of Corsican scenery, and not a little Sicilian in character, the drive from the ruined and dreary Algayola to Calvi, the long cape and light-house near which are now visible. A succession of pictures of exquisite interest delights the eye as the road passes along new basins or crescents at the foot of high hills, bare at their tops, then terraced into corn-fields all the way down from those rocky heights to the shore; the grain all ripe, and the fields full of busy reapers, dotted with grand old olive trees, standing, not in continuous groves, but singly, or in massive and picturesque groups, some of the trees being quite the finest I have seen in the island. Farther on a ruined castle crowns one of the highest points, as you continue to drive through this beautiful scenery, with the wide sea ever on your right hand, until after leaving the coast by an ascent of short duration, the road comes suddenly in full view of the bay of Calvi, that town and citadel on its farther side shining out like a gem above the purple water, by the side of a plain running up to the foot of magnificent mountain ranges, some of them the highest in Corsica. Assuredly the Genoese were wise to cling so long and so fondly to this, as it seems to me, fairest part of the island.

May 30. Belgodére
I resolve to avail myself of an introductory letter given to me by the Préfet to the Maire, M. Malaspina.

From this gentleman a most friendly welcome is forthcoming; with Corsicans – as in days I well knew of old, with Calabrians and Abruzzese – there is very little compliment and much sincerity. 'I am only too glad the inns are full, and that you are thus obliged to give me the pleasure of receiving you, although it so happens that my family are away for the day, and therefore you will not fare particularly well' – was said gravely and evidently in earnest, as M. Malaspina took me to his house – one of the largest in the place – and told Flora and Company where were his stables.

The first floor is that resided in by the family, and that above it contains what may be called the guest rooms, and which are so well and handsomely fitted up that one seems in Paris. A more perfectly comfortable little bedroom than that allotted to me could not be found, and – for the day has been hot, and the landscape painter far from well – I am glad to get some rest in it till six p.m., when I join the Maire and his uncle, both intelligent and gentlemanly men, the latter an elderly person who has passed many years in different parts of Italy.

Landscape being my main object in coming to this island, I have throughout avoided all arrangements by which delays to my work could be occasioned, and thus have allowed myself to see but little of the Corsicans, a circumstance I in some senses regret, for whenever I have done so, the making their acquaintance has been invariably a source of pleasure, and on the present occasion particularly so. At seven dinner was announced, and we descended to the family dining-room, where were the wife of the Maire's son (he himself is a widower) and his two daughters. I was carried forcibly back to days of Abruzzo travelling by the friendly ways and hospitable anxieties of these amiable people, who live in a plentiful and patriarchal style, and whose dinner, profuse and of excellent quality, gave ample evidence of a well-managed household. They insisted on the Suliot sitting at the same table, spite of his appeal to me, and as the service was limited, I thought it best to acquiesce.

What though there were dishes of hare, roast fowl, creams, and many other good things, only my host the Maire partook of animal food, the rest of the family eating snails or vegetables only, as it was a vigil or fast day; none the less, however, was their attention to their guest unremitting. Their home-made wine was thoroughly good, but they had two other sorts of Corsican vintage; altogether the entertainment was a very pleasant oasis in these days of doubtful *locande*, and well it is for me that M. Géry gave me this introduction. Later, accompanied by the three ladies, who were all unaffected and well bred, we adjourned to the well-furnished drawing-room, to which coffee was brought, and here we talked till 9.30, when this kindly family wished me good night.

These people are quite *au fait* regarding all European intelligence; and their remarks on Turkey, Italy, and other subjects, were free from the prejudice and violence so frequently met with in proportion to the ignorance of the speakers. Of their own island they are acquainted with the minutest details of both present and past condition, physical or political; and the wide interest shown upon European and cosmopolitan topics in so remote a mountain district contrasts curiously with the apathy and blank ignorance noticeable in many similar positions. There is, however, this difference respecting the Corsican's broad intelligence regarding contemporary history: his own island and people have been for so long a time actors in the principal European events, that it is but natural he should become acquainted with facts which are, so to speak, a part of his own interests, whereas to all other countries they are only outside occurrences.

June 1. Vivario
The hotel in the little back alley at Vivario, is, as when I came through here on the 20th, quite full, but I get two rooms in an adjoining house. The ladder entrance to the public eating-room at the inn is not prepossessing, nor is the appearance of the room itself without need of a balance of compensation, which some opine to be a universal law of nature. Such there certainly was at the hotel of Vivario, where it came in the form of a very jovial and pleasant landlady and of two surprising daughters, the sudden appearance of whom from an inner chamber was most astonishing. For not only were these two girls of extreme beauty, both in face and figure, but they were dressed in the best Parisian taste, their coiffure arranged with the utmost care, and altogether they were a very unexpected sight in so rude a mountain village; these damsels, however, take no part in the hotel *ménage*, but only beam forth at occasional intervals.

Of Miss C. the landlady here speaks with the greatest

enthusiasm, and adds, *'C'est si remarquable qu'elle soit si gaie, parceque toutes les autres Anglaises qu'on voit sont tristes et froides et superbes'*,* a general accusation of my countrywomen I very positively oppose as untrue. My hostess, however, it is but just to say, excepts the Hon. Mrs A. B., who it seems has lately been here, from this sweeping condemnation, and, like all the rest who have seen that lady, goes into raptures about her beauty.

June 3. Col de Verde

While waiting for the driver's return, some *cantonniers* come and beg me to enter and rest in their little wayside house; these good people do not perceive how much more agreeable it is to sit or lie beneath a chestnut tree contemplating the wide and beautiful landscape than to encounter the disagreeables of a close room; the more so, in the present case, that besides the *cantonniers* there is a party of charcoal burners, who do not seem to be either of the apathetic, or civil and well-bred nature, so characteristic generally of these islanders, two or three of them having been closely examining the luggage for some time past, and having made themselves not a little disagreeable. Towards ten o'clock, however, Domenico returns, and proceeds to shoe the pony, by no means assisted in his work by the riotous group about him, most of these being 'elevated' by drink, and one of them apparently an idiot. These fellows profess to help my driver by holding up the pony's foot, but in the middle of the shoeing they purposely give it a jerk, and every time the shoe comes off again by this manoeuvre they dance round the carriage roaring with drunken laughter; which game goes on in a very irritating fashion, in spite of the *cantonniers'* interference, so that I fear a serious quarrel may ensue. When Domenico's patience is nearly exhausted by these practical jokes, it is thought better to drive off with the shoe only partly nailed on; a sign of defeat on our part greeted by loud shouts of derision, and especially by the idiot, with the wildest shrieks and gestures. I confess I should not have been pleased to have been obliged to pass the night with the society I have just left; nevertheless, this is the one and only instance, in two months of Corsican touring, of my having received the least molestation, even in the most out-of-the-way places. This vast valley, scantily populated above Guitera and

---

* 'It's so remarkable that she should be so gay, since all the other Englishwomen one sees are sad and cold and proud.'

Zicavo, leads only to Ghisoni by the forests of Verde and Marmano, seems very little frequented, and thus far in it I have not seen a single mounted gendarme, who are generally met with in pairs from time to time on all the roads.

June 4. Col St Georgio
Soon the *maquis*-grown crescent of hills beyond the Col is passed; then the familiar village of Cauro, and the far view of Ajaccio is seen on the horizon; the run down to the Piana dell' Oro follows; and I am soon once more in Ajaccio, where the squadron of ironclads enliven the the bay, if, indeed, any place may be said to be enlivened by those specimens of naval architecture. My journeys in Corsica are ended; much more there is to see, but time is up, and the glass of Corsican travel is run out; close, therefore, the note-book of research, and lock it up in the closet of resignation.

After the fresh mountain air how hot does Ajaccio now seem! and above all the small rooms of the Ottavi Hotel!

Flora and Company are dismissed with esteem. No better nor more careful coachman could be found anywhere than the youth Domenico, who, by the by, is an amateur, having, as he told my servant, property to the amount of 20,000 francs, and who drives about to see the world by choice – '*per piacer di veder il mondo, fuori di Corsica no – ma tutta l'isola.*'* Farewell, spotty little beast of excellent qualities – Flora, best of dogs!

---

*   'for the pleasure of seeing the world, not the world outside Corsica – but the entire island.'

Appendix

Lear and Natural History

The Visibly Vicious Vulture,
who wrote some Verses to a Veal-cutlet in a
Volume bound in Vellum.

Lear and Natural History

In the 1830s Lear worked as an illustrator in zoology, playing his part in the huge nineteenth-century enterprise of classifying and categorizing the natural world. He did not himself write any of the descriptive texts in this brief selection, but he was the illustrator for all the animals featured; and it is not difficult to imagine connections between these little life stories of eccentric, endangered, transplanted creatures and the narratives of remarkable fauna in his nonsense writings.

Lear's illustrations for the books on Knowsley Hall (1846) and on tortoises (1872) were done between 1831 and 1837, though the books were not published until many years later.

A Monograph of the Ramphastidae, or Family of Toucans by John Gould (1834)

RAMPHASTOS TOCO, Auct. Toco Toucan
This magnificent species is one of the largest of the genus, and is remarkable for possessing a bill perhaps more disproportionate in size than is found in any other, by which circumstance and the rich colouring of the mandibles it may be at once distinguished. I would also here observe, that it seems to differ slightly from the rest of the Toucans, in having an unusually short and square tail, covered at its base by large white feathers. A few years ago this was a species rarely found in cabinets of natural history; latterly, however, it has been brought over more abundantly, and may now be met with in every museum of any extent. Though the *Ramphastos Toco* has the

widest range of any species, being distributed through the whole of the wooded districts from the River Plate to Guiana, it is but thinly dispersed, and according to the information afforded me by my friend Dr Such, is extremely shy, and not procured without considerable difficulty, keeping to the tops of the highest trees, and exercising the utmost wariness and caution.

As with the rest of the genus, fruits compose the principal part of its food, and among these, it is said to be extremely partial to the banana.

The sexes offer little or no difference in colour, but the female may be always distinguished by her smaller size, and the comparatively inferior dimensions of the beak. The general colours of the young are also similar, but the beak is of course less developed, and is a considerable time before it attains its rich colouring and perfect size.

PTEROGLOSSUS INSCRIPTUS, Swainson. Lettered Araçari
It appears to be a bird of the greatest rarity, and only to be found in the remote and untrodden parts of the country destined by nature for its abode; and which, according to the best information I can collect, is Guiana, the low and swampy districts of which, abounding in luxurious palms, etc., afford it a retreat, from which there will doubtless be yet obtained many ornithological productions at present unknown.

The Lettered Araçari takes its specific character from the peculiar markings of the mandibles, which in some measure resemble Hebrew characters, and these, with its diminutive size, distinguish it from every other species.

Inhabits Guiana.

The Birds of Europe by John Gould (1837, 5 volumes). Volume 1, Raptores

From EGYPTIAN NEOPHRON
Of the family of *Vulturidae*, which is so extensively spread over the hotter portions of nearly every part of the globe, the present is the only species which has ever been taken in England; and of this fact, only a solitary instance is on record. It appears that the example alluded to was killed near Kilve in Somersetshire, in the month of October 1825, and is now in the possession of the Reverend A.

Matthew of the same place. When first discovered, it was feeding upon the body of a dead sheep, with the flesh of which it was so gorged, as to be either incapable of flight, or, at all events, unwilling to exert itself sufficiently to effect its escape; it was therefore shot with little difficulty. Another bird, apparently of the same species, was at the same time observed in the neighbourhood, but escaped its pursuers. The circumstance of this example coming so far north, must be attributed entirely to accident, its native habitat being exclusively the southern provinces of Europe, and the adjoining districts of Asia and Africa.

The traveller who visits Gibraltar, the adjacent parts of Spain, the islands of the Mediterranean, Turkey, and the northern coasts of Africa, cannot fail to have his attention attracted by this remarkable bird, one of the *Vulturidae*, which is there often found associating in flocks. Like the rest of its family, it is one of nature's scavengers, being ever on the search for carrion and putrid offal, upon which it greedily feeds, seldom if ever attacking living prey.

from TENGMALM'S OWL
In all probability this little Owl extends its range over the whole of the Arctic Circle, in which inhospitable region it appears to represent the Noctua Nupidae, a species inhabiting more temperate parts, and with which it has more than once been confounded. The Noctua Tengmalm is abundant in Russia and Norway; it is also found, but more rarely, in Germany and France, and it has been captured two or three times in the British Islands. Mr Selby mentions one example in particular, which was killed near Morpeth in Northumberland in 1812, and forms a part of that gentleman's collection. In the 'Fauna Boreali-Americana' Dr Richardson states his belief 'that it inhabits all the woody country from Great Slave Lake to the United States. On the banks of the Saskatchewan it is so common that its voice is heard almost every night by the traveller wherever he selects his bivouac. Its cry in the night is a single melancholy note, repeated at interludes of a minute or two; and it is one of the superstitious practices of the Indians to whistle when they hear it. If the bird is silent when thus challenged, the speedy death of the enquirer is augured; hence its Cree appellation of Death-bird.'

When it is disturbed or accidentally wanders abroad by day, it is so dazzled by the sun that it becomes stupid, and may be easily taken with the hand.

Zoology of Captain Beechey's Voyage (1839)

from PTEROPUS PSELAPHON, Lay's Pteropus

Mr Collie makes the following observations of its habits: – 'During the day, these bats were frequently observed hanging or climbing among the branches of the trees, the head almost always lowest and at right angles to the body, suspending themselves by one or both hind claws. They not infrequently came down close to our men, and were caught. Sometimes they alighted from an adjoining tree, at other times they ran down a branch to pick off one of the adjoining fruits. In all cases, I believe, they ascended by climbing, and they never seemed to be aware that they were taking a short branch, until they came to its termination, when they tried all round for something to cling to, seldom trusting themselves to their wings on such occasions. In the night we heard a loud and frequent screeching, which we attributed to these animals.'

Gleanings from the Menagerie and Aviary at Knowsley Hall by J.E. Gray (1846)

AMERICAN EMU, Rhea Americana

Inhabits the East Coast of South America.

Until lately it was believed that there was only a single species of American Ostrich; but Mr Darwin, in a letter to Professor Henslow, states that he was led, by the account he heard from the natives, to believe that the kind found in Chili differed from those which inhabited the plains of the east coast; and specimens of different ages which have lately been received from Mr Bridges and deposited in the British Museum collection, prove the truth of this idea.

The following are extracts taken from Lord Derby's notes: –

'The six Rheas of last year are doing well, though one has somehow lost an eye.' – May 16, 1845.

'The Rhea has begin to lay.' – May 23, 1845.

'My Rhea eggs have hatched ill this year; out of twenty-six, twenty-three proved bad, and the other three had dead birds in them. But I have three later still to hatch: I hope they may prove more lucky.' –Sept. 18, 1845.

'My Rheas have laid about thirty eggs.'

'Out of my new young Rheas we hope *certainly* to succeed (accidents barred) with six of them. My young Rheas are progressing well.'

'The Rhea has laid about forty eggs, but no incubation yet.' – July 2, 1846.

'The *Rhea Americana* has bred here twice, and at this moment I have, I believe, upwards of forty eggs, laid partly, I believe, by those bred here.' – July 21, 1846.

'My African Ostrich has laid four eggs.' – 1846.

'My Emu is sitting on fourteen eggs, and we have one Rhea egg.' – May 31, 1845.

'My female Emu has laid about twenty eggs, but still the male shows no symptoms of sitting.' – April 9, 1846.

'It is rather provoking our Emu will not sit, while at Wentworth their male is waiting to sit and has no egg. John thinks of sending our eggs to them. Would you advise this?'

'My only doubt about sending the Emu eggs to be hatched by the Wentworth male is, whether the carriage might not spoil them.'

Tortoises, Terrapins and Turtles (1872)

TESTUDO AREOLATA, Thunberg
Habitat. South Africa, Madagascar
The front legs are covered with very large scales, and have only four claws on the forefoot; the first vertebral and cortal plates are much longer than broad, and the others much broader than long, the lateral margin revolute.

Mr Bell says: – 'This species is easily familiarized. I have repeatedly had them so tame as to take food easily from the hand, and even to eat from one hand when held on the other.'

EMYS DECUSSATA, Bell
Habitat. North America
Mr Bell says that 'This is the species most commonly brought alive to this country. They are voracious, like their congeners, tearing in pieces and greedily devouring meat, frogs, small fish, or any other food of this kind. On being teased, they snap at any object held near them with considerable quickness and force.'

TRIONYX GANGETUS, Cuvier
Habitat. India; Ganges; Pegu
Hunting them in hill-streams – when pulled out – sometimes, when the animal is large, or the water deep, a stake is held over the animal's back, and, with a few well-delivered blows of a mallet,

driven through both shells. Woe betide the limb, however, which comes in reach of the infuriated animal! I saw the top of one man's toe bitten clean off by a trionyx plagyry which was being staked; as these animals are both active and ferocious, it is always advisable to set a bullet through their brain as soon as possible. So tenacious of life, however, are these creatures, that their heads bite vigorously after being completely dissevered from their bodies. From Theobald, *Journal of the Linnaean Society*.

Index of Nonsense Verse First Lines

Cold are the crabs that crawl on yonder hill,   82
He only said, 'I'm very weary.'   113
'How pleasant to know Mr Lear!'   108
In dreary silence down the bustling road   4
King and Queen of the Pelicans we;   96
Mr and Mrs Discobbolos (Climbed to the top of a wall,)   62
Mr and Mrs Discobbolos (Lived on the top of the wall,)   109
Mrs Jaypher found a wafer   106
O dear! how disgusting is life!   107
O my agèd Uncle Arly! –   111
On the Coast of Coromandel   64
On the top of the Crumpetty Tree   87
Once Mr Daddy Long-legs   51
Our mother was the Pussy-Cat, our father was the Owl   106
Said the Duck to the Kangaroo,   28
She sate upon her Dobie   94
She sits upon her Bulbul   28
The agèd hens of Oripò,   8
The Broom and the Shovel, the Poker and Tongs,   49
The Nutcrackers sate by a plate on the table,   61
The Owl and the Pussy-cat went to sea   47
The Pobble who has no toes   89
The Scroobious Pip went out one day   83
There was a Young Lady of Bute,   9
There was a Young Lady of Dorking,   17
There was a Young Lady of Hull,   13
There was a Young Lady of Lucca,   25
There was a Young Lady of Norway,   15
There was a Young Lady of Parma,   19
There was a Young Lady of Portugal,   24
There was a Young Lady of Sweden,   15
There was a Young Lady of Troy,   14
There was a Young Lady of Tyre,   12
There was a Young Lady whose bonnet,   23
There was a Young Lady whose eyes,   10
There was a Young Lady whose nose,   77
There was an old Derry down Derry,   1
There was an Old Man in a barge,   70
There was an Old Man in a tree, (Who was horribly bored by a Bee;)   23
There was an Old Man in a tree, (Whose whiskers were lovely to see;)   77
There was an Old Man of Berlin,   11
There was an Old Man of Cape Horn,   18
There was an Old Man of Corfu,   12
There was an Old Man of Dumbree,   74

There was an Old Man of Dunluce,   70
There was an Old Man of Kildare,   20
There was an Old Man of New York,   18
There was an Old Man of Peru,   14
There was an Old Man of the Nile,   19
There was an Old Man of Whitehaven,   26
There was an Old Man on the Border,   73
There was an Old Man who said, 'O! –   22
There was an Old Man who said, 'Hush!   26
There was an Old Man who said, 'See!   21
There was an Old Man who said, 'Well!   27
There was an Old Man who screamed out   72
There was an Old Man whose despair   68
There was an Old Man with a beard,   22
There was an Old Man, who when little,   68
There was an Old Person in black,   69
There was an Old Person of Anerly,   27
There was an Old Person of Blythe,   75
There was an Old Person of Bray,   76
There was an Old Person of Bree,   71
There was an Old Person of Chester,   10
There was an Old Person of Cromer,   25
There was an Old Person of Crowle,   76
There was an Old Person of Deal,   69
There was an Old Person of Grange,   74
There was an Old Person of Gretna,   13
There was an Old Person of Harrow,   78
There was an Old Person of Ischia,   16
There was an Old Person of Nice,   75
There was an Old Person of Philæ,   24
There was an Old Person of Sheen,   72
There was an Old Person of Shields,   71
There was an Old Person of Skye,   78
There was an Old Person of Tartary,   11
There was an Old Person of Troy,   16
There was an Old Person of Ware,   73
There was an Old Person whose legs,   20
There was an Old Person whose mirth,   21
There was an Old Sailor of Compton,   17
They went to sea in a Sieve, they did,   58
Two old Bachelors were living in one house;   98
What makes you look so black, so glum, so cross?   43
When awful darkness and silence reign   100
When the light dies away on a calm summer's eve   6
Who art thou – sweet little China Man? –   7
Who, or why, or which, or *what*, Is the Akond of SWAT?   90

Index of Places

Abruzzi 123, 126–38, 140, 143, 148, 155, 156, 158, 243, 244, 337
Acroceraunia see Khimára
Agnano 260, 263
Agrafa 230
Ain Gedi 284
Aïtone 324, 328
Ajaccio 307, 310–16, 321, 325, 328, 329–30, 332, 340
Akhridha 170, 177, 181–3, 191
Alba, Lake 134, 152
Albania 167–234, 290, 309
Aléssio 194–5, 198
Algayola 336
Ametrice 162–3
Antrodoco 140, 158, 159, 160
Apennines 129, 137
Apollónia 201
Apulia 239, 278
Aquila 137, 141, 143, 155, 163
Arabeh 285–6
Ardhénitza 201–2
Arghyró Kastro 222–3
Ariano 274
Arta 170, 223
Arya 224
Ascoli 158
Aspromonte 240
Athens 170, 228
Athos, Mount 170, 175, 176, 223, 233
Avellino 274–7
Avlóna 200, 202–4, 215, 219, 220–1

Bacucco 155
Bagaládi 242
Bagnara 240
Baltalimán 174
Balzorano 149
Bantja, River 222
Basilicata 239
Basilicò 268, 272
Bastìa 333–4
Bavella 322
Belgodére 337–8
Bazzano 253

Bebék 174
Benitza 302
Bérat 181, 185, 199–201
Bigonzi 253
Bocognano 330–1
Bonifacio 317, 322, 323
Borbona 159
Borghetto 158
Bosnia 173
Bosphorus 174
Bova 243, 244, 255, 269
Buyúkdere 174

Calabria 235–79
Calore, River 274
Caléssio 197–8
Calvi 336
Campagna 118, 119, 129
Cánalo 260–3
Cannes 308–9, 310, 329
Cap Corse 334–5
Capestrano 162
Capistrello 131
Capo dell' Armi 269
Caprera 317
Carghésé 327
Carsoli 129–30, 136
Casalabriva 323
Castel del Monte 277–8
Castelnuovo 265–6
Castel Vetere 253–8, 263
Catanzáro 241
Cauro 316–17, 324–5, 340
Cavaliere 127–9
Celano 130, 131, 134, 151–2
Cervara 118
Città di Penna 153–6
Civita D'Antino 131, 132, 134, 136, 149–51
Civita Ducale 139, 160
Civitella di Subiaco 118–19, 127
Cocullo 153
Col de Verde 339–40
Col St Georgio 340
Colle d'Oro 155

Collepardo 119
Constantinople (Stamboul, Istanbul)
    170, 173–4, 175, 176, 177, 186, 192,
    215
Corbara del Conte 143
Corfú 206, 222, 233–4, 286, 299, 300–2
Corneto 194
Corsica 123, 305–40
Corte 332–3
Cosenza 241

Dead Sea 285
Delvino 215–16
Draghiádhes 205–6, 207, 208–9, 215
Dukádhes 206, 208–10, 211–12, 215,
    220

Ed Deir 289, 290
Edéssa 176
Elbassán 177, 184–7, 191, 203
Epirus 170, 181, 223, 301
Episkopí 223
Es Zuweirah 284
Etna, Mount 241, 244, 269
Evisa 324

Fano 159
Fozzano 321
Frascati 119, 157
Frigento 275–6
Fucino, Lake 133–4, 152

Gebel Haroun 287
Gebel Musa 287
Gerace 244, 250, 255, 259, 260, 263,
    264–5
Ghegheria 181, 183
Ghisonaccio 321
Gioiosa 255, 256–7, 258–61, 263, 275
Girano 120, 126, 127
Gran Sasso 155
Greece 169, 171, 176, 222, 224, 226,
    230, 231, 234, 320
Grosseto 322, 325
Grotta Minarda 274–5
Guadagnolo 126, 127
Guitera 339

Hebron 283, 284, 285

Hor, Mount 286–7, 288, 289, 291

Ile Rousse 335–6
Ioánnina 223
Ionian Islands 297–303
Isola 155

Kalabáka 229
Kamarína 224
Kandilí 174
Kánina 204–6
Kastráki 228–30
Katerína 176, 231
Kaváya 199, 200, 201
Khasmé 290, 292
Khimára (Acroceraunia) 169, 170, 203,
    204–6, 207, 208, 212, 214, 215, 216,
    217–20
Khórmovo 221
Kiáfa 227
Koniah 186
Króia 170, 192–4, 198
Kúdhesi 212
Kukues 183–4

Lárissa 232–3
Leonessa 161–2
Leustri 201
Liris, River 149
Lliáttes 214
Luri 335

Macedonia 170, 176
Magliano 131, 148–9
Magnesia 233
Malta 223, 228, 273, 274
Marsica 130, 131
Meano, River 255
Melfi 275
Mellili 330
Mélito 242, 269, 272
Mentorella 123, 126–7
Messina 240, 241, 268–9, 272, 273–4
Metéora 228, 230
Métzovo 228
Missolonghi 221
Monastír 176–7, 179–81, 186
Mongibello 242
Montebello 137, 242, 269, 272

Monte Corno 155, 158
Montefuscolo 274
Monte Lungo 318
Monte Vergine 274
Monte Voltore 278
Montorio 163
Motta San Giovanni 240, 242

Naples, Kingdom of 124, 131, 139–57,
    158–63, 235–79
Nicótera 274
Novito, River 250, 260, 261, 263
Nukb-es-Sufâa 285

Olévano 206
Olmeto 322
Olympus, Mount 177, 230, 232
Ostia 118
Ostrovo 179

Palása 213, 220
Palizzi 246–7
Palmi 274
Párga 227–8, 233
Passo del Mercante 260, 261
Paterno 152
Patrás 226, 233, 234
Pentedatilo 269
Petra 283, 284, 285, 286, 287, 288, 289,
    295
Pietrapennata 247, 248
Pizzoli 163
Platamona 176
Polístena 266, 267
Porto Vecchio 320–1, 322, 324
Prata 274
Pratola 274
Prévezya 223, 234

Rapallo 312
Reggio 240–3, 255, 266, 268, 269, 270,
    271–3, 274
Rieti 139–40, 158, 161, 163
Rocca di Corno 142
Rocella 250–2, 255
Romano, River 260
Rome 117, 118, 119, 120, 123, 126, 131,
    156, 159, 163, 194, 197, 198, 237, 250,
    266

Sagona 326
Saloníki (Salonica) 170, 173, 174,
    175–6, 177, 192, 200, 231
San Angelo di Bianco 244
San Giorgio 266, 267
San Luca 244, 249
San Quirico 158, 159
Sant' Anatolia 143
Sant' Angelo de' Lombardi 275
Santa Maria di Polsi 244, 249–50
Santa Maria Zicché 325
Santa Maura 302
Santa Severa 335
Santo Stefano 273
Sardinia 311, 317, 320, 323
Sarténé 317–20, 322–3
Sayádes 233–4
Scanno 152–3
Scútari 174
Scylla 240, 274
Siciliano 127
Sicily 237, 241, 328
Siderno 250–2, 260, 261
Sigillo 158
Skódra 177, 181, 182, 195–7
Skopo, Mount 303
Skumbi, River 184, 186, 187, 199
Solenzaro 322
Solmona 134, 145
Sora 131, 149
St Florent 335
Staíti 244, 247–8
Stamboul *see* Constantinople
Stilo 253–4, 255
Subiaco 118, 119, 120, 123, 126
Súli 224, 225–7, 234

Tagliacozzo 130, 131, 140, 141, 146,
    148
Tavaria, River 317–18
Tchíka 206, 208, 212–13
Tchúka 199, 201–2
Tempé 230–1
Tepeléni 221–2
Teramo 137, 155, 158, 163
Terminillo 159
Terra di Lavoro 250
Tervitzianá 225

Thames Tunnel (Rotherhithe Tunnel) 140, 141
Therapia 174
Thessaly 170, 173, 230, 233, 290
Tiber, River 118
Tirana *see* Tyrana
Tivoli 118, 120, 157
Tjermí 199
Tomóhr (Tomóhrit) 185, 187, 199, 200
Trasacco 134, 149
Trebushín 221
Tufo 156–7
Turano 143
Turkey 169, 173
Tyrana (Tirana) 182, 187, 188–92, 194, 198
Tzikurátes 226

Ucciani 331

Valdoniello 324
Velino 130, 134, 135, 137, 139, 152, 158–9
Venosa 278–9
Vescovato 333

Via Egnatia 176
Via Salaria 159–60
Vico 324
Vivario 338–9
Viósa, River 222
Vittolo 327
Volo 233
Vunó 213, 214–17, 220

Wady Fikkreh 286
Wady Mousa 287, 295, 296
Wady Nemula 296
Wallachia 173

Yannina 176, 199, 223, 224, 231, 233
Yenidjé 176, 178
Yenikoi 174

Zagori 290
Zálongo 224, 234
Zante 302–3
Zermí 225
Zicavo 325, 340
Zítza 223

Fyfield*Books*

Two millennia of essential classics

The extensive Fyfield*Books* list includes

Djuna Barnes *The Book of Repulsive Women and other poems*
edited by Rebecca Loncraine

Elizabeth Barrett Browning *Selected Poems* edited by Malcolm Hicks

Charles Baudelaire *Complete Poems in French and English*
translated by Walter Martin

The Brontë Sisters *Selected Poems*
edited by Stevie Davies

Lewis Carroll *Selected Poems*
edited by Keith Silver

Thomas Chatterton *Selected Poems*
edited by Grevel Lindop

John Clare *By Himself*
edited by Eric Robinson and David Powell

Samuel Taylor Coleridge *Selected Poetry* edited by William Empson and David Pirie

John Donne *Selected Letters*
edited by P.M. Oliver

Oliver Goldsmith *Selected Writings*
edited by John Lucas

Victor Hugo *Selected Poetry in French and English*
translated by Steven Monte

Wyndham Lewis *Collected Poems and Plays* edited by Alan Munton

Charles Lamb *Selected Writings*
edited by J.E. Morpurgo

Ben Jonson *Epigrams and The Forest*
edited by Richard Dutton

Giacomo Leopardi *The Canti with a selection of his prose*
translated by J.G. Nichols

Andrew Marvell *Selected Poems*
edited by Bill Hutchings

Charlotte Mew *Collected Poems and Selected Prose*
edited by Val Warner

Michelangelo *Sonnets*
translated by Elizabeth Jennings, introduction by Michael Ayrton

William Morris *Selected Poems*
edited by Peter Faulkner

Ovid *Amores*
translated by Tom Bishop

Edgar Allan Poe *Poems and Essays on Poetry*
edited by C.H. Sisson

Restoration Bawdy
edited by John Adlard

Rainer Maria Rilke *Sonnets to Orpheus and Letters to a Young Poet*
translated by Stephen Cohn

Christina Rossetti *Selected Poems*
edited by C.H. Sisson

Sir Walter Scott *Selected Poems*
edited by James Reed

Sir Philip Sidney *Selected Writings*
edited by Richard Dutton

Henry Howard, Earl of Surrey *Selected Poems*
edited by Dennis Keene

Algernon Charles Swinburne *Selected Poems*
edited by L.M. Findlay

Oscar Wilde *Selected Poems*
edited by Malcolm Hicks

Sir Thomas Wyatt *Selected Poems*
edited by Hardiman Scott

For more information, including a full list of Fyfield*Books* and a contents list for each title, and details of how to order the books, visit the Carcanet website at www.carcanet.co.uk or email info@carcanet.co.uk